A SERBIAN VILLAGE

A SERBIAN VILLAGE

By JOEL MARTIN HALPERN

Illustrations by BARBARA KEREWSKY HALPERN

Columbia University Press, New York 1958

COPYRIGHT © 1956
COLUMBIA UNIVERSITY PRESS, NEW YORK
FIRST PUBLISHED IN BOOK FORM 1958

PUBLISHED IN GREAT BRITAIN, CANADA,
INDIA, AND PAKISTAN
BY THE OXFORD UNIVERSITY PRESS
LONDON, TORONTO,
BOMBAY, AND KARACHI

LIBRARY OF CONGRESS
CATALOG CARD NUMBER: 57–11449
MANUFACTURED IN THE
UNITED STATES OF AMERICA

CLARKE F. ANSLEY AWARD

THIS STUDY, prepared under the Graduate Faculties of Columbia University, was selected by a committee of those Faculties to receive one of the Clarke F. Ansley awards given annually by Columbia University Press.

FOREWORD

OUR KNOWLEDGE of the folk base of civilization and its various national traditions continues to grow. In growing it gives us a surer basis of comparison of the civilizations of the world and a better understanding of the currents of social and cultural change flowing from metropolitan centers of invention and elaboration into the countrysides of Europe, the Americas, Asia, and Africa. The inherited ways of life that have shaped folk and peasant tradition continue to exert themselves, and there seems less fear to think they will disappear. Rather, there is today more expectancy that they will continue, in transformation to modernity, to exercise some of the particularizing force that has given us the richness of national and regional peculiarities. If the world now in emergence combines old and new, and somehow merges the ancestral and the modern, the view of a changing Serbia that we get here by looking from the village outward and upward will serve us well as a foretaste of the future of those countries which will combine peasant persistence and urban sophistications, technical, political, or cultural.

That we can have such foretastes we owe to the continuing scholarly use, in social and anthropological science, of the community study method. Dr. Halpern worked within the anthropological tradition of the lone investigator. Although he was bolstered by a courageous and helpful young wife and by stout advice and encouragement from Yugoslav scholars who were fairly close by, he worked by himself without the complex apparatus of team work among survey specialists and technicians so common today. There are advantages in the continuance of the tradition in which a lone investigator takes on a whole small community. What persons and events he himself can reach represent to him a whole round of life and exemplify in their own activities and interrelationships a living and changing culture. Insight, sharpness of detail, sympathy, verisimilitude, a sure grasp of the real connections among forces are some of the rewards as they are here. If an overview of national or world influences is difficult to keep before oneself when one is immersed in the "grass roots" of real lives of real persons in a real and intensely particular village and countryside, the book one writes after one comes home, with field work backed with sound reading, can weave together the local and the national. Dr. Halpern's *A Serbian Village* is such a book. Looking upward and outward from the village gives one the indispensable realistic view from below of these influences which no other method can so well obtain.

It is encouraging, thus, to realize that community studies like this one, sounding in depth, are giving us deeper and truer knowledge of the ways of life of so many modern countries. Britain, France, Spain, Germany, our own New England, West, South, and Middle West—in recent years these have been sounded through community studies in the anthropological (or, as Europeans say, the "ethnographic") tradition of objective and comparative social research. Coupled with the many problematic studies current in such countries and areas, these community studies enrich our perception of social and cultural realities. They substitute truth and clarity for our previous too-easy self-images and our sometimes too-hasty national prejudices about ourselves and our neighbors. The gain accrues both to social science in the abstract and to its application in private and public problem solving.

It is the abstract gain that is of most importance to the future of social and cultural studies and anthropology in the widest sense. Here Dr. Halpern's foray into one of the heartlands of the Yugoslav national spirit, and one of the hearths of European man, is most welcome. Much of older cultural anthropology implicitly and explicitly contrasted the European or Western world with the outer lands of alien or primitive civilization. It took a long time before the comparative story of Man and the comparative analysis of his cultures and societies embraced more than the preliterate and "barbaric" lands outside high civilization. Today the gain for inclusiveness has been won. The civilizations of China, Japan, India, the Moslem world, known at first only to culture historians and orientalists, are under study today as human cultures and as social systems, with techniques ranging from community study and local surveys up to an analysis of art and literature. Anthropology's treatment of human achievement and adaptation, in its immense variety, now includes high civilizations other than the European.

But the full comparison will not be possible, and the record not complete, until the same techniques of cultural study have been turned upon the European world as well. Today cultural anthropology and comparative ethnology are completing the record and thereby conveying to us the real place of European ways of life, peasant or not, in the history and variation of mankind. This account of Serbian village life takes its place in that perspective.

CONRAD M. ARENSBERG

July, 1957
Trappe, Maryland

PREFACE

YUGOSLAVIA was chosen as the locale for a study of cultural change for several reasons. Because the area on which it lies has always been a meeting ground of cultures, it affords an excellent laboratory for the study of cultural dynamics. For the anthropologist interested in Slavic studies, Yugoslavia is at present the only country open to American investigators who wish to work *in situ*, a condition preferable to working with emigrant informants. It is an area which has been little studied by Western anthropologists, although Yugoslav ethnologists and human geographers with a somewhat different orientation have been actively working there for over half a century. Most notable among these are Jovan Cvijić and his students, who have been concerned chiefly with various types of environmental adaptations and population movements.

A decade ago practically nothing was said about field technique. Field methods were evidently viewed as something of an art, and every anthropologist seems to have kept his own counsel, like a prize chef with his favorite recipes. Since the end of the Second World War, however, this tradition has broken down and discussions of field techniques have become more frequent. Nevertheless, field methods still retain something of the aura of an occult art. These facts were brought home to the author as a fledgling anthropologist on his first major field research project.

The village of Orašac in the region of Šumadija was originally selected because it had been chosen as the village for the People's Republic of Serbia to be the site of a projected United Nations program in community development. It was also sufficiently far from Belgrade and any other big town so as not to be directly influenced by them. In August, 1953, my wife and I went to Orašac

after spending over a week in Jarmenovci, another village in the
same general area, with Professor Borivoje Drobnjaković, Chairman of the Department of Ethnology at Belgrade University, and
two of his assistants. This period with the Serbian ethnologists
was very helpful, although their methods and interests, focusing
largely on material culture and origins of the population, are
somewhat different from those of most American anthropologists.

With a letter from the official Yugoslav Commission for Cultural
Relations with Foreigners we went by train to the rural county
seat of Arandjelovac, about 50 miles south of Belgrade. Our letter
was addressed to the County Cooperative Union, since we had
evidenced an interest in the United Nations program in Community Development, a joint project of the United Nations Technical Assistance Administration and the Central Union of Yugoslav
Cooperatives. When we arrived at the Cooperative's county headquarters, the President of the Orašac Cooperative happened to be
there. He decided to allow us to return with him to his village,
several miles away. Upon our arrival in Orašac, a conference as
to where we would be lodged was immediately held among the
leading officials: the Director of the school, the President and
Secretary of the Village Council, and the President of the Village
Cooperative. The house of the Secretary of the Village Council
was unanimously agreed upon, and there we remained for our
year's stay.

His house had the disadvantage of being located some distance
from the center of the village. This was more than compensated
for by the fact that there were six members—three generations—
in the household: his parents, his wife, and his young son and
daughter, all of whom were very friendly and later proved themselves to be eager and dependable informants. Since our host was
Secretary of the Village Council, however, many of his attitudes
and those of his family could not always be called typical. For
example, he was more in favor of the present government and was
to a greater extent susceptible to urban influences than was characteristic of the village on the whole. Although much valuable
material was obtained from the members of this family we con-
tacted as many other people as possible, by means of conventional

participant-observer techniques and by extensive interviewing of selected individuals.

Whatever measure of merit this work may have was due in large part to the extreme friendliness with which we were received by almost everyone. From the beginning we were welcome guests wherever we went at any time, mainly because of the traditional attitudes of Serbian hospitality toward strangers. In fact, as we began visiting different households, chatting with people, casually interviewing them, and just "sitting around," we found that others were offended because we had not yet come to their homes. For two people in a village of over 400 households this was a difficult situation. Naturally, our selection of informants was based on their position in the culture, reliability, and other qualifications, of which an elucidation to the average villager was a nearly impossible task.

The usual cautions were observed, one of the most important being noninterference in the internal affairs of the villagers. From the outset we made it clear to Communists and non-Communists alike that our purpose was to collect data about their way of life and not to meddle in their politics. Some exception to this was made during the Trieste crisis in October, 1953, when villagers asked us about the American position. But by that time we were sufficiently established in the village so that our status was not affected, although we were subjected to earnest and persistent questioning. Our acceptance in the village was often based not so much on the fact that we were foreigners in general but rather Americans in particular. This always ensured a warm reception and a very friendly relationship. It gave rise to some minor discomfort, however, when I was on numerous occasions enthusiastically embraced by stalwart peasants who, following Serbian customs of camaraderie, rubbed their grizzly cheeks against mine in impulsive demonstrations of affection.

Another factor which I believe aided us on two counts—avoiding suspicion and being able to approach people easily—was that at the time of the field work, 1953–54, my wife and I were both in our early twenties. Because of our youth, we were obviously not to be taken too seriously according to the peasant ethos. This inspired some interesting attitudes on the part of several older men who addressed me as "*Vi, dečko*" (You [formal form], Boy). In spite of this, to the villagers the fact that we had traveled the great distance from America to Orašac meant that we had some sort of importance.

In explanations of our stay in the village, historical circumstances worked in our favor. The statement that we had come to study their history was often satisfactory by itself, for Orašac was the site of the First Revolt against the Turks in 1804, where Karadjordje—the founder of one of the two Serbian royal dynasties, which lasted intermittently until the Second World War—organized his forces. Any additional explanation was provided by the statement that we wished to learn about their interesting customs. This usually had a very positive effect on a people so consciously patriotic as the Serbian peasantry.

A typical first encounter was taken up mostly by the informant questioning us, about ourselves and America, and then revealing spontaneous expressions of interest in America and gratitude for United States economic aid to Yugoslavia. It is considered good form for the fieldworker not to project his personal background into the situation, but we adopted the policy of not going to the extreme of concealing ours. Since we were received in an open and friendly manner we decided to act similarly, and although the remarks were in no way solicited, of course, it would have been impolite to ignore them. We consciously tried, however, to express a minimum of value judgments regarding their culture and not to take sides in any controversial discussions which did not affect us directly.

On the latter point, it was necessary to yield somewhat when it was a question of establishing better *rapport*. It was not our intention to be adopted into the culture, for such was not their ethos— the peasants preferred us for what we were. We came to the village equipped with old clothes for tramping around over fields and muddy lanes, but I was discreetly informed that I should dress "like an American." So for most of our stay in Orašac I had to wear shoes instead of old boots, and trousers in place of Army fatigues. Yet at other times we were able to blend convincingly into the scene, as when one old man refused to believe I was an American but rather an official from Belgrade who had come down to work on the "Plan." And my wife was approached several times by bachelors from neighboring villages when she went to the market town with the young women from Orašac.

All work was done in Serbian, which we studied intensively for almost two months in Belgrade before starting field work. Our knowledge of the language was far from flawless, but it improved considerably in the field. The fact that it was never completely perfected did not turn out to be a handicap.

Written material was a source of supplementary information. Several essay contests were held for the school children, and the winners were given small prizes. They wrote on such topics as "My Childhood," "What I Want to Be," and "My Favorite Holiday." Several men wrote their autobiographies, and a number of women were interviewed extensively—they seldom had the free time or schooling to write personal histories. No questionnaires were used, although I believe much valuable data could have been gained from them. This was again because the two of us could not cover the entire village adequately. An agency in Belgrade expressed interest in sponsoring such a survey, but action was never taken.

The physical and cultural landscapes and the yearly cycle of activities were recorded in over 500 photographs. Tape recordings of folk songs and instruments were made. Quite a bit of attention was given to the material culture, especially house furnishings and costumes, since an ethnographic collection was made for the American Museum of Natural History.

From county and village records numerous statistics were collected, and all local officials and some county ones were interviewed. In the majority of cases they were anxious to be of help and supplied me with all data requested, although the full accuracy of their material cannot be confirmed. The Statistical Office of the People's Republic of Serbia provided much valuable data, particularly the complete Orašac census reports for 1948 and 1953, from which material on social organization and nonagricultural employment was obtained.

I am deeply grateful to Professor Milenko S. Filipović, of the Ethnographic Institute of the Serbian Academy of Sciences and currently of the University of Sarajevo, for his constant interest and insights into Serbian peasant culture. The other ethnologists at Belgrade University and the Ethnographic Museum of Belgrade, particularly Miss Bosiljka Radović, were all extremely helpful.

In general, the Yugoslav authorities, on the national as well as on the local level, were quite cooperative. A mild form of pressure was applied by some county officials, who made it clear that they were being helpful because they assumed I would write a sympathetic report. Contact with a few of the formerly wealthy peasants, now looked upon with disfavor, was discouraged although never prohibited.

This study is in a sense something of a restudy, since the area (all the villages in pre-war Jasenica County, now mostly in Orašac County) has been covered in a monograph by Jeremije M. Pavlović, *Život i Običaji Narodni u Kragujevačkoj Jasenici u Šumadiji* (Peasant Life and Customs in Jasenica Region of the Kragujevac District in Šumadija), published by the Serbian Royal Academy of Belgrade in 1921. Jeremije Pavlović was a village schoolteacher interested in ethnology. He lived in the region prior to the First World War, and his work is almost entirely descriptive but with broad coverage. His study is valuable chiefly for comparisons on various details, but it is also strongest in the sphere where this study is weakest—namely folklore and oral literature. Another publication bearing directly on this area is *Jasenica*, by Professor Drobnjaković, also published by the Serbian Royal Academy, in 1923. A monograph in the series *Naselja i Poreklo Stanovništva* (Settlements and the Origin of Populations), it follows the pattern established by Jovan Cvijić in his *La Péninsule Balkanique*, and gives, for every village in the county, including Orašac, brief descriptions of the topography and origin of each clan group. Also included in *Jasenica* is a brief history of the general area from prehistoric times and a detailed discussion of the various waves of migration which settled the county. Still another valuable monograph is the massive work on the ethnography of the neighboring region of Gruža, compiled by Petar Petrović and based on field work there in the 1920s. It was published by the Serbian Academy of Sciences in 1948. This, too, is largely a compendium of neatly categorized facts without much attempt to synthetize or evaluate, but it is nevertheless useful for supplementary documentation, although there are some minor differences between Gruža and the region dealt with in the present study.

Milisav Lutovac's *Privredno-Geografska Karakteristika Sliva Jasenice* (Economic-Geographic Characteristics of the Jasenica Basin), published by the Serbian Academy of Sciences in 1951, provided helpful information. The only works on Šumadija approximating community studies are by a physician, Dr. Aleksandar Petrović. Published by the Central Hygiene Institute in Belgrade, they deal with the villages Banjane (1932) and Rakovica (1939) and emphasize public health and nutrition, with an attempt to integrate other aspects of culture. Some additional publications, by Cvijić, Jovan Erdeljanović, Tihomir Djordjević, and others have been used as references, since the general region in which Orašac is located has been relatively well studied by Serbian scholars for over half a century, although not by the "community study" approach.

It is impossible to fully acknowledge here all those who helped in one way or another to make this study possible. Certainly most significant were the warmhearted, cooperative people of Orašac. In addition to the ethnologists in Belgrade, Tihomir Kostić aided enormously in the translation of songs and old church documents. Edwin Henson, a community development expert with the United Nations, helped in the selection of Orašac as the site for my study.

Several Serbs originally from Šumadija now residing in New York checked innumerable details and discussed general impressions obtained in the field. To Budimir Sreckovich I owe a special debt of gratitude for his great patience and aid throughout the preparation of my manuscript.

I am grateful to Professors Milorad Drashkovitch, Harvey Moore, Philip Mosely, Harry Shapiro, Jozo Tomasevich, and Charles Wagley, to M. B. Filipovic and others for helpful comments, and especially to Professor Conrad Arensberg, who encouraged and guided this project.

To my parents, Nettie and Carl Halpern, I am indebted for

both their faith and financial assistance, enabling me to spend a year in the field and a year writing up my material. My wife, Barbara, in addition to sharing field experiences and collecting useful information, helped during all stages of preparing the manuscript. Especially invaluable was her assistance in drawing the illustrations, preparing maps and diagrams, and assuming some of the thankless and laborious tasks connected with compiling statistics—but most important of all were her inspiration and enthusiasm in this project.

This book is a somewhat condensed version of my doctoral dissertation under the Department of Anthropology, Columbia University; a limited prepublication edition of this study has been issued by Human Relations Area Files, Inc., New Haven, Connecticut, in 1956.

JOEL MARTIN HALPERN

Luang Prabang, Laos
April, 1957

CONTENTS

TABLES

FIGURES

MAPS

ILLUSTRATIONS   *follow* 198

A SERBIAN VILLAGE

*Cultures are infinitely perfectible
and everything indicates that all cultures
are in a constant state of change.*

RALPH LINTON, *Acculturation
of Seven American Indian Tribes*

NOTE ON PRONUNCIATION

IN THIS STUDY all proper names and other Serbian words are given in their customary form in Latin characters (Croatian), except for names with established English equivalents, for example, Yugoslavia (Jugoslavija), Belgrade (Beograd), Serbia (Srbija).

CHAPTER 1

THE SETTING

A DIRT ROAD winds over gentle slopes. In the summer it is
a ribbon of powdery dust, and when it rains the wheels of cow
carts cut deep ruts and ridges into the mud. Small fields of wheat
and corn, and meadows, where sheep graze, stretch across the
rolling landscape. Studding the fields are whitewashed cottages
topped with red tiled roofs. Neat plum orchards, now rows of
bare-branched trees, now obscuring the cottages in clouds of pink-
white petals, now hung with purple fruit, surround each homestead. The road dips down toward the new Cooperative Home
and a cluster of peasant cottages, and there, where it bends around
Preseka Hill, Orašac village lies, its homes sprinkled over slope
and plain.

Orašac is in the region of Šumadija in Serbia. Its people think
of themselves primarily as Serbs rather than Yugoslavs. Their way
of life is characteristic of that of central Serbia and represents a
picture of the largest—and possibly the most homogeneous—
ethnic unit in the cultural mosaic that is the modern Yugoslav
nation.

GEOGRAPHICAL BACKGROUND

A glance at Map 1 serves to emphasize one of the most critical
factors in the shaping of the culture of the Yugoslavs: a geographic location between the Eastern and Western worlds, which
has given rise to Yugoslavia's characterization as a halfway station,

Map 1. Yugoslavia, Showing Region of Šumadija in Central Serbia

not only in modern times but also in historic and to a certain extent even in prehistoric periods.

Beginning in the sixth and seventh centuries, there occurred migrations of Slavs from the Carpathian regions, who in turn either eliminated older inhabitants or else amalgamated with them. After a period of competition between the Bulgarian and Serbian kingdoms began the wars with the Turks, culminating in the defeat of the Serbs at the Battle of Kosovo in 1389.[1]

But different parts of Yugoslavia have different backgrounds. Slovenia, in the north, bordering on Italy, Austria, and Hungary,

[1] Although preeminent in traditional Serbian literature, this battle is more of psychological than historical significance; the Battle of Marica in 1371 had a greater military significance. It was not until 1459 that the Serbs were completely subdued.

was under the Hapsburg Empire until the First World War (as was Croatia, its neighbor to the east). Today one of the six republics of the Federated People's Republics of Yugoslavia, Slovenia has a predominantly Roman Catholic population of approximately 1,500,000, who in personality, attitudes, and material culture resemble more nearly the neighboring Austrians than they do their fellow Yugoslavs. Croatia, with a population of 4,000,000, and neighboring Serbia are the two largest ethnic and political units in Yugoslavia.[2] Although they speak a common language, the Croats write mainly in the Latin alphabet and are Roman Catholics while the Serbs use chiefly the Cyrillic and are Eastern Orthodox. Antagonism between the Serbs and Croats was one of the major disruptive factors in Yugoslavia prior to the Second World War. In fact, the tension was so strong that Yugoslavia was never consolidated from an internal point of view. Aside from the Austro-Hungarian influence, which was strong in the interior, the control of Italy and Mediterranean culture was dominant along the Dalmatian Coast.

Serbia is the largest republic and ethnic unit, with a total population of some 7,000,000. There are two autonomous areas within Serbia. The province of the Vojvodina, the flat plains area north of the Danube, was, like Croatia, under the Hapsburg Monarchy (the Hungarian part) until the First World War. The Vojvodina, which has a population of 1,714,000, has the richest farm land in the whole of Yugoslavia and is inhabited mainly by Serbs, although it has large groups of Hungarian and Rumanian national minorities. In addition, scattered throughout the province are villages of Slovak, Czech, Russene (Ukrainian), and German minority groups.[3] Serbia also has the autonomous region of the Kosmet (Kosovo-Metohija), center of the Albanian minority, which has a population of 800,000. They speak their own language and are of the Moslem faith for the most part.

The remaining three republics are Bosnia-Herzegovina, Montenegro, and Macedonia. Bosnia is populated by Catholics, Or-

[2] From the twelfth to the fifteenth century Croatia was united with Hungary and later became part of the Hapsburg Empire.

[3] Most of the Germans left Yugoslavia during or soon after the Second World War.

thodox, and Moslems, all of whom speak Serbo-Croatian. The
Moslems are part of the original Slav population which accepted
Mohammedanism at the time of the Turkish conquest. This area
was ruled by Austria-Hungary, which succeeded the Turks in
1878, until the First World War.

Montenegro, with its population of less than 500,000, is a small
mountainous country bordering on Albania. Its people managed
more successfully to resist conquest by the Turks because of their
security within the rocky, rugged terrain. In language, religion, and
general culture they are Serbs; although never directly ruled by
the Turks they were nevertheless influenced by them.[4] Montenegro
was independent until the end of the First World War.

Macedonia, a center of the medieval Serbian state, remained
under Turkey until 1912, when her withdrawal was forced by
Montenegro, Serbia, Bulgaria, and Greece. It is here that the
Turkish influence was strongest and persisted for the longest time.
The old section of Skoplje, the capital, is more "Turkish" today
than much of Istanbul. Macedonia's population of some 1,300,000
is a mixture of Moslem and Orthodox.

This very brief summary, then, gives some idea of the cultural
diversity of present-day Yugoslavia. An understanding of this
diversity is essential in placing the village of Orašac in any perspective, or, for that matter, in understanding the village itself, for
the inhabitants of this village, unlike some of their fellow farmers
in other parts of the world, are acutely conscious of national differences and of what they consider to be their place in the national
and international picture.

In contrast to the differences underscored above, the Republic
of Serbia (exclusive of Belgrade and the two autonomous regions)
has in general a very homogeneous population; this is especially
true of the region of Šumadija, in which Orašac village, in Orašac
County,[5] is situated. Here anyone who is not an Orthodox Serb
is something of a peculiarity, although this situation has been

---

[4] There are, however, many minor distinctions related to environmental and historical differences, both in cultural traits and psychological orientation, between the
Serbs of Montenegro and those of Serbia proper.

[5] Unless otherwise specified, in this book Orašac always refers to the village.

altered slightly since the Second World War, with its accompanying population movements. This cultural homogeneity and central geographic location explain why the area is called the "heart of Serbia." There are also important historical reasons. It is in Šumadija, in fact in the very village of Orašac, that the first revolt against the Turks began.

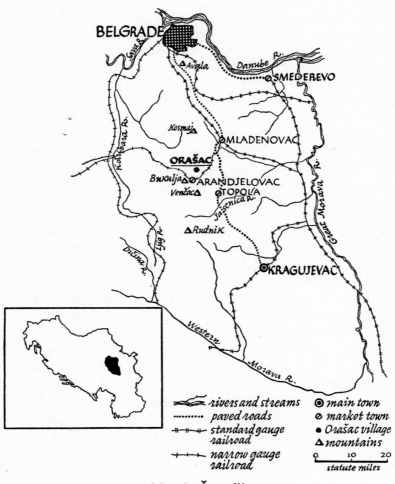

Map 2. Šumadija

Šumadija derives its name from the Serbian *šuma*, or woods, for at the turn of the nineteenth century, when its intensive settlement began, the entire region had a rich oak forest cover. Today only small scattered patches of the original forest remain.

Šumadija is bounded on the north by the Sava and the Danube and on the east and south by the Great Morava and the Western Morava; within the region's western border lie the valleys of the Kolubara, Ljig, and Dičina Rivers (see Map 2). Its area is about 3,500 square miles, approximately one half the size of New Jersey. Šumadija is on the margin of the basin occupied by the vast Pannonian Lake of the Neocene. Pleasant rolling hill country, the region actually consists of three distinct topographical features: enclosing and transversing river basins, mountain massifs, and glacial lake terraces, which gradually decrease in elevation from south to north, to the Danube. The tops of the mountain massifs were islands in glacial times. Shoreline terraces are still visible today to an altitude of about 2,000 feet, almost to the summits of the small mountains. Kosmaj, Bukulja, Venčac, and the highest massif, Rudnik (3,714 feet), still rise clearly above Šumadija's undulating fields and meadows. Overlaying the crystalline core and the semicrystalline Cretaceous limestone of these massifs are Neocene sediments, horizontal layers of clay and yellow-colored sand.[6]

On the lower slopes of the mountains are thin stands of oak and beech, and above a thousand feet there is a thicker coniferous cover. The rolling lowlands below, where most of the villages are located, can be characterized as mixed deciduous forest. Except for an occasional patch of oak, acacia is seen everywhere, in groves, bordering roads, and lining paths.[7] In addition, there is a variety of cultivated fruit trees, especially plum.

Šumadija has a marked continental climate, like that of most of inland Central Europe. The nearest meteorological station is Bukovička Banja, about four miles from Orašac. Its records indicate the general meteorological pattern for Šumadija and give specific data on the immediate area of Orašac. July is the warmest

[6] Lutovac, *Privredno-Geografska Karakteristika Sliva Jasenice*, p. 1.
[7] This is not part of the aboriginal forest cover but was introduced into Šumadija in the nineteenth century.

month, with an average temperature of 74°F., while January is the coldest month, with an average of 35°F. Rainfall is constant all year, with maximum precipitation in May and June. The average annual precipitation is 30 inches.

Within this pattern, however, there is a good deal of variation. Readings as high as 109°F. have occurred in the summer and as low as −17°F. have been recorded in the winter. Total annual precipitation often registers as little as 23–25 inches and sometimes as much as 38 inches. It is estimated that the average date for the first frost is October 21, and an extreme for the region is the end of September. The last frost occurs about April 13, with extreme records for the first week in May. Again, the area is subject to great variation, but in general an eight-and-a-half-month growing season prevails, from the middle of March through November. In spite of the many deviations from average conditions, the occurrence of maximum rainfall during this period is, of course, very favorable for agriculture.

At the beginning and end of winter, and often before the first frosts, a bitter cold, dry wind called the *košava* blows into the region. Coming from across the flat, wind-swept plains of the Vojvodina, it loses much of its force as it passes through the hill regions of Šumadija. Often it blows steadily for a few days and sometimes for longer periods, causing damage to agriculture, especially to the fruit trees.

Šumadija, still overwhelmingly a land of peasants, contains a few small commercial and industrial centers. These originally developed during the period when the railroad came through in the latter part of the nineteenth century, although they may have existed previously as peasant villages. This is the case for Mladenovac (population 6,206), Topola (population 4,588), and Arandjelovac (population 5,746), the towns nearest Orašac. In Arandjelovac, about four miles south of Orašac, small factories producing refractory material and porcelain insulators for electrical equipment have recently begun operations and are largely responsible for the population increase. The town is also endowed with natural mineral springs, around which a wooded park and several inns have been built. Yugoslav city folk come from as far away as Macedonia

to enjoy the hot springs. This development, unlike the new factories, has had little effect on the peasants, and the primary function of Arandjelovac is as a county seat and market town for the
twenty-odd villages in the surrounding region.

PREHISTORY AND EARLY HISTORY

Yugoslavia in general, and Serbia in particular, is rich in antiqui-
ties and reveals evidences of human occupation even from as early
as the paleolithic period.[8] The regions surrounding Orašac village
have many archeological remains. In Lipovac, about seven miles
south of Arandjelovac, there is a large neolithic site. The finds from
Lipovac are closely comparable to those from the famous site at
Vinča, on the Danube near Belgrade, and are analogous to finds
at other neolithic sites in the Moravo-Danubian area. The material includes fluted and ribbed ware and incised and burnished
decorated ceramics in the form of bowls, cups, and large storage
vessels. There are also clay figurines, celts, knife blades, scrapers,
and milling stones. Bones of domestic cattle and pigs have been
found.[9]

It has been suggested that the present day economic structure
of the Moravo-Danubian area reflects a heritage derived from
neolithic times, that the neolithic pioneers found a physical en-
vironment essentially similar to that of the present day, that the
Slavic emigrants adopted the traditions established here by their
neolithic predecessors, and that the culture of the present Šumadijans still reflects much of the aboriginal mode of life.[10] Undoubtedly,
most of the crops and animals raised by the peasants today, as well
as some of their implements and techniques, had their origin in
neolithic times. But what specifically the contemporary peasant
population has received directly from the prehistoric inhabitants
of Šumadija is something else again. Although this area has been
inhabited in neolithic and Roman times, there is a long period of

---

[8] Knowledge of paleolithic cultures in Serbia is at present imperfect, but in 1955 a
site near Arandjelovac was excavated by Brodar and identified as Mousterian, by
associated artifacts and accompanying Pleistocene fauna, according to a communication from Professor Brodar.

[9] Fewkes, "Neolithic Sites in the Moravo-Danubian Area," *American School of Prehistoric Research Bulletin*, No. 12 (May, 1936), pp. 5–82.

[10] *Ibid.*, pp. 8–9.

history, up to and including part of the early Middle Ages, for which there is little or no record of settlement. It would seem, therefore, that a direct tradition would be hard to trace. Probably what is meant is the general basis of the peasant economy, a combination of sedentary agriculture and stock breeding, supplemented by hunting and fishing. In Šumadija today, however, the latter are almost negligible.

In the second and third centuries the neighboring region of Rudnik was an important Roman mining center and was relatively well settled. The Jasenica drainage basin, in which Orašac is situated, was also settled by the Romans at this time, and both were part of the province of Moesia. Peasants from Orašac and several nearby villages have found Roman coins in the course of their plowing, and many Roman sites have been discovered by professional archeologists.

From the recorded history of Belgrade, it is known that the city was held by the Illyrians. In the fourth century B.C. they were replaced by the Celts, who lived there for over three hundred years. It was under the Celtic name of Singidunum that Belgrade later became a Roman trading center. Before the arrival of the Slavs, the Belgrade region was fought over by the Huns and Avars as well as the Romans. Then, with the Slav migrations, the area was settled again. This Belgrade region was all frontier territory, and if the locale of Orašac, some sixty miles still further south, experienced these vicissitudes at all, there seem to be no records of it. Nor are there many reliable records for the area for the next thousand years.

POPULATION MOVEMENTS TO THE NINETEENTH CENTURY

Because Šumadija[11] was a frontier and subject to almost constant warfare, the population fluctuated greatly. According to Drobnjaković, an authority on population movements in Šumadija, the development of the region's population in historic times can be divided into three phases.[12] The first phase was after the defeat at

[11] The name Šumadija dates only from the eighteenth century.
[12] Drobnjaković, "Sur la composition ethnique de la population de la Šumadija," in *Comptes rendus du III Congrès*.

Kosovo in 1389. People migrated north to Šumadija from the Turk-invaded areas and presumably mingled with earlier inhabitants. At this point there is little data, probably due to the lack of sources, but all indications, including the historic records of several churches in this area, point up the fact that the section was relatively well populated at the beginning of the fifteenth century.[13]

This northward migration to Šumadija continued until 1459, when the Turks conquered Smederevo, the last Serbian feudal stronghold. At this time, conditions evidently became increasingly difficult for the peasantry, resulting in the beginning of the second phase. The majority of the population emigrated to other areas, namely, farther north to Hungary and west to Bosnia and the mountainous Dinaric regions. It is estimated that less than 10 percent of the people stayed behind. In the second decade of the sixteenth century a traveler wrote of the area as being completely deserted, without any villages.[14] Yet a century earlier, in the 1420s, another traveler crossing the same general area had noted the many prosperous towns and villages.[15] The immediate area of Orašac village appears to have been largely uninhabited during the fifteenth and sixteenth centuries.

During the periods 1683–99 and 1716–19, Serbia was the scene of continuous warfare between the Austrian and Turkish Empires. This was a time of constant population movements, the greatest of which occurred in 1690 and was known as the Great Migration, when about 30,000 Serbs crossed the Danube into Hungary. The Hapsburg Empire welcomed these newcomers and used them to populate their border regions and fight against the Turks.[16]

Upon defeating Turkey in 1718, Austria occupied Šumadija from that time until 1739, and large-scale repopulation occurred. Orašac is not mentioned in the detailed Austrian records of this

[13] A parish priest in the village of Bukovik, near Orašac, wrote a local history in which he claims that according to tradition his present church is built on the foundations of one dating from the time of Stevan Lazarević (1389–1427).

[14] Drobnjaković, *Jasenica*, p. 225.

[15] Drobnjaković, "Stanovništvo u Srbiji za Vreme Prvog Ustanka," in *Srpskog Geografskog Društva*, special publication, No. 32, p. 37.

[16] Tomasevich, *Peasants, Politics, and Economic Change in Yugoslavia*, p. 36.

period, so it is fairly safe to assume that it was not founded until the latter part of the eighteenth century.[17]

With the ending of Austrian rule the Turks again came back to power in their former Pashaluk of Belgrade. Despite the return of Turkish control, the mid-eighteenth century seems to have witnessed a substantial build-up in the population of Šumadija by immigration into the area. This was no doubt brought about by pressures in the overpopulated Dinaric mountain areas from which most of these immigrants came as well as by the return of many inhabitants who had fled during the previous war.[18]

But again, mass depopulation occurred in the period of the Austro-Turkish War of 1788–91. Before this war there were approximately 80,000 households in Serbia; after the war the number dropped to 20,000.[19] In the same tradition of the Great Migration, many emigrants crossed the Danube and went north to the Vojvodina, some of them remaining permanently to form the basis of the present Serb population there.

Immediately after the war a temporary period of stability set in. Once more repopulation of Šumadija occurred. This is what Drobnjaković refers to as the third phase. Many returned from the Vojvodina, and larger numbers of new settlers came from the mountain regions to the south and west. This constant returning of settlers to Šumadija would appear to be an eloquent tribute to the attractiveness of the area. Despite the constant wars it seems to have been more habitable than the relatively barren mountains or even the Vojvodina, which was at that time still full of swamps and marshland.

SETTLEMENT OF ORAŠAC

It was in the period between the two Austro-Turkish wars that Orašac was settled. The first recorded mention of the village is in

[17] Some villages in the vicinity of Orašac existed at this time: Donja and Gornja Šatornja had ten households, Topola six, and Lipovac two. See Popović, *Srbija i Beograd*, p. 23.

[18] T. Djordjević, *Iz Srbije Kneza Miloša: Stanovništvo-Naselja*, p. 24.

[19] Filipović, "Selo u Srbiji Krajem 18 i Početkom 19 Veka," in *Srpskog Geografskog Društva*, special publication, No. 32, p. 74.

an account written by an Austrian officer who was making a pre-war reconnaissance in Serbia. This was in 1784, and at that time he states that Orašac had fifteen Christian (Serbian Orthodox) households and a well-built log inn, or *han*, where local Turkish officials resided.[20] Additional supporting evidence is found in the traditional family histories. According to the descendants of the Maričević clan, which is generally conceded to be the oldest in the village, their ancestors first settled in Orašac around 1750. By this time some degree of stability existed in Šumadija; at least, despite future wars, many of the ancestors of the present population of Orašac had begun to establish permanent homesteads.

The people who came to Orašac in the latter part of the eighteenth century were mainly from the Dinaric regions to the southwest, that is, from the general region where the present-day southern Serbia and the Republics of Bosnia-Herzegovina and Montenegro meet, particularly from around Sjenica and Bjelo Polje.[21] The reason for their movement was primarily economic and ecological. The mountain regions where they had lived were capable of sustaining only a limited number of people and seem to have been overpopulated.

Immigrants to Orašac did not arrive as a group but rather as small family units, usually brothers accompanied by their wives and children. Because they were settling in a new homeland these pioneers founded clan groups. Their descendants derived their family name from the first name of the ancestor who originally settled in the village.[22] Occasionally a woman would be the founder of a clan if she were a widow when she came to Orašac. This is what happened in the cases of the present day Nedić and Anić clans, the names being derived from the widows Neda and Ana.

[20] The fact that Orašac existed at this time is confirmed by another source, stating that a certain Milosav Milošević of Orašac went to the Vojvodina to fight against the Turks in 1788. Arsenijević, *Istorija Srpskog Ustanka*, I, 394.

[21] Some authorities think that Sjenica was a concentration point for future immigrants to Šumadija rather than a place of origin. Other regions from which the ancestors of the Orašac population came are Novi Pazar in the Sandjak region and Nikšić Župe in Montenegro. With regard to the origins of its population, Orašac is typical of the entire Jasenica region within Šumadija.

[22] The clan name is formed by adding the suffix *ić*, *ović*, or *ević*—Nedić from Neda, Stojanović from Stojan, Matijašević from Matijaš.

The case of Neda is fairly typical; according to Nedić family tradition, she arrived in Orašac in 1786. She and her husband had originally come from the region of Sjenica, and they first went to the village of Rogača in Kosmaj County. After her husband was killed by the Turks, she fled to Orašac with her children and possibly with some widowed sisters.[23]

During the period from 1790 to 1810, Orašac and Šumadija in general received the heaviest influx of immigrants. Once settled in their new homes the pioneers encouraged relatives who had remained behind in the Dinaric mountains to join them. The first settlers constructed their homes in the section now known as *centar* (center of the village). These were small log huts built in a glen to conceal them from the Turks. But having come from mountainous regions, where people were accustomed to living far apart, they evidently wanted more breathing space and before long started to scatter their homesteads. Several of those who arrived after 1800 established their homes directly in the outlying sections.

TURKISH RULE IN SERBIA AND ITS EFFECTS

Although Orašac was founded when Turkish rule in Serbia was in its final phases, an understanding of the present-day inhabitants and their culture would be incomplete without giving some attention to the preceding period of almost five centuries, when the Turks ruled not only Šumadija and Serbia but most of the Balkan peninsula. While it is true that Orašac as a village did not exist for most of this period, the inhabitants' ancestors were greatly influenced by Ottoman rule, even those who were not under its direct control (as in Montenegro, for example). It is impossible to converse with a Serbian peasant without having him mention the *pet stotina godina pod Turcima* (five hundred years under the Turks)[24] —whether as a reason for the low standard of living, a comment on national history, or an excuse for a neighbor's behavior.

As was the case with most of the rest of Europe, what is today

[23] Although a few clans are named for widows, most bear the names of men. The usual Serbian pattern is to trace descent through the male line.
[24] Actually it was closer to four hundred years, since it was not until the fifteenth century that Turkish rule was consolidated.

Yugoslavia was during the Middle Ages controlled by feudal lords. At times parts of Yugoslavia were united by strong rulers, such as Stevan Nemanja and Stevan Dušan. These empires were short lived, although Nemanja founded the dynasty which ruled Serbia intermittently until the Battle of Marica in 1371. The expansion of the Serbian state during this period gave impetus to the development of feudal forms which, although built upon a Serbian cultural base, were copied from Byzantine models but which also had some West European influences. The system was crystallized in the Code of Tsar Dušan in 1349, at the height of the Serbian medieval state. At this time all lands in actual ownership belonged either to the ruler, the Church, or the feudal lords, although the ruler possessed the right of eminent domain over all the land. These estates were worked by serfs whom Dušan's Code bound to the land. By virtue of its ownership of huge estates, the Church had tremendous wealth and secular power but was nevertheless under the control of the temporal king. The feudal lords had even less independence than those of the Church, being subject to economic and military levies from which Church estates were exempt. It was during this period that many of the famous Serbian monasteries were built. This era saw a flowering of Serbian culture, especially in religious art.

But all this was changed by the Turkish conquest. The importance of the date of conquest would be hard to overestimate. Every peasant today, even if he is illiterate, is aware of its significance. It is an interesting commentary on Serbian character that the date is preserved as a national holiday, *Vidovdan*, when the names of all those who have died in the nation's wars are read in the parish churches.

There are several reasons for the peasants' acute awareness of their national history. First, there is the *guslar*, closely akin to the wandering medieval bard of Western Europe, only the guslar chanted heroic ballads exclusively. Accompanied by his *gusle*, a single-stringed instrument played with a bow, he would travel from village to village reciting the long epic poems for which the Serbs have become famous. These ballads dealt with heroic deeds in the struggles against the Turks. The defeat at Kosovo gave rise to a

whole cycle of epic poems, and Tsar Lazar, the leader of the
Serbian troops, became a national hero. Although the wandering
guslari no longer exist, the gusle is considered the national instrument of Serbia, and many village men know how to play it. Almost
without exception, all villagers can recite parts of the ballads and
children learn them at home and in school.

Historically Kosovo was not the end of the Serbian state, for it
survived almost another seventy years, until the fall of Smederevo
in 1459, but to the Serbs it has always symbolized the loss of their
independence and the onset of Turkish rule. With the Turkish
conquest, Serbian nobility was for all practical purposes completely
eliminated as a class. These nobles either migrated to the West or
to Hungary, blended with the peasantry, or, as was particularly
true in Bosnia, accepted Islam. Yet despite the elimination of the
Serbian state and all its governmental forms, the peasantry retained
most of its traditional culture and its consciousness as a national
entity.

The epic ballads helped to achieve this, but perhaps even more
important was the role of the Church. It functioned on a local,
village level and not on the basis of a centralized hierarchy, for
all national organization was eliminated or made completely sub-
servient to the conquerers.[25] A church building, which could
easily be destroyed by the Turks, was not absolutely necessary,
while those which did exist were widely scattered throughout the
countryside. The most significant ceremonies were performed by
peasant priests at the individual village homes. Each household
had its own patron saint, presumably a survival from pre-Christian
times. The observance of the Saint's Day, or *slava*, was one of the
high points of the year and the occasion for much formalized
ritual in the home. The tradition carries over to the present, when
the home rather than the parish church is the most important
ceremonial center.

Yet an even more vital factor was the manner of Turkish rule.
The Turks were not particularly interested in proselytizing or in

[25] Around 1459 the Serbian church was incorporated in the Patriarchate of Con-
stantinople. In 1557 the Serbian Patriarchate was revived and played a great role in
preserving Serbian national consciousness, but its power was very limited as all political
control was in Turkish hands.

establishing settlements with their families. Rather, they wanted to consolidate their conquests by subduing all active resistance and extracting as much in taxes from the *rayah* as was possible.

In contrast to the obliteration of all national institutions, village organization remained intact. This is most significant in the evolution of Serbian peasant culture and comes into play on several other occasions. With the introduction of Christianity in the Balkans (through the nobility and sometimes by force) a new national Church came into being. On the village level customs from pre-Christian times remained and were blended with the new religion.

Fundamental to the preservation of local autonomy was the fact that the Turks lived in the towns while the Serbs occupied the countryside almost exclusively. Those few Serbs who lived in the towns came under strong Turkish influence. "The Serbs have no people other than peasants. The few Serbs who live in the towns are called *varošani* [town dwellers] and wear Turkish clothes and live according to Turkish customs."[26]

Serbia, known as the Pashaluk of Belgrade, was ruled by a governor or pasha who resided there. Locally there were *spahis* who, in return for rendering service as cavalry officers in time of war, had a claim to a percentage of the peasants' produce. They were the Turkish version of feudal lords and were closely analogous to holders of military fiefs in Central and Western Europe. They were very unlike Western nobility or the old Serbian aristocracy since they did not live in the countryside but congregated in the towns. And, unlike some of their Western counterparts, they possessed no titles to their lands but acted as tax collectors for the Empire, naturally taking a rather generous commission for themselves in return for their services in time of war.

As to the Church, the Turks did not insist on conversion and at times even went so far as to officially proclaim religious toleration. Though the Church was allowed a certain amount of autonomy in regulating its own affairs, the high Church offices were closely bound to the ruling Turks, and in fact they were valued chiefly for their pecuniary rewards.

[26] Karadžić, *Iz Istorije Prvog Srpskog Ustanka*, ed. by Perović, p. 38.

On the village level, there was the *seoski knez*, or village headman, chosen by his fellow villagers from among the Council of Village Elders. By common agreement he and the Council assessed the taxes among the villagers. He also exercised all police and judicial functions of a purely local nature. For a group of villages there was an *oborknez*, a district chief, who in turn was responsible to the Turkish administration, usually to a spahi.

Aside from the usual taxation in kind, the Turks' treatment of their conquered rayah took several other forms. There was a head tax, or *harač*, from which all Turks were exempt. In addition *corveé* was used to varying degrees. Besides these economic measures there was a long series of regulations designed to humble the peasantry and preserve the status of the ruling class. The peasants were forbidden to carry or possess arms, and their dress was severely regulated; anything the Turks considered beautiful or desirable they reserved for themselves. According to a contemporary account,

no Servian dared to ride into a town on horseback; he was only allowed to appear on foot. To any Turk who might demand it, he was bound to render personal service. When meeting a Turk on the road it was his duty to halt and make way for him; if he happened to carry small arms in defence he was obliged to conceal them . . . to suffer injuries was his duty; to resent them was deemed a crime worthy of punishment.[27]

From the beginning of the sixteenth century until the nineteenth century, when Serbia again became an independent state, the Turks were faced with almost constant guerrilla warfare. The occupiers took many severe repressive measures, but the Serbs never ceased harassing their conquerors. Most troublesome to the Turks were the *hajduci*, who today are legendary figures in Serbian folklore. Originally they seem to have been peasants who, like Robin Hood, took to the woods and plundered wealthy caravans and travelers. These highwaymen then turned to making surprise attacks on the Turkish soldiers, and for much of this period the Turks had all they could do to keep the main highways open. At times the hajduci even became powerful enough to take certain towns

[27] Ranke, *History of Servia*, p. 52.

and hold them for short periods. Some of them later achieved immortality in Serbian history as the leaders of the first successful revolt against the Turks early in the nineteenth century.

Their lives and deeds still live today in the epic poems of Serbia. The following extract from *Starac Vujadin* depicts the hajduke as symbols of challenge to the Turkish rulers and heroism to the Serbian people. It is translated here directly from the form in which it was chanted by an Orašac villager in 1954, accompanying himself with the lamenting, mournful strains of his gusle.[28]

> Oči moje, da ne bi gledale!
> Sve gledaste sinoć ne videste,
> Kad prodjoše Turci Lijevljani,
> Provedoše iz gore hajduke,
> Provedoše starca Vujadina,
> Vujadina sa obadva sina;
> Kad su bili prokletu Lijevnu,
> Progovara starac Vujadine,
> "Deco moja, dva rodjena sina,
> Vidite li prokleto Lijevno?
> Onde će nas biti i mučiti.
> Ne odajte krčmarice mlade,
> Kod koji smo rujno vino pili,
> Kod koji smo zimu zimovali."
> U tom reći u Lijevno stigli,
> Baciše ih nadno u tamnicu,
> Tamnovaše tri bijela dana,
> Kad četvrto jutro osvanulo,
> Izvedoše iz gore hajduke,
> Počeše ih biti i mučiti,
> Prebijati i noge i ruke.
> "Kaži, kurvo, starac Vujadine,
> Kaži, kurvo, te jatake mlade,
> Kaži, kurvo, krčmarice mlade,
> Kod kojih si rujno vino pio,
> Kod koga si blago ostavljao!"
> Prebiše mu i noge i ruke,

[28] A more complete and slightly different version is given in Karadžić, *Srpske Narodne Pesme*, III (Belgrade, 1929), 327–29.

Kad stadoše vadit' oči čarne,
A govori starac Vujadine,
"Ne ludujte, Turci Lijevljani—
Ja ne kaza za noge junačke,
I ne kaza za bijele ruke,
A da kažem za oči lažljive,
Koje su me na zlo navodile!"

Oh my eyes, that you hadn't seen
All that you saw last night,
When the Turks from Lijevno[29] passed by
Leading the hajduke down from the mountains
Leading the old man Vujadin,
Old Vujadin and both his sons.
When they neared wretched Lijevno
Old man Vujadin spoke out,
"My children, my own two sons,
Do you see the cursed Lijevno?
There they will torture and beat us.
Do not reveal the young maidens at the inn
Where we drank red wine
And where we spent the winter."
With these words, they reached Lijevno,
And the Turks threw them in a dungeon.
They remained in the dungeon for three days,
And when the fourth morning dawned
The Turks led the hajduke from the mountain
And started to beat and torture them
And break their legs and arms.
"Tell us, you scoundrel, Old Vujadin,
Tell us, scoundrel, who your young helpers are,
Tell us, scoundrel, the names of the young maidens,
Where you drank red wine,
And where you left your treasure!"
They crushed his legs and arms,
And when they began to poke out his eyes
The old man Vujadin spoke out,
"Don't be fools, you Turks of Lijevno—

[29] A Turkish fortress in Bosnia.

I didn't reveal them to spare my heroic legs,
I didn't reveal them to spare my white arms,
And I shall not reveal them to spare my treacherous eyes,
These eyes which led me to misfortune!"

CHAPTER 2

SERBIA AND ORAŠAC IN THE NINETEENTH CENTURY

VILLAGE LIFE AT THE TIME OF THE FIRST REVOLT

WE HAVE SEEN how and under what circumstances Orašac was founded, and we have examined the historical traditions of the region and the general way in which the peasants were governed by the Turks. What follows is a picture of everyday life in Orašac and in Serbian villages on the whole at the beginning of the nineteenth century,[1] to provide some background necessary for understanding the village itself and essential for examining the process of culture change.

Some folk memories of this period are still preserved, but they concentrate mainly on the part played by family members in wars and politics rather than on old customs and traditions. The Serbian peasants, like some of their counterparts in other parts of the world, are very proud of their history, and although limited literacy is fairly common, book- and newspaper-reading is not. Old men are still looked upon as the preservers of tradition and are eagerly listened to by the younger people. It is from one of these village elders, now in his mid-seventies, that we obtained an

---

[1] In this period of its history Serbia was limited in area to include little more than Šumadija, the present heartland, and the names Serbia and Šumadija can almost be taken as synonymous. For a map of the Pashaluk of Belgrade at the beginning of the nineteenth century, see Novaković, *Ustanak na Dahije, 1804.*

account of what life was like in Orašac "at the time of the First Revolt."[2]

According to tradition the present village of Orašac is not a very old settlement. It is considered that the village was first settled at most twenty to thirty years before the First Revolt. At that time it was located in a forest . . . and populated by refugees from Montenegro and other places, who brought their customs with them. This migration was caused by Turkish tyranny, and it was the only way to preserve the life of the people. The first settlers in this rolling, wooded place lived far from the main road and here found both personal and economic security. They made their homes and outbuildings of wood, cleared as much land as they needed, and used the vast forests to graze the livestock because the woods belonged to everyone. . . .

At the time of the First Revolt, in 1804, there were some twenty houses, with three to eight able-bodied men in each, plus the women and children. Men were courageous and hard-working. The head of a *zadruga*[3] was the oldest man in the household, who was obeyed unconditionally by the others. . . . Men built their own homes and other buildings and made barrels and kettles and tools of wood. Women wove colored woolen fabrics and flax, which was the material for clothing. Clothing and food were very simple. All the houses and buildings were of wood, of which they had plenty. They warmed themselves around a fire. . . . Corn bread was the main food. They had plenty of livestock because they had plenty of space. There were neither schools nor literate people, and religion was the most important thing in their lives. The religious laws were strictly observed. It was considered a sin not to forgive and not to fast on a fast day. Fast-day meals consisted of corn bread, boiled beans, potatoes, onions, vinegar, sour cabbage, and peppers. On other days cheese, *kajmak*,[4] eggs, and bacon could be eaten. Meat was for important holidays. The poor people didn't even have this. Goods were cheap but people were always short of money. Nobody stole, nobody cursed. An oath was the best guarantee and nobody dared break it.

[2] Formerly the clerk of the village Council, he had four years of schooling and had done some reading on local history; he had an exceptionally keen mind. This selection is translated from his own written account based largely on recollections of his family elders.

[3] This is an extended family group characteristic of the South Slavs, consisting of a man, his wife, and their married sons and families, sometimes including the man's brothers and their families.

[4] A loose cheese made from compressed and salted skins of scalded milk.

They were very superstitious. Some of the things they did were good and some were bad, and these matters were never discussed. To make the godfather angry was a great sin. Godfatherhood was inherited from father to son. The godfather named the children without asking the parents for their approval. Nobody asked the bride and groom if they wanted to marry—this matter was usually settled between the heads of the zadrugas. It was compulsory for everyone to go to church and confess at least once a year. All this which I have written happened at the time of the First and Second Revolts, that means before 1850.

A reasonable figure for the size of Orašac at the beginning of the nineteenth century seems to be about thirty-five households.[5] With usually at least five people per household the population of Orašac probably amounted to about two hundred, an average size for a village at that time. The whole area was thinly populated, however, and houses were spread out over a large area, giving rise to the oft-quoted statement of a Serbian peasant who, when told about the size of Vienna, replied with a lofty wave of the hand that his village was larger—*veće od Beča* (bigger than Vienna).

In view of the constant warfare and the pioneering nature of settlement in this region, little more than a primitive, largely subsistence type of economy could be expected. That is exactly what we find at this period. It is clearly reflected in the homes. In the case of the poorer peasants, these were wattle huts covered with straw or bark. The richer peasants had a one-room log cabin with dirt floor and a hearth in the center. Here all the cooking was done, and the head of the zadruga, or *starešina*, and his wife had the privilege of sleeping on the floor near the fire. Surrounding the main house were little log huts, or *vajati*. Each subsidiary nuclear family slept in its own vajat summer and winter, without any fire for warmth. In addition, there were numerous other outbuildings for storing wine and brandy, grain, dairy products, and for the various kinds of livestock. Karadjordje, leader of the First Revolt and founder of the dynasty that ruled Yugoslavia intermittently until the Second World War, lived in such a house in the village

[5] The accounts of the peasants and the local histories written by the parish priest give figures ranging from twenty to forty households, and about twenty original kin groups are known to have been in the village at the time of the First Revolt.

of Topola (about eight miles from Orašac), now a county seat but
then a village of forty houses. He was the wealthiest man in his
village and one of the most prosperous peasants in all Serbia. His
house was distinguished from the others in that the main building
was better constructed, with thick walls, and he had about ten
different types of outbuildings.[6]

In the early nineteenth century Šumadija's dense oak forests
were broken occasionally by scattered clearings of isolated homesteads surrounded by fields newly wrested from the forest. Land
was free for the taking, and a family used as much as it could
clear and cultivate. Even more important than agriculture was the
raising of livestock—sheep, goats, cattle, horses, and especially
pigs. The pigs were fed on the acorns in the forest and represented
the main source of cash income. The woods were the peasant's
greatest asset. Aside from providing grazing ground for the swine
and other animals and wood for fuel and construction, they also
offered shelter from the Turks, for in times of danger the peasants
fled to *zbegovi*, shelters hidden in the forests.

Yet the tracts of forest land do not seem to have been completely
free, for "each village had common woods where the pigs were
pastured."[7] There were also private pastures in the village, but if
a man wished to assert his ownership he had to enclose them. Outside of this all other land was free for grazing, but this freedom
appears to have been limited to the inhabitants of the individual
village; when herders from a distant area would graze their stock
on the village's land they paid for these rights "according to the
nearness to towns."[8] Apparently what we have here is a transitional
situation as far as landholding is concerned, because as the number
of settlers increased so did the enclosed land, until common land
disappeared in Šumadija.

Each household had its own herd of pigs, the poorest having at
least twenty to thirty animals and the wealthier folk from one
hundred to two hundred. Swineherds left the village in spring,

[6] Filipović, "Selo u Srbiji Krajem 18 i Početkom 19 Veka," in *Srpsko Geografsko Društvo*, special publication, No. 32, p. 83.

[7] Drobnjaković, *Smederevsko Podunavlje i Jasenica*, p. 206.

[8] Lutovac, "Privredno-Geografske Prilike i Saobraćajne Veze Srbije Prvog Ustanka," in *Srpsko Geografsko Društvo*, special publication, No. 32, p. 54.

sometimes not returning until winter, when the pigs were kept in the woods outside the village. The swineherds had their own huts there and often spent the better part of the year away from home. Frequently many members of the zadruga were engaged in this task. Occasionally pigs' feed was supplemented with corn, which the peasant brought to his herd in the woods. But acorns were most important; in fact, the standard greeting when one Šumadijan met another in the forest was, "Do you have acorns?" Some writers go so far as to claim that since the better part of a household's labor force was engaged in herding pigs, agriculture was neglected.

Although swine were the most important livestock for trade, each household also had from twenty to fifty sheep, which were chiefly for subsistence, to supply the family with wool for clothing and blankets and, to a lesser extent, with food. Each family also had a few goats and several head of cattle whose milk was converted into cheese and kajmak. In addition, most households had at least one horse and the larger zadrugas had two or three.[9]

The people of Orašac were fortunate in that nearby were the small mountains of Venčac and Bukulja (see Map 2), on whose slopes they pastured their pigs. They were not limited to this area and often went rather far afield. In the county of Tahovo there is a section of woods named after the Orašac swineherds who grazed their animals there.

Although agriculture was distinctly secondary, it was nevertheless vital to subsistence. During this period corn was the chief crop and cornbread the staple of the peasant diet. Earlier wheat had been more important, and it again became significant during the First Revolt, when it was needed by the army and so became an important cash crop. Oats and barley, rarely grown, were for the market rather than home consumption.

Hunting was of some significance, as a source of both food and clothing. The woods had bear, deer, marten, and other game which have long since become extinct in most of Šumadija.

Around each homestead was a small orchard of plum trees, and

[9] Interestingly enough, there were more horses per capita than there are now. They provided the chief means of transportation as few roads were passable with oxcarts, and they were also used for threshing.

the traditional *rakija*, plum brandy, was distilled at home. Some
of the richer peasants had vineyards for wine. Vegetable gardens
yielded kidney beans, onions, cabbage, and garlic as well as some
turnips, beets, and peas. Potatoes had only recently been introduced. There were apple, pear, peach, and cherry trees, but plums
were decidedly the most important fruit.

As for the social organization, the classic patriarchal zadruga
seems to have been most prevalent. Vuk Karadžić, the most famous
Serbian historian of the time, describes the role of the starešina as
follows:

He runs the house and decides what work is to be done and when. He
deals with the Turks and goes to the village meetings. He does the buying
and selling for the household, controls the cash, and pays the taxes. He
leads the family prayers. When there is a guest he talks with him and eats
with him in the main house, and when they have finished the other men
and then the women and children eat. The starešina is not always the
oldest one in the household. When he becomes too old he turns over the
leadership to his most intelligent brother, son, or nephew. If the starešina
proves to be an incompetent leader the household selects another.[10]

Nuclear family households were rare, and Serbian peasants
lived in zadrugas comprising as many as four or five married men
with their families. Certainly large households were necessary to
manage the herds of livestock and cultivate the crops. This was
men's work, while the women cooked, worked around the house,
and helped with the work in the fields. The schedule of women's
work was usually arranged by the *stanarica*, wife of the head of the
household, all the women of the family alternating farm work with
housework. In addition, each woman spun and wove and prepared
cloth and sewed her own husband's and children's garments.
Aside from these everyday tasks, most peasants, especially the poor
ones, built their own homes. For certain jobs specialists, such as
the coppersmith, gunsmith, wagon-maker, rope-maker, carpenter,
and tailor, were needed; some of these craftsmen were peasant
specialists in the village while others worked in the small towns.

The village Council of Elders or *kmetovi*, from among whom
was selected the village headman, was composed only of the stare-

[10] Karadžić, *Iz Istorije Prvog Srpskog Ustanka*, ed. by Perović, p. 37.

šine. The headman acted as the intermediary between the local peasants and the Turks, for collecting taxes and for other functions.

An interesting point with regard to peasant culture during this period was the extent to which it involved a cash or commercial economy. At first glance it would appear to be insignificant, in view of the lack of roads, the primitive technology, the pioneering nature of the settlement, and the recurrent wars. However, even though the economy was chiefly a subsistence one, a very small but significant amount of produce found its way into commercial channels. The chief reason for this was the large number of taxes levied by the Turks—even assuming that these peasants, like their brethren in other parts of the world, managed to avoid a good share of them. In addition to taxes, the peasant needed money to pay for the services of craftsmen and to purchase such items as salt and gunpowder. The chief item of peasant trade was lean pigs, which were exported, mainly across the Danube and the Sava to the Austrian territory of the Vojvodina. These were fed on acorns and were easier to drive than corn-fattened swine.

In addition to exports abroad, there was a certain amount of internal trade limited to peasant markets. Since there were very few towns in Šumadija at this time, fairs were often held at monasteries, which during the time of Turkish control had become traditional gathering places for the peasants on the most important religious holidays. Among the more famous of these fairs was the one held three times a year at the monastery of Trešnja on Kosmaj, not far from Orašac.

With village houses widely scattered, and the villages themselves far apart and sparsely settled, meeting friends and relatives was a big event. Family life in the village was centered almost exclusively in the home, as there were few churches, and schools and village taverns were nonexistent. The popular village diversion was to gather round the guslar or the *gajdaš* (bagpipe player) and listen to them play.

Peasants either had to travel a long way to the nearest church or have the priest come to their homesteads for special occasions such as sickness, death, and birth. If a family needed the priest they had to go and find him. This could often be very difficult since he might be out visiting other families, and it was sometimes days before he could be located. There were set fees for his services, and in addition each married mother of the household gave him a certain amount of wheat or corn called *bir*. Even so, the priest was barely able to make a living and had to do some farming himself in order to have enough for his family to live on.

The peasant household occasionally had a guest. He was always welcomed, be he priest, monk, trader, or Turk. Upon his arrival his horse was immediately stabled and fed, while he was invited into the main house to eat and drink with the starešina. If there were no rakija in the house they would send to a neighbor or however far it was necessary to obtain some. Traditions of hospitality would not permit the guest who had spent a night with his host to continue on his way until he had eaten another meal.

Orašac probably had more than its share of visitors since the first mention of the village (1784) notes the existence of an inn, which would seem to indicate that a road of some sort ran through the village. This is confirmed by several local folk histories.

THE FIRST AND SECOND REVOLTS

The First Revolt was an event in Serbian history destined to have a profound effect on the peasants of Šumadija and on all of Serbia. It was an historical turning point, the drawing to a close of almost half a millennium of Turkish rule. This was not a revolt in which intellectuals played any significant role; rather, in the tradition of European peasant rebellions, resistance broke out when conditions became so bad as to be unbearable.

> Bože mili čuda velikoga
> Kad se ćaše po zemlji Srbiji,
> Po Srbiji zemlji da prevrne
> I da druga postane sudija,
> Tu knezovi nisu radi kavzi,
> Nit' su radi Turci izjelice,
> Al' je rada sirotinja raja,
> Koja globa davati ne može,
> Ni trpiti turskoga zuluma;

I radi su božji ugodnici,
Jer je krvca iz zemlje provrela,
Zeman došo, valja vojevati,
Za krst časni krvcu proljevati,
Svako svoje da pokaje stare.[11]

Oh Lord, what a great miracle
When Serbia began to change,
A revolt in the land of the Serbs
That others should rule it.
The knezovi[12] do not want to fight,
Nor do the Turkish plunderers,
But this is a fight of the poor peasants
Who can no longer bear their burdens,
Who can no longer bear the Turks' oppression;
And the holy saints want it,
Whose blood is boiling from the earth.
The time has come to fight,
And to shed our blood for the holy cross,
And to avenge our ancestors.

Events leading to the First Revolt began with some liberal gestures by the Turks, when Suleiman III ascended the throne in 1789 as a reforming sultan, at the end of the Austro-Turkish War. Taking advantage of the treaty concluded in 1791 he excluded the Janissaries from Belgrade. Among all the troops of the Sultan, these were perhaps the most intensely hated on account of their brutality toward the peasant rayah. At the same time he sent a pasha to Belgrade, one Mustapha who was sympathetic toward the Serbs and was in fact sufficiently liked by them that he became known as *Srpska Majka* (Mother of the Serbs). He even went to the length of organizing the Serb peasants as an armed militia in order to enable them to fight the Janissaries, should the need arise. When it is realized that the disarming of the rayah was a fundamental principle of Ottoman rule, we can appreciate that this was

[11] "Početak Bune Protiv Dahija" in *Prvi Ustanak: Srpske Narodne Pesme*, ed. by Stanić, p. 3. Ballad attributed to Filip Višnjić, famous Serbian guslar. (The *dahija* were the leaders of the Janissaries.)
[12] District headmen.

a startling innovation. But this situation did not last long. In 1799, driven by his own domestic necessities, the Sultan forced Mustapha to readmit the Janissaries to the Belgrade Pashaluk.

Deeply resentful of their previous exclusion, these warriors began to avenge themselves on the rayah, openly flouted all the other Turkish officials, and in 1801 murdered Mustapha. The matter was brought to a head when the Janissaries began to murder district and village headmen. This situation as it affected the villagers of Orašac was described by one of the peasants in the following manner:

When the Janissaries gained power in the Pashaluk of Belgrade, they appointed their own men, the so-called *subashe*, in each village. The subasha for Orašac was a Turk named Ibrahim, whose han was built by the inhabitants near today's church. He had a certain number of armed men who took over village government. All their expenses were paid by the villagers. They were forced to give them as much as they (the Turks) wanted. The Turks committed many crimes of violence. For example, they forced the head of a household to lead a horse while the Turk rode it, or they made him carry a Turk's sandals. The women had to prepare meals and serve the Turks. Whoever disobeyed was killed without mercy or trial, and if a man raised a hand in defense of his home, his house was immediately set on fire, his wealth confiscated, and his wife and children were taken away and never again heard from.

The Serbs had previously appealed to the Sultan, and the uprising originally began in an attempt to right these wrongs rather than to set up an independent Serbian state. It is at this point that the village of Orašac came into its moment of brief but lasting glory in Serbian history. The leaders of the revolt chose Orašac as their meeting place for planning the uprising, and the beginning of the fight against the Turks was symbolized by the burning of Ibrahim's han. It is hard to overestimate the importance of these incidents for the whole of Serbia, and for Orašac village in particular—for the events that took place so long ago are discussed by the local peasants as if they had happened only yesterday, and every Serbian schoolchild is familiar with the name of Orašac.

The year that these observations were made in Orašac (1953–54) was that of the One Hundred and Fiftieth Anniversary of the First Revolt. Besides the celebrations and exhibitions in the capital city on February 14, the day the uprising began, a delegation headed by the President of the People's Republic of Serbia, several army generals, and other government officials visited Orašac. Speeches were delivered to a crowd of villagers in front of the local school, and later a "banquet" was held in the Cooperative Home, officially opened on this occasion. A similar type of celebration was held in 1904, the One Hundredth Anniversary; the school building in Orašac was later built specifically as a monument to the First Revolt.

There are no local written records from the 1804 uprising, and the time span of a century and a half more than suffices for the construction of a rather elaborate folklore concerning the exact events. Even so, the main developments are fairly clear. Although they may not be historically precise they serve to show the origin of Serbia as a peasant state and throw some light on the peasant culture and social organization of that period.

The first meeting was held on Archangel Michael's Day in the autumn of 1803. To disguise themselves Karadjordje and the others dressed as members of an Orašac wedding party. Later they retired to a nearby glen and made plans to prepare the people in the different parts of Serbia for the revolt. The priest from neighboring Bukovik administered an oath of secrecy, to which they swore on bread and salt. That winter, while they made plans, the Turks became increasingly oppressive, proceeding with their plan of executing the village headmen. The Turks also learned of the secret meeting in Orašac. Immediate action became imperative for the Serbs, and on February 14, 1804, the hajduci and village headmen from the surrounding villages as well as from more distant parts of the country gathered once more in Orašac, this time at the home of Marko Savić, one of the Orašac elders. Again they used a peasant wedding to mask their intentions.

Although they were acknowledged leaders, all those present were peasants. Among them were leading peasant merchants, particularly useful since in the course of their activities they acquired guns and ammunition from Austria. According to various estimates the group included from sixty to eighty armed men.[13]

Now that they had decided to revolt, one problem remained—choosing a leader. Several men were proposed, including Teodosije Maričević, the rich trader from Orašac, but they all declined, claiming they lacked the ability. Then Teodosije proposed Karadjordje. At first he too refused, saying that he was an impulsive man and would punish injustice by death. At this the men cried, "We want exactly such a man!" The priest once more administered the oath. They began the revolt at once by burning down the han. Then couriers were sent out from the village with the message, "Each of you kill the subasha in your village, and send your women and children to hiding places in the woods!" According to the heroic ballad,

> Kad to čule srpske poglavice,
> Namah oni poslušaše Djordja:
> Svi skočiše na noge lagane,
> Pripasaše svijetlo oružje,
> Svaki svoga ubiše subašu,
> Žene, djecu u zbjeg odvedoše.

> When the Serbian headmen heard this
> They obeyed [Kara] Djordje,
> Jumped to their nimble feet,
> And buckled on their gleaming weapons.
> Each killed his village subasha,
> And women and children were sent to the woods.

What happened to the Turks in Orašac? There are several versions of the story. The one commonly accepted by the villagers is that they were warned by the widow Ana, with the pre-arranged signal of a golden apple, and fled in time. She is supposed to have lived with one of them, and because of this the family which bears her name (Anić) is considered by some to have a rather shady reputation in the village today.

The revolt thus begun was very successful at first, since most of the Turks were taken by surprise. The Serbs were also aided by

[13] This account is based on local tradition and a number of published sources.

the fact that from 1806 to 1809 Turkey was engaged in a war with Russia. Later, however, the tide began to turn; in 1812, when the Russians, who had become allies of the Serbs, were faced with an invasion by Napoleon, they hastily concluded peace with the Ottoman Empire and left the Serbs to the Turks' mercy.

The following year Karadjordje, it seems, buckled under the strain and fled across the Danube. The Turks began to avenge themselves on the peasantry in their traditional manner, and on Palm Sunday, 1815, another revolt broke out in Šumadija. This Second Revolt was under the leadership of Miloš Obrenović, who, like Karadjordje, was a wealthy trader. Unlike Karadjordje, he also had considerable skill as a diplomat as well as a fighter. In 1817 he was formally elected by the headmen as their leader. Karadjordje picked this inopportune moment to return to Serbia, and he was promptly murdered by Miloš, who at this time was conducting negotiations with the Sultan. In the same year Miloš became Prince of Serbia, and in 1830 the Sultan designated him hereditary Prince.

So began the conflicts between the Karadjordjević and Obrenović dynasties which ended only in 1903, with the murder of the last Obrenović king. In 1817 Miloš also concluded an agreement with the Sultan whereby the Pashaluk of Belgrade attained a degree of autonomy. In 1830 Turkey allowed the Serbs to assume completely their own internal administration; Turkish landlords sold their holdings and their troops were confined to a few special garrisons. Not until 1867 were all Turkish troops finally withdrawn from Serbia, and in 1882 Serbia was officially proclaimed an independent kingdom.

THE ESTABLISHMENT OF THE SERBIAN STATE
AND ITS IMPACT ON THE PEASANTRY

With the successful completion of the revolt against the Turks and the establishment of a national government in Serbia, the life of the villager began to change in many ways. Miloš Obrenović, like his predecessor Karadjordje, was a successful livestock trader who had grown up under the Turks, and his government clearly reflected this background. Although both the First and the Second

Revolts were organized and carried out by peasants, once a formal government became established its leaders went to live in the towns. They also inevitably began to develop interests which were at least in part directly opposed to those of the mass of the peasantry.

In Serbia there was no native middle or upper class. The people had little contact with the outside world; they knew only of the Turks who had ruled them for so long and something of the Austrian Empire to the north. Even in the First Revolt the separation of the peasant leaders from the other peasants became evident —familiar only with Turkish traditions of government, they saw nothing wrong in enriching themselves, often at the expense of the poorer peasants. When Karadjordje began to replace local headmen with chiefs of his own choosing, this separation became formalized.

Under Miloš both these processes were greatly developed and expanded. After peace with the Turks was established, one of Miloš's first acts in 1817 was to replace the village leaders with his own appointees.[14] This affected the peasants directly and was very much opposed by them.

This was only one side of the character of the new government, however, for to paraphrase a common expression, the first business of this government was private business. Miloš, keen livestock trader that he was, became the richest man in Serbia during his reign. According to some writers, during his rule it was hard to differentiate the state enterprises from the private enterprises of the head of the state.

These traders and merchants, most of whom had grown up in the villages, came to look upon the peasant as someone from whom they could profit. The first of many conflicts between the town merchants and the peasants came about shortly after the Second Revolt, when some of the peasants began to open their own crafts shops in the villages. As early as 1818 Miloš issued an edict against them, but as a result of peasant appeals he vacillated in this policy; he finally solved the problem in the 1830s by allowing peasant shops to open but imposing a large tax on them. Conflict was

[14] T. Djordjević, *Iz Srbije Kneza Miloša*, p. 270.

destined to increase as the peasants began more and more to participate in a money economy.

It would be a mistake to assume that as a result of Miloš's autocratic rule he was uniformly hated by the peasants and that he always sided with the merchants against them. In addition to his desire to amass wealth, he was also a clever politician and clearly realized that the basis of his power lay not with the new townsfolk and bureaucrats but with the peasantry. A most important reason why peasant opposition to Miloš never became significant, despite his many decrees, was that in the most basic question of all, that of land tenure, early in his rule he proclaimed the principle that "the land belongs to those who till it." Considering their historical traditions, it does not seem that it could have been otherwise.[15] In 1833 the spahis were officially eliminated as land owners, and thus established, Serbia continued as a nation of peasant small holders until the Second World War.

No sooner had villagers officially become the owners of their land than their ownership was threatened by another factor, peasant indebtedness. Villagers needed money to buy goods and especially to pay taxes. Not having a ready supply of cash on hand, the peasant was forced to go to the local merchants to borrow at high rates of interest. The merchants probably took advantage of his illiteracy, so that once indebted it was very hard for the peasant to sever the bond of dependency. In 1836 Miloš established a protected minimum homestead, consisting of a house, a small amount of land, two oxen, and a cow, which could not be confiscated for debts. In later years this concept was often revised and enlarged as peasants' debts continued to be one of the crucial problems of Serbia until well into the twentieth century.

Despite the emergence of traders and a centrally controlled bureaucracy, Serbia continued to be a peasant state with strong Turkish influences. Prince Miloš himself slept on the floor until 1834, and at that time he was the only one in the country to own a carriage. Tables and other Western urban household furnishings were unknown, as was Western dress, for the city people dressed in Turkish-type clothing. Churches were rare, and although a few

[15] Tomasevich, *Peasants, Politics, and Economic Change in Yugoslavia*, p. 38.

schools were established the great majority of the population, including Miloš, was illiterate. At this time (1834) only 6.5 percent of the total population lived in the towns.[16]

While Miloš was a rather arbitrary autocrat, his rule ushered in a welcome period of peace and stability. The country began to develop economically and the standard of living of the peasants began to rise, very slowly but steadily. One of the clearest evidences of this new stability was the growth in population, which increased from 700,000 in 1829 to 1,200,000 in 1839. In the Jasenica region the most intensive settlement occurred from 1809 through 1815; unfortunately we have no figures for this period, but during Miloš's reign and the period immediately thereafter the size of Orašac more than doubled, increasing from forty-seven households in 1818 to one hundred in 1846.[17]

As a result of the population increase, free land was occupied, and in 1839, during the reign of Aleksandar Karadjordjević (son of Karadjordje), the boundaries of land were established and formally divided into private, village, and government sectors. This also marked the end of most immigration to the area. All later settlers had to obtain their land from the government or purchase it from earlier settlers. This formal enclosure of the land, at about the midcentury, marked the turning point of Šumadija from a pioneer area into the heart of a growing national state.

In the second half of the nineteenth century commerce increased, the railroad came through, some villages became towns, schools and churches began to appear in the villages, and the peasant personally began to learn of the world outside his village as a result of compulsory army service. At the same time, increasing numbers of peasants left the village permanently to seek their fortune in the expanding towns, as the ensuing decades saw the transformation of Serbia from a Turkish province into a European state.

[16] Protić, *Razvitak Industrije i Promet Dobara u Srbiji za Vreme Prve Vlade Kneza Miloša*, p. 10.
[17] Drobnjaković, *Jasenica*, p. 230.

CHAPTER 3

ORAŠAC VILLAGE TODAY

THE VILLAGE, THE MARKET TOWN, AND THE COUNTY
ACCORDING TO local tradition the name Orašac, from *orah*, walnut, derives from a grove of walnut trees which in earlier times stood near the site of the present graveyard. The village spreads over an area of some 2,264 hectares (about eight and a half square miles) and is located approximately sixty miles south of Belgrade by road or rail. The train trip takes over five hours, since a standard gauge track from the capital runs only to Mladenovac. From there it is necessary to switch to a narrow gauge line which meanders through fields and woodlots to Arandjelovac, get off at the station for Kopljare or Vrbica villages, and hike in to Orašac (Map 3). A trip by bus is shorter, following the Belgrade–Kragujevac highway past Mladenovac to the turn-off for a "second-class" dirt road which runs through Orašac. The road is not always useable, and because of its unreliability and the shortage of motor transport, the railway is the main line of communication for both people and goods.

Attractive vistas open up as the road curves around Orašac. North of the village, some fifteen miles away, Mount Kosmaj looms prominently on the horizon. Mount Venčac, with its rounded twin humps, is to the south, and beyond, still further south, is the Rudnik massif. Evergreen-clad Mount Bukulja, just five miles southwest of Orašac, cannot be seen from the road, for Preseka

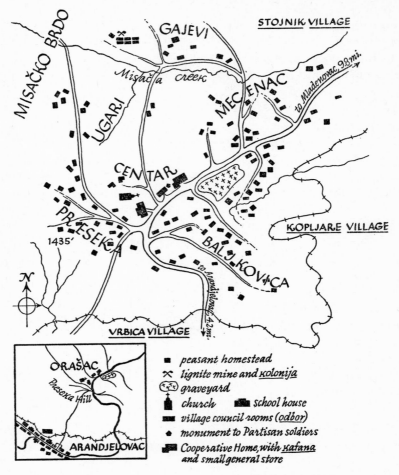

Map 3. Orašac, Showing Scattered Settlement Pattern,
Centar (*Center of the Village*) and Neighboring Villages

Hill, rising directly behind the stone schoolhouse, blocks it from view.

At the so-called center of the village, the school, church, village council rooms, and the Cooperative Home all hug one side of the bend in the road. A few cottages are nearby, and scattered homesteads, many of them a good hour's walk from the road, are reached by a network of lanes and footpaths.[1] The paths are used all year around, although wet weather churns them into practically impassable courses of famous sticky village mud.

In spite of the extremely dispersed settlement pattern, it is interesting that buildings for formal governmental and religious and some social functions are clustered in one place. On his weekly market trip almost every villager passes by the center and frequently stops in at the *kafana* for a glass of plum brandy or pauses to exchange pleasantries with the priest or the men at the village offices. Business or ceremonial errands—paying taxes, buying or selling produce at the Cooperative, a meeting at the Cooperative Home, a christening or a funeral at the church—bring Orašani to the center of the village. Few people attend church on Sundays, but often some of the older men congregate in the sun in front of the tavern to smoke and discuss the weather, crops, and local gossip. Sometimes late on Sunday afternoons there are *kolo* dances to the accompaniment of accordion and flute, and occasionally the same square of packed earth between the church and the priest's house serves as a *futbal* (soccer) field for village youths. In the autumn, almost every Sunday the church is the scene of several gala, shouting wedding parties. Yet with all this, the center of the village is merely the area where most village institutions happen to be located and serves as a convenient meeting-place; by far the most important place for the individual villager is his own homestead.

With the village only four miles from its market town, it may seem strange that Orašac should have such a relatively independent and flourishing life of its own and not have become a satellite of its larger neighbor. Orašac does not border directly on Arandjelovac; unlike Bukovik, it has avoided becoming a suburb providing homes for the increasing labor force in Arandjelovac's new factories. Also, the few miles become considerably longer when we consider the fact that Arandjelovac is strung out along a narrow valley with Orašac located above and beyond in the surrounding

---

[1] Gajevi, the most distant neighborhood in the village, is a sort of subsidiary center with its own one-room school. There is also a small graveyard, and near Gajevi is the local lignite mine with its administrative building and workers' houses.

upland. The winding, uphill return trip to the village by a lumbering cow-drawn wagon often takes two hours.

In one important respect, trade and commerce, Orašac is almost entirely dependent on the town. There is a Cooperative store in the village, but it is not very well stocked. Further, the Cooperative purchases only a relatively small proportion of the peasants' marketable goods. This is partly by design rather than through inefficiency, for the village store was established only after the last war, and it is not easy to compete with the variety which the town has to offer or to break long-established habits. Orašac is also completely dependent upon Arandjelovac for communication with the rest of Serbia. There is no telephone or telegraph in the village, and mail is fetched from the town post office two or three times a week.

Cultural, social, and economic conditions are relatively uniform throughout Šumadija, but even on the county or local level there are differences among villages which are worth mentioning if we are to understand the extent to which Orašac may be taken as representative. In most of its basic features Orašac is not readily differentiated from its neighbors. With them it shares the pattern of dispersed settlement, each house surrounded by its outbuildings and orchard.[2] Culturally, too, the differences within the county are practically negligible, although between neighboring counties there are minor variations in language, dress, and the details of certain customary observances.

Perhaps the major atypical feature of Orašac itself is its lignite mine. Except for the period immediately after the Second World War, when ethnic Germans from the Vojvodina were brought in briefly, the mine has been operated by local peasants who continued to till their land and live in the traditional way.

POPULATION AND VITAL STATISTICS

In 1953 Orašac village had a population of 2,182 living in 480 households. The population statistics given in Table 1 clearly show the increase that has occurred since the first record of Orašac in

[2] This is, in fact, a common pattern throughout much of the western part of the Balkan Peninsula, but as soil in this region is fairly fertile, villages here are more closely grouped than those in marginal regions where livestock raising is of greater importance.

1784. Until 1844 no figures for the total population are available. Since all earlier figures were gathered exclusively for tax purposes, they should be accepted with some caution. It is only in 1866 that there are the beginnings of a regular census. The population has

Table 1. Population Growth in Orašac, 1784–1953

Year	Number of Households	Percent Increase over Previous Census	Total Population	Percent Increase over Previous Census
1784	15	. . .	. . .	. . .
1804	30	100.0	. . .	. . .
1818	47	56.7	130[a]	. . .
1819	51	8.5	158[a]	. . .
1822	54	5.9	174[a]	. . .
1844	100	85.2	833	. . .
1866	142	42.0	1,185	42.3
1874	159	12.0	1,212	2.8
1884	188	8.9	1,320	18.2
1890	214	13.8	1,469	11.3
1895	225	5.1	1,538	5.0
1900	248	10.2	1,628	5.9
1905	278	12.1	1,835	12.7
1910	293	5.4	1,949	6.2
1921	282	−3.7	1,570	−19.4
1931	344	22.0	1,894	20.6
1948	496	44.2	2,234	17.9
1953	480	−3.2	2,182	−2.3

Sources: Serbian Statistical Bureau; Drobnjaković, *Jasenica*, p. 230; Gavrilović, *Rečnik Geografsko-Statistiki Srbije*, p. 185; M. Petrović, *Financije i Ustanove Obnovljene Srbije do 1842*, II, 541.

[a] All males between ages 7 and 80, based on head tax records.

been constantly increasing except for the period immediately after the First World War, in 1921, and again in 1953. The first decrease was a direct result of a long period of war and accompanying epidemics.[3] There were at least sixty deaths in the village directly attributable to the Second World War. No census was taken in 1941 because of the war, leaving a seventeen-year gap (1931–48) for which there are unfortunately no records. Increases in both the total population and the number of households have followed the erratic pattern indicated in Table 1. The greatest increase

[3] There was a severe influenza epidemic in the village at this time. The 1953 decrease was the result of the departure of several hundred Germans who had worked at the mine.

came in the period between 1844 and 1866,[4] and the second great-est increase from 1921 to 1931. The percentage increases are not strictly comparable, of course, because of the gaps in the available data; the table does serve to indicate the general pattern of Orašac population growth.

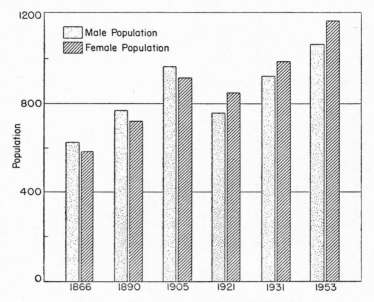

Figure 1. Sex Ratio of Orašac Population
for Census Years 1866–1953

Source: Serbian Statistical Bureau.

There has always been a larger number of men than women leaving to seek a livelihood outside the village. This plus war losses would seem to explain the sex ratio after 1921, as shown in Figure 1.

Despite the fact that the population of Orašac has shown a steady increase for over a century and a half, the factors causing that increase have been quite different in the nineteenth century as opposed to the twentieth. In the early part of the nineteenth

[4] Historical data seems to indicate that in the first few decades of the nineteenth century population growth was even greater because of the heavy influx of settlers at that time.

century increases were primarily due to large scale immigration to Orašac from other regions, while in the latter part of that century most of the increase can be attributed to a high birth rate. Since 1900 the population has continued to increase in spite of a declining birth rate and emigration from the village. It is due largely to the declining death rate. Births per 1,000 population have declined from 39.5 for the period 1884–95 to 24.5 for the period 1948–53. The death rate for the same period, however, has declined by almost 50 percent, from 22 to 11.6. This is not sufficient to offset

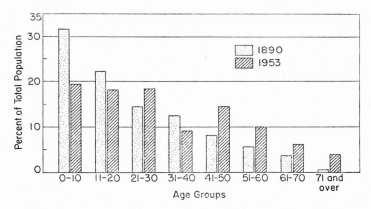

Figure 2. Percentage Distribution of Orašac Population by Age Groups, 1890 and 1953

Sources: Serbian Statistical Bureau and *Statistika Kraljevine Srbije*, I, 272–75.

the decrease in the birth rate, so that the rate of natural increase has dropped from 17 to 13.

The decrease in the death rate has resulted in a change in age structure of the population, with larger percentages now found in the over forty-one group and smaller numbers proportionately in the under twenty category. The extent of these changes is shown by comparing the age composition of the Orašac population in 1890 and 1953 (Figure 2).

Comparing death statistics, the most dramatic change is in infant mortality. Infant deaths (one year and under) accounted for 43 per-

Table 2. Annual Births and Deaths in Orašac, 1881–1953

Year	Births	Deaths	Year	Births	Deaths
1881	58	30	1918	23	66[b]
1882	53	22	1919	33	38
1883	55	20	1920	68	21
1884	55	28	1921	68	33
1885	55	21	1922	62	32
1886	44	30	1923	71	28
1887	62	25	1924	61	23
1888	54	28	1925	72	15
1889	63	30	1926	69	32
1890	60	36	1927	62	22
1891	66	37	1928	60	30
1892	41	49	1929	61	41
1893	64	47	1930	56	23
1894	65	25	1931	49	23
1895	58	26	1932	47	29
1896	78	49	1933	60	25
1897	45	29	1934	44	34
1898	46	19	1935	33	32
1899	61	43	1936	31	27
1900	70	32	1937	51	33
1901	74	20	1938	48	29
1902	57	29	1939	33	37
1903	78	26	1940	45	36
1904	60	40	1941	49	22[c]
1905	57	39	1942	21	28[c]
1906	74	47	1943	37	30[c]
1907	73	44	1944	30	34[c]
1908	55	47	1945	29	21[c]
1909	67	45	1946	51	36
1910	79	36	1947	43	20
1911	59	30	1948	41	34
1912	50	27	1949	46	23
1913	34	47	1950	73[d]	23
1914	49	90	1951	52[d]	27
1915	28	153[a]	1952	68[d]	27
1916	20	26	1953	43[d]	18
1917	14	17			

Source: Records of Orašac Village Council.
[a] Typhus epidemic.
[b] Influenza epidemic.
[c] For the Second World War period an additional 50 deaths are estimated.
[d] Includes a total of 16 births in the hospital in Arandjelovac.

cent of the total deaths in 1881–82; they only made up 26 percent of the deaths in 1951–52. Interestingly enough, although deaths of persons over sixty-one accounted for only 11 percent of the total in the earlier two-year period, that group represented the majority of deaths, over 57 percent, in 1951–52, because of the increased numbers of older people in the 1950s.

A record of village births and deaths from 1881 to 1953 is presented in Table 2. In essence these data represent a local Serbian example of a general European trend of declining birth and death rates.

POPULATION COMPARISONS

Orašac, with its population of 2,182, is one of the larger villages in the area, exceeded in size in 1953 by only four of the nineteen other villages that make up Orašac County. The range in village size is considerable, varying from 1,035 for Jelovik village to 3,614 for Venčani. There has also been much variation in rate of growth of the various villages. The greatest increase has occurred in the *varoš* (market town), the county seat of Arandjelovac, where the population more than tripled between 1890 and 1953, increasing by a third in the period between 1948 and 1953 alone. By contrast, Orašac increased only a little over 51 percent in the past sixty-three years.

Many changes which have occurred in Orašac village are closely analogous to those which have taken place throughout Serbia as well as all of Yugoslavia.[5] This is particularly true of the decline in birth and death rates and infant mortality. The birth rate was about 40 per 1,000 up to First World War, with that of Orašac between 38 and 40 during that period. In 1950 the national rate was 30, although the 1948–53 average for Orašac was only 24. Orašac's death rate of 27 per 1,000 in 1890–94 was below the national average of 30 per 1,000 for the same period. The death rate today follows a similar pattern; the national average for 1948–52 is 13 deaths per 1,000 while the Orašac average is 11 for approximately the same period.[6]

The growth of Orašac has paralleled the population increases in Šumadija, the latter having increased from 62,800 in 1834 to 147,077 in 1884 and to 248,300 in 1950.[7] For Orašac, there is no

[5] As Yugoslavia did not exist as a national state prior to the end of First World War, all figures preceding this period are based on composite estimates.

[6] Myers and Campbell, *The Population of Yugoslavia*, pp. 3, 18, 24.

[7] *Stanovništvo Narodne Republike Srbije od 1834–1953*, pp. 22, 42.

record of the population in 1834, but in the period 1884 to 1950 the village population increased from 1,320 to 2,234, representing an identical rate of 69 percent for both Šumadija and the village. It should be remembered, however, that the towns in Šumadija have increased at a much faster rate than the villages.

NATIONALITY COMPOSITION

Until the Second World War there were virtually no non-Orthodox Serbs in Orašac. The census of 1890 listed but three non-Serbs out of a total population of 1,436, and only twelve men were not born in the village. In 1921 all of the 1,570 village inhabitants were listed as Orthodox Serbs. The whole county, including Arandjelovac, was only slightly less homogeneous at that time.[8]

This situation changed considerably for a brief period after the Second World War. The large influx of German miners has already been mentioned. In 1948 they and their families numbered 220, or almost 10 percent of the total village population of 2,234, and there were 23 other non-Serbs in the village at this time. But by 1953 only 36 of the Germans remained; the other 31 non-Serbs included 19 Slovenes and a few Croats and Montenegrins. Almost all of them worked at the mine and lived nearby with their families at the *kolonija*, in houses built by the government. Their contact with the villagers is quite limited. The only exceptions are two Croat clerks at the local Cooperative store and their families, and the village priest, who is from Montenegro, and his family. At the time of this study less than 4 percent of the population was not of Serbian extraction, so that with the exception of the brief period after 1948, the Orašac population has remained extremely homogeneous.

PHYSICAL TYPE

In view of this fact one cannot help wondering whether there are any physical characteristics which distinguish these people from other ethnic groups in Yugoslavia or from peoples in other parts

---

[8] In 1890 only 0.5 percent of the total population of Jasenica County (22,108) was composed of non-Serbs, and in 1921 only 54 out of 36,097 were non-Serbs, less than 0.2 percent. In the same year in the whole of the District of Kragujevac, which included almost all the southern part of Šumadija, the percentage was 0.3 percent.

of the Balkans. As might be expected, there is considerable variation in an area which has seen so many migrations and been subject to many diverse cultures. Defining these differences precisely
is another matter. The Serbs were at one time thought to belong
to the so-called Dinaric subdivision of the white race. According
to Carleton Coon, the Serbs (as well as the Croats) have an average
stature of 5 feet 7 inches and a cephalic index of 85. Serbs are
darker, 45 percent with pure brown eyes and only 20 percent with
light; 10 percent has light hair while more than 50 percent has
either black or very dark brown hair.[9] Personal observations, however, in general confirm Coon's statements concerning hair and
eye color and complexion. Although the author made no systematic
observations of physical type, it did seem that in the Jasenica area
of Šumadija the percentage of blonds was higher and blue-eyed
brunettes were quite common. Stature was also variable, with
tall males (over 5 feet 9 inches) not uncommon. This is not too
surprising when we recall that little more than a century and a
half separates many of these people from their Montenegrin ancestors, considered to be the tallest people in Europe.

LANGUAGE

The people of Orašac speak the *Štokavština* variety of the Serbo-
Croatian language. This in turn is broken down into three sub-
areas, and most Serbs, including those from Orašac, speak the
dialect known as *Ekavština*.[10] Although there are some differences
between the speech of the villagers and literary Serbian they are
relatively minor. This is due in no small measure to the fact that
modern literary Serbian owes its development largely to the efforts
of Vuk Karadžić, who, early in the nineteenth century, compiled
the first Serbian dictionary using the language as it was actually
spoken in the villages. Previously all writing had been in Serbian
Church Slavonic.

A few of the distinctions between the speech of the villagers and
that of the more educated townsfolk are, however, worth mentioning. In literary Serbian both the first and second syllables of certain

[9] Coon, "Racial History," in *Yugoslavia*, ed. by Kerner, p. 28.
[10] Noyes, "The Serbo-Croatian Language," in *Yugoslavia*, ed. by Kerner, p. 289.

words are usually given equal stress, while in the village one syllable is strongly accented. There is also a tendency to substitute *v* for *f*, as in *vamilija* and *ovicir*. An important difference is the universal use of the informal *Ti* form. Almost without exception *Vi* is used in the village only as the plural pronoun.

CHAPTER 4

MAKING A LIVING

THE AGRICULTURAL POPULATION

TODAY THE PEOPLE of Orašac, like the majority of their countrymen throughout Yugoslavia, depend on the land for their living. Theirs are small farms producing chiefly for their own needs, although in areas such as Orašac they have been marketing at least a portion of their produce for some time. We have seen how, at the time of the Turkish conquest, Serbia was a land made up almost entirely of peasants and how, as a result of economic development in the nineteenth and twentieth centuries, the proportion of peasants in the total population has slowly decreased. It should be made clear here that rural or village inhabitants are not synonymous with the agricultural and livestock-raising population, nor is urban population synonymous with nonagricultural population. The agricultural population is, however, almost synonymous with the private-land-owning population.[1]

In 1948, 84 percent of Orašac County was directly dependent on agriculture. Table 3 summarizes the situation for the twenty-one communities in the county. In Orašac and Misača villages, where small-scale mining enters the picture, the percentage of the agricultural population is under 80. Except for Arandjelovac and Bukovik nearly or well over 90 percent of the populations of the other villages are agricultural. Within the town itself 6 percent of the people are engaged in agriculture. By 1953 the percentage of

---

[1] For 1948 the number of landless agricultural laborers is insignificant in Orašac (16, or 0.4 percent of the total population).

MAKING A LIVING

Table 3. Agricultural Population of Orašac County, by Villages, 1948

		AGRICULTURAL POPULATION	
VILLAGE	TOTAL POPULATION	Number	Percent
Arandjelovac	4,278	244	5.7
Banja	1,924	1,659	86.2
Blaznava	1,335	1,307	97.9
Bosuta	1,358	1,347	99.2
Brezovac	1,375	1,230	89.5
Bukovik	1,532	1,179	77.0
Donja Šatornja	1,065	980	92.0
Garaši	1,254	1,191	95.0
Gornja Trešnjevica	1,546	1,492	96.5
Gornja Šatornja	1,331	1,297	97.4
Jarmenovci	1,754	1,557	88.8
Jelovik	1,031	993	96.3
Kopljare	1,364	1,254	91.9
Misača	1,299	1,031	79.4
ORAŠAC	2,234	1,729	77.4
Partizani	3,229	2,689	83.3
Ranilović	2,039	1,975	96.9
Stojnik	1,736	1,630	93.9
Venčani	3,503	3,345	95.5
Vrbica	1,854	1,634	88.1
Vukosavci	1,028	965	93.9

Source: Orašac County Statistical Bureau.

the agricultural population decreased slightly, a decline less than that in Yugoslavia as a whole where population in agriculture dropped from 71 percent in 1948 to 61 percent in 1953.[2] In spite of the decrease these statistics show that Yugoslavia is one of the most agricultural countries in Europe, so that in describing agriculture in Orašac we are also presenting the manner in which the overwhelming majority of Yugoslavs make their living.

SOIL, LAND, AND VEGETATION

The basis of the soils in the Jasenica region are Neocene sediments deposited by the Pannonian Lake, altered by geological, hydrographic, and vegetation changes.[3] The most fertile soil in the area, fine river mud, is not found in Orašac. Chernozem soils (*smonice*), the second most fertile type, are widespread in the village. Although

[2] Myers and Campbell, *The Population of Yugoslavia*, p. 81.
[3] See Lutovac, *Privredno-Geografska Karakteristika Sliva Jasenice*, p. 8, for a discussion of soil types in the Jasenica basin.

rich in humus they are underlain with a layer abundant in lime, which the peasants claim is difficult to plow. Another rich soil occurring commonly is the chestnut-brown (*gajnjača*) type. The potential fertility of the chernozems and chestnut-browns is high, but actual productivity is often reduced by insufficient soil moisture. Despite this and the lack of modern soil conservation methods, the soils in and around Orašac, on the level and gently rolling areas, may be considered fairly fertile.

Steep hills are uncommon in Orašac. Gently sloping ones are the rule, with level land at a premium, and consequently much of the cultivated land is on the sides of these hills. During the annual thaw and the rainy months of May, June, and October considerable erosion occurs, forming unchecked gullies which constantly increase in size. The only truly level land in Orašac is along Misača Creek. Flooded by rains and poorly drained, it is swampy most of the year and used only for pasture.

Willow trees are common here, as well as scattered alder, aspen, and ash. On the hillsides are patches of ash and linden with fragments of the original oak cover. In higher places hazel and beech are seen, although no point in Orašac is high enough to support the evergreens found on neighboring Mount Bukulja. More important than these occasional clumps are the acacia trees so characteristic of every photograph and painting of the region. They mark property boundaries, help to some extent to prevent erosion, and provide the peasant with a source of wood.[4]

LIVESTOCK

Before moving on to a detailed discussion of agriculture in Orašac we will consider the passing of hunting as an occupation, the decline of livestock breeding, and typical livestock holdings today. Since there are no sizeable streams near Orašac there is no fishing, although in the Jasenica River and in other parts of Šumadija there is local trout-fishing. Hunting decreased as the virgin forest disappeared, although at the time of the First Revolt and well into the nineteenth century it was a fairly important supplement to the

---

[4] Acacias are planted and cut after about five years. This wood only partially supplies the peasants' fuel needs, and the leaves are used as winter feed for the sheep.

two main economies. Today it is almost entirely a sport with practically no economic significance. In fact, the only profit one can derive is the occasional bounty received for a wolf; the 6,000 dinar reward is rarely made because wolves are today uncommon in the region.

The decline in hunting has not been due entirely to "natural" geographic factors such as the cutting down of the woods. Government regulation has also played a part. A little over forty years ago every householder owned a rifle. About the turn of the century the Serbian government began to require permits for guns, and later, during the First World War, invading German armies confiscated many of them. Now one must pay a 1,200 dinar fee for a permit to hunt during the proper season, and as a result in 1954 only thirty-six men in the whole village took out hunting licenses, less than one man in every ten households. Those who do hunt concentrate mostly on rabbits and foxes, eating the former and selling the fox skins.

The basis of the economy remains today as it had been originally in neolithic times, a mixture of agriculture and livestock breeding. Although these two economies have continued to exist side by side, the past century has brought changes to the relative importance of each. At the time of the First Revolt livestock breeding was distinctly primary and the source of the major part of the peasants' cash income, with agriculture used only for subsistence. Today the situation is reversed. Livestock breeding is still important, but one of the two main crops, corn, is raised to be used as fodder, and the animals are fed by-products of agriculture— corn husks and stalks, hay, and bean vines—since the amount of pasture land has been much reduced.

The change in Orašac closely paralleled that which took place in Serbia in general. Toward the end of the nineteenth century a marked drop in per capita livestock holdings occurred, with a gradual decrease in livestock numbers on down to the present. Bulls and oxen have become almost extinct in the village, dwindling from 260 in 1866 to only 30 today. On the other hand, after a slight decline the number of horses has started to increase again, so that horses per capita are almost the same as they were in 1866.

Relative to the increasing population there are only about half as many cows per capita in 1953 as there were in 1866 and less than one third as many sheep and swine.

The changes which have occurred and the contemporary significance of livestock breeding are best examined by considering each type of livestock separately, since the ecological and economic factors vary. Vuk Karadžić and other writers describing economic conditions in Šumadija in the early nineteenth century mention that most households had at least one and often two or more horses. They were essential at that time for transporting goods and people, since there were no roads, and for threshing and plowing as well. Today, however, possessing a horse is usually limited to those households which have between 5 and 10 hectares of arable land, for with the decreasing size of peasant landholdings feeding horses has become a problem (oats and barley are grown only on the larger holdings). Horses are also less necessary since the introduction of mechanical threshers. To own a horse is today a sign of wealth and luxury, for although used for plowing and drawing wagons, the horse serves an even more important function in the eyes of the owner. It is something to show off, to brush and to decorate with fancy bridle, bells, and streamers, to ride on to a wedding or other celebration, so that all the world can see. The horse may be hitched to a *čeze* (an open shay) for going to the market in style or to a *fijaker* (fiacre) borrowed for the most festive occasions.

Replacing the glamorous horse is the prosaic cow, now economically the most important livestock. Cows are today used for plowing and harrowing, for hauling wagons, for milking, and occasionally for meat. They also bring a very good price on the market. Of all the livestock, excluding horses, they have suffered the smallest percentage decline. Oxen were formerly used for plowing, with two yokes often needed to break the hard chernozem soil with the primitive wooden plow. With the introduction of the metal plowshare at about the turn of the century, combined with the decreasing amount of pasture land and feed, oxen gradually were replaced by cows until today they are quite rare. From the time when each household had at least two cows, today this is true for only one third of the households in the Jasenica region, while one third has only one and another third has neither cattle nor horses.[5]

Swine have had the greatest decline of all. As we have already seen, they were formerly the most important livestock, fattened on the acorns in the then-abundant oak forests. Then, as the forest disappeared, the number of pigs decreased drastically. In the latter part of the nineteenth century it was not uncommon for a household to have 30 to 50 swine, while today the wealthier households and larger zadrugas have from 10 to 20 and the general village average is from two to four. Swine are grazed in the summer, fed the residue from the plums after brandy has been made and the grape skins left over from wine-making. Corn has replaced acorns as the main feed. Most households carefully heat up kitchen slops in the winter before feeding it to their pigs. Swine are still of considerable importance, providing the household with lard, grease for soap-making, and dried meat, one of the winter staples. They are also roasted on special feast days. In addition, pigs are marketed in relative quantity, for with the coming of the railroad both lean and fattened ones could be sold to other markets. In absolute numbers there are fewer pigs to be marketed, but they are of greater value per head.

After swine, sheep experienced the largest percentage decline, for as the amount of land brought under cultivation was increased there was naturally less room for grazing. Sixty years ago a large zadruga in Orašac had about 40 sheep, whereas today, although one zadruga has 30, the average is three to six to a household. Unlike cattle and swine, sheep are kept almost exclusively for home consumption. Their chief value is in their wool, providing most of the material for clothing needs. Sometimes their milk is used, and they, too, may be roasted on important holidays. It would seem that their numbers will decrease still further as the price of manufactured woolen goods slowly continues to go down relative to the peasants' income.

Goats were never important in this area and, because they did not require pasture, were usually kept only by the poorest families.

[5] Lutovac, *Privredno-Geografska Karakteristika Sliva Jasenice*, p. 45.

They were injurious to the remaining woods and have recently been prohibited by law, so that today their numbers are negligible.

Poultry (including chickens, turkeys, ducks, and geese) were formerly raised for home consumption only. They have become increasingly significant as an item of trade as their numbers have multiplied. Most families occasionally eat chicken or turkey, either roasted or in a soup or *paprikaš*. Goose down is collected, usually to sell to the townsfolk. Unlike the other animals, both the care and marketing of poultry is almost exclusively in the hands of the women.

According to one authority, bee-keeping was the peasants' most important source of income early in the eighteenth century, during the time of Austrian rule. The population was, of course, small, and it is estimated that there was approximately one beehive per capita.[6] Honey was the only sweetening substance, but as sugar gradually became more easily available the number of hives decreased. Today in Orašac there is an average of one hive for every three households. Since those who keep bees usually have several hives the statistics actually indicate that the great majority of the peasants have none.

In the past few years a few Orašac women have raised silkworms for the purpose of making their own embroidery thread.

There are a number of causes for the general decline in the importance of livestock, perhaps the most basic being the increase in population. Extensive livestock raising as it was practiced in Šumadija requires a large amount of land and was not capable of supporting even a moderately dense population. This, combined with the fact that the region is fairly fertile, made the shift to agriculture almost an inevitable conclusion. In Yugoslavia today livestock raising is the primary economy only in those marginal regions such as the Dinaric uplands which are not suitable for agriculture. In Šumadija, accompanying the increase in population was the disappearance of common woods and pastures as the land came under individual, private ownership.

Along with these changes was a general decline in the size of the household group. The number of households increased faster

[6] Lutovac, *Privredno-Geografska Karakteristika Sliva Jasenice*, p. 49.

than the population (Table 1), so the amount of land held by each household decreased. At the beginning of this century holdings of twenty or more hectares were not unusual, while at present only a few of the largest landholders have that much. To combine agriculture and livestock raising on a large scale in a peasant economy necessitates not only much land but also a large labor force, so it is not surprising that the decline in livestock raising and the decrease in household size occurred simultaneously.

Since 1900 wars have been significant in preventing any increase in the number of livestock. During the occupation of this region in both the First and Second World Wars, Austrian and German troops confiscated much of the livestock. These various factors, then, all help to explain why raising livestock is a distinctly secondary economy in Orašac today. But most important has been the emergence of agriculture as the main economy, representing the changed relationship between man and the land, as a result of a growing population.

AGRICULTURE: CROPS, YIELDS, AND HOLDINGS

The shift from livestock raising to agriculture began about a century ago, but the past fifty or sixty years have witnessed several basic changes. Most important is that the amount of cultivated land in Orašac has doubled, from 678 hectares in 1895 to 1,354 in 1953. The amount of arable land per capita has increased at the same time; in 1895 there were 0.43 hectares per capita, and in 1953, 0.63.[7] The present population density, approximately one hundred persons per square kilometer for the Jasenica region (ninety-seven for Orašac), represents about the maximum the land can support under contemporary methods of cultivation.[8]

The increase in cultivated land in Orašac is most evident in the amount of land sown in corn and wheat. In 1893 these crops occupied 300 and 350 hectares respectively. The average for 1950–53 was 513 hectares in corn and 569 in wheat. More cultivated land

[7] This compares with 1949 figures of 0.59 for Serbia, 1.41 for the Vojvodina (the richest agricultural region in Yugoslavia), 0.66 for Yugoslavia as a whole, 1.12 for Germany, 1.80 for France, and 6.58 for the United States. See Tomić and Šević, "Poljoprivreda," in *Proizvodne Snage NR Srbije*, p. 143.

[8] Lutovac, *Privredno-Geografska Karakteristika Sliva Jasenice*, pp. 18–19.

was made available by the decrease in pasture areas as well as by the cutting down of the woods.[9]

Corn was formerly grown for bread flour as well as for livestock feed, while wheat was almost exclusively a cash crop—"The wheat was sold, putting away only enough for seeds and holidays."[10] Poorer peasants sold their wheat crop right away, in order to have enough money to pay taxes, and they used surplus cash to buy corn, which was cheaper.[11]

In the last few decades, and particularly since the Second World War, there has been a shift in the corn-wheat pattern. Formerly *proja*, or corn bread, was eaten every day and bread made with wheat flour was baked only on special occasions. Today the opposite is true; this development is most significant, for bread is the mainstay of the peasant diet. This change is also considered by the peasants themselves to be very important; in virtually every autobiography written by the older men of Orašac there is mention of looking forward to the various holidays in their youth as a time when wheat bread would be enjoyed. An important reason for the change is that owing to post-war government land reforms and other policies most villagers no longer have the desire to amass money to purchase more land, once the prime goal in a peasant's life. Further, the relatively low prices of agricultural products and the comparatively high cost of consumer goods appear to have discouraged the peasant from marketing a maximum amount of grain. Then too, he has become increasingly self-conscious of what he himself calls backwardness; eating wheat bread seems to him one way in which he can raise his own living standard and become more *kulturan*. Corn bread is, however, still the basic staple in several of the poorer households in the village.

Depending upon the quality of the soil and the extent to which

[9] The richest pasture land in Orašac, along Misača Creek, may yield as much as 10,000 kilos of hay per hectare (the average is from 3,000 to 5,000). These fields are mown three to four times during the season, the hay being used almost exclusively for feeding the livestock of the individual owners of this land.

[10] Pavlović, *Život i Običaji Narodni u Kragujevačkoj Jasenici u Šumadiji*, p. 13.

[11] The coming of the railroad to this area in 1882 helped to make wheat a cash crop, and from that time it became increasingly important as such. At the same time corn was well suited to the climate, and it had a greater yield per hectare than wheat or any other grains.

it has been fertilized, wheat yields today vary from a low of 700 kilos per hectare to over 3,000. Those for corn are somewhat higher with approximately the same range. Yet even the poorest yields are much higher than the best of those at the turn of the century. According to one of the older village men, "if a man had a total yield of 500 kilos of wheat from his land he was considered a *gazda*." Peasants today who have only very small amounts of land (about two hectares or less) grow just corn, since it gives a greater yield per hectare than wheat. The usual practice on most holdings, however, is to rotate crops after a period and grow forage on part of the cultivated land for several years. Although they realize this will help the land regain fertility, many peasants claim they cannot afford to practice rotation. Other grains such as barley, oats, and rye are secondary.

Although there has definitely been an increase in yields since the last century, no significant changes seem to have occurred in the last thirty years. This is true of Orašac as well as for all of central Serbia.

Flax, cultivated by the women, has long been one of the traditional crops, but its importance has varied with the availability of manufactured cloth. During the past war growing flax greatly increased, and then it tapered off when cloth again became available in the town. It is usually planted in rows between the major field crops or in the vegetable gardens, so that the amount of land devoted to it is difficult to estimate.

Near every homestead is a vegetable garden. Vegetables are raised chiefly for home consumption, but here, too, the trend is more toward a market economy. Vegetables grown are peppers, garlic, onions, cabbage, snap beans, tomatoes, and potatoes. Carrots, cucumbers, scallions, peas, cauliflower, eggplant, and radishes are raised on a much smaller scale. Vine plants, including beans, pumpkins, squash, and watermelons, are commonly planted between the rows in the vegetable patch or cornfield.

A characteristic pattern in Šumadija is the plum orchard surrounding the household unit. Plums are overwhelmingly the most important fruit, accounting for over 90 percent of all the fruit trees in Orašac. Today there are also some apple, pear, walnut, peach, sour cherry, sweet cherry, apricot, quince, and medlar trees in the village. There are no records of most of these before the turn of the century, indicating that their numbers were negligible at that time. During the past fifty years there has been an increase in the size of orchards which has kept pace with the increasing population. Orašac had 24 plum trees per capita in 1897 and 26 in 1953. On a much smaller scale, there have been corresponding increases in the number of apple, pear, and walnut trees.

The major use of plums is for rakija. *Pekmez*, a thick prune jam, is also prepared. Brandy and fresh and dried plums are sold in the market, and plums from all over Šumadija have become one of Serbia's main exports. Almost without exception the other fruits are strictly for home use. They are eaten fresh in season. Discarded and rotten fruit is fed to the pigs. Every household usually prepares a small amount as *slatko*, the sweet preserves traditionally served to guests.

Just as there has been an important growth in the size of orchards, the same holds true for vineyards. In the nineteenth century, grapes and wine of the Jasenica region were exclusively for home consumption, but in the last fifty years wines, and later grapes, have become a significant element in the village economy. A *ružica*, or rosé wine, is the most common type in Orašac. Orašac grapes, although not of the outstanding quality of those from nearby Banja and Topola, are marketed in other parts of Yugoslavia and even abroad.

AGRICULTURAL TECHNOLOGY

Mechanization is of only minor significance in peasant agriculture as it exists in Orašac today. Two households own old tractors, and two have threshing machines operated by gasoline motors. Simple power threshers were first introduced into this area about forty years ago; the two in Orašac were manufactured in Hungary in the late 1930s. Three seeders, acquired through UNRRA after the Second World War, and three selfbinders complete the list of more modern machinery. There are also some hand-operated items such as sprayers and grape presses. In addition to a few grain mills in the county, powered by water or by gasoline generators,

there is a small, privately owned gasoline-powered mill located up
the road in neighboring Kopljare.

The two basic items of agricultural equipment remain the wagon
and the plow. The number of wagons, in terms of units per number
of households, has increased during the past eighty-five years,
while at times the number of plows has not kept pace with the
growth in number of households. It should be emphasized here
that all equipment, with the exception of the few items of machinery
mentioned above and some newer types of plows, is handmade
locally or in the towns by special craftsmen.

Figure 3*a* illustrates the old-type single-handled *ralo*, or lister,
used in parts of Šumadija at about the turn of the century. Plowing
today is done with the *plug*, a simple double-handled wooden plow
with metal colter, mold-board, and asymmetrically shaped plowshare (Fig. 3*b*). A wooden peg fastener (Fig. 3*c*), a leather strap,
or, more recently, a metal chain, serves to link the plow-shaft to
the shaft connected to the yoke. The simple oxbow type of *jaram*,
or yoke, used today in many parts of Yugoslavia, is no longer seen
in Orašac; instead, the type now found has two carved and orna-
mented horizontal bars with removable pegs (Figs. 3*d*, *e*).

Additional fundamental farming implements are shown in Figure 4. The rakes, axes, shovels, hoes, scythes, pitchforks, and other
tools used by Orašac villagers are made by local craftsmen, and
their form has remained substantially the same for the past century (Figs. 4*a-d*, *f*, *g*). Every farmer prepares his own horn and
flint (Fig. 4*e*). Crude but efficient rollers as well as simple harrows
are made by certain of the village men (4*h*, *i*).[12]

Important in Orašac economy are the implements associated
with wine and rakija production, as illustrated in Figure 5. Formerly a branched stick served as a grape crusher (5*b*), but today
several types of hand-cranked rollers do the job (5*a*). In many
parts of Orašac County the old-type still for making rakija can be
seen (5*c*). The plum mash is heated in a kettle suspended above a

[12] Many of these implements are closely analogous to those used by peasants in other
parts of the world. For example, for rural Brazil a harrow almost identical to the one
used in Orašac is described, with hoes, axes, and listers roughly equivalent to those
of Orašac. Cf. Donald Pierson, *Cruz Das Almas: A Brazilian Village* (Smithsonian Institution: Institute of Social Anthropology, No. 12, 1951), pp. 52–53.

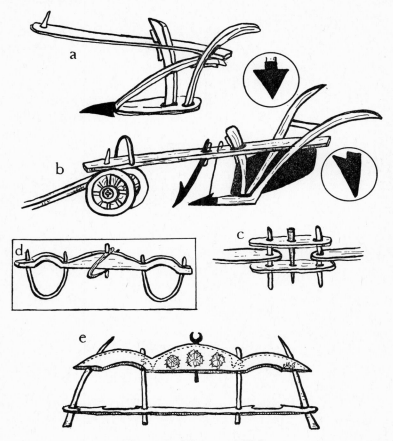

Figure 3. Plows and Yokes

(*a*) *Ralo*, old-type single-handled wooden plow, with symmetrical metal plowshare shown in inset. (*b*) *Plug*, contemporary double-handled wooden plow with metal colter, mold-board, and asymmetrical plowshare. (*c*) *Krpele*, linking plow-shaft to shaft connected to yoke. (*d*) *Jaram*, old-type yoke. (*e*) Contemporary yoke with ornamental carvings. (Figs. *c* and *d* after P. Petrović, *Život i Običaji Narodni u Gruži*, p. 35.)

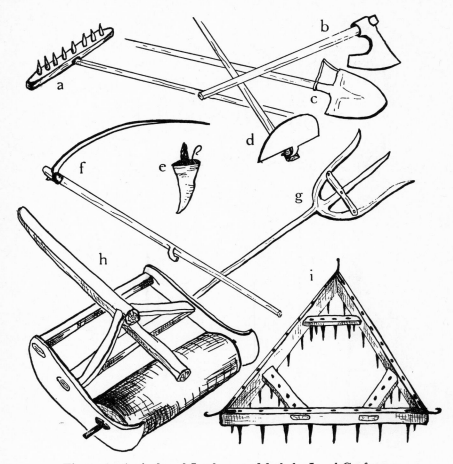

Figure 4. Agricultural Implements Made by Local Craftsmen

(*a*) *Grabulje*, wooden rake. (*b*) *Sekira*, ax. (*c*) *Ašov*, shovel. (*d*) *Motika*, hoe. (*e*) *Vodir i brus*, horn and flint. (*f*) *Kosa*, scythe. (*g*) *Vile*, wooden pitchfork. (*h*) *Valjak*, roller. (*i*) *Drljača*, harrow with metal spikes.

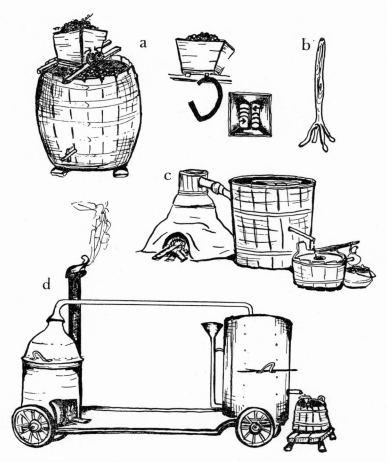

Figure 5. Apparatus for Making Wine and Brandy

(*a*) *Muljač za vino*, grape crusher. (*b*) Old-type grape crusher. (*c*) *Kazan za rakiju*, old-type still for making brandy (after P. Petrović, *Narodni Život i Običaji u Gruži*, p. 56). (*d*) Modern distilling apparatus.

permanent outdoor oven. The vapors pass into and condense in a large water barrel, and finally the distillate goes through a series of crude filters. The process is essentially similar to that which takes place with the more modern, portable *aparat* except that the latter has a much larger capacity and a more effective spiral condenser (5*d*). Entirely of metal, the "apparatus" is considered by the peasants to be a streamlined piece of equipment indeed; it is made in town by the *kazandžije*, or coppersmiths.

Considering Orašac agricultural methods as a whole, the hand tools are of much greater significance than the few elementary pieces of mechanical equipment available to the peasant. The Orašac farmer still wrests a living from his small plot of land by the strength of his back.

THE AGRICULTURAL CYCLE: SPRING

For a people who live intimately with their land and are completely dependent upon it for their existence, the yearly cycle of farm duties forms an orbit in which all life revolves. The Šumadijan peasants are constantly attuned to the changing seasons. Even as the cover of snow is melting from the fields, tiny green blades of winter wheat, planted the previous autumn, have begun to push through the earth. The bleating of newborn lambs is heard in the sheep hutch, and litters of piglets appear now, to be raised especially for sale around Easter time. Everyone loves the young animals, and many a stalwart peasant pauses on his way to the fields to pick up a spindly legged lamb and strokes it endearingly.

Early March is the time for spring plowing, to prepare the land for the corn which must soon be sown. Those who raise oats and spring wheat plant at this time. In the vegetable patch potatoes, onions, and garlic are planted, to be ready by early summer. Plowing is usually done by the men, with a child leading the cows. Only the more prosperous households have horses. Those who have no plow or draft animals and relatively little land have a neighbor plow their land for them and make arrangements to return an equivalent amount of work at the neighbor's at some future date. Seeding is the next chore. Most of the villagers do it broadcast, from a sack slung over the shoulder. Next, the vineyards are attended to; they must be hoed and trimmed, and new vines are set out.

The able-bodied members of the household are intensely busy in the fields, and the care of the livestock falls to the very young and the very old, for in Orašac communal herdsmen are unknown. Young boys and girls often meet to herd their families' flocks together. The pasturing of the cattle is entrusted to older people. If a man wishes to graze his stock on another's land, he does so for a fee or in exchange for labor.

With the arrival of April and better weather the tempo of work increases—now must be done all the jobs which the peasant had hoped to accomplish in March but was, in spite of his efforts, prevented from completing because of unpredictable rains. Two weeks after corn has been sown the villager turns his energies to the first hoeing, called *prašenje*. In May the *okopavanje*, or second hoeing, takes place, and a final hoeing of the cornfield, *ogrtanje*, is done in June. Spring is a busy season, and the tasks require a lot of labor. Often it happens that within the individual household there is insufficient manpower to do all the work. A *pozajmica*, literally a loaning of labor, is arranged. Neighbors and relatives, often several from the same households, go to help, and in return the recipient or adult members of his own household agree to return the equivalent number of man-days to each helper.

April is the most difficult month of the year as far as food is concerned. Supplies from the last harvest have been used up and no new crops have matured. Snap beans and cabbage are planted, and tomato seedlings which have been carefully nurtured indoors are set out. Again the vineyards are dug, and the garden requires more and more work.

SUMMER

As the days become longer the race continues, to finish one chore before the next one must be done. This is the time when the women of the house must rise early, sometimes at three o'clock, to milk the cows, feed the stock, prepare breakfast, and help the men get an early start off to the fields. One by one the garden vegetables

mature, and fresh fruits and vegetables are abundant. When work
around the house is done, women often join the menfolk in the
fields.

Late June is haying time, and then, during July, starts the big
job of reaping the wheat. A scythe is the standard tool used, and
under a blazing sun men laboriously cut swathes through the tall
wheat. The women follow behind, gathering and binding the
grain. Reaping by this method is very strenuous work, and a man
will often call together a *moba*. Unlike the pozajmica, which is
simply a labor pool, the moba combines mutual help and merrymaking. When the day's work in the fields is done, the helpers
relax, eat supper, drink, sing, and dance at the home of their host.
Here the return of labor is not formally a necessity, but most
peasants regard it as an obligation. Occasionally a worker or two
must be hired for reaping, and because it is such difficult work he
is paid more than the usual daily wage for agricultural labor.[13]

One huge chore done, attention turns to threshing. The two
village men who own threshers rent them out to others during the
season and are repaid in kind, sixty kilos of wheat for each ton
threshed. A pair of cows pulls the old machine around from field
to field, while men and women once more gather to help one another. Wheat is fed into the grumbling machine by hand, and at
the other end women with bright kerchiefs bound over nose and
mouth fork aside the straw and dust that come spurting out. The
grain is caught in large hand-woven sacks. The owner of the
machine and the man who raised the wheat weigh each sack together ceremoniously, to ensure honesty on both sides. Work over,
twenty to thirty workers sit down to a hearty lunch of thick stew,
bread and rakija, served on cloths and sacks spread on the field.
For the next week or two everyone is busy returning the labor given
him by friends and relatives, and finally all the wheat is threshed.

About this time the household sheep are sheared. Each animal
has its wooly coat clipped away by a pair of sturdy scissors handmade by a Gypsy smith.

No time to stop and rest—the corn is ready to be harvested.

[13] A typical daily wage for agricultural work is 300 dinars, while a hired reaper gets
500 dinars a day.

This is the time of the *komišanje*, the annual husking bee, and again helpers join in to make the work go faster. At about sunset, a musician or two arrives. Corn is husked at a furious pace, amidst much singing, joke-telling, and tossing of corn. When work is done there is dancing in the courtyard, with helpers of all ages participating. The more thrifty peasants do not call a komišanje at their homestead, for many of the husks are lost in the course of the fun, and they cannot afford to waste this important cattle feed.

In the meantime, golden *dinje* melons and orange and pink watermelons have ripened on the vine. Bean vines, cut and stacked to dry the month before, are spread on the ground and flailed with long sticks, to burst the pods. There is a scramble to pick up every one of the small white beans which form one of the basic elements of the winter diet.

AUTUMN

Hot, dusty late summer days give way to fall, and again attention turns to the crops. Once the grains are in, the orchards, heavy with small purple plums, present the next job. Picking plums is relatively easy work, and children usually help their elders, literally eating their way through the task. Arrangements are made for a rakija-making still to come around, and for days there is plenty of sampling and singing as the new plum brandy is made.[14] The owner of the distilling apparatus receives pay at the rate of two liters of brandy for every barrel produced[15] and supervises the over-all operation. Someone from the household is on hand constantly, to chop firewood and feed the portable oven and to rake aside waste pulps and skins to be fed to the swine.

October days bring another pleasant chore. It is grape-picking time, and this work, perhaps more than all the others, is a family affair. Everyone crouches in the rows of the vineyard, stripping off

[14] Rakija is the name usually applied by the peasant to ordinary plum brandy, but the word may be used for any distilled beverage made from fruit. In literary Serbian the word *šljivovica* refers specifically to plum brandy which, although considered the national drink of Serbia, is a term not commonly used in the village. Plum brandy which is distilled several times and consequently has a higher alcoholic content is called *ljuta rakija* or simply *ljuta;* it brings a much higher price on the local market.

[15] Barrels used have a twenty-three liter capacity.

clusters of ripe green and purple grapes. Wagonloads of the fruit are carted home and carefully sorted, for those with especially fine flavor and appearance are purchased by the local Cooperative and sent to Austria and England. The rest of the grapes are poured into crushers and the juice runs down into huge barrels, where it is left to ferment. A mug is left hanging on the spigot of the barrel, and adults and children alike sneak sips and comment on the wine's progress.

The stock is especially well fed at this time of year; one swine is singled out and put in a special pen to be fattened. When it is glutted with corn and can no longer eat, it is slaughtered. The lard is cubed and rendered, to serve as cooking fat and shortening for the coming year.

There is a tang in the air, and the oak and ash trees in the glens turn brown and yellow. But work in the fields is not yet over. The wheat fields are plowed and later, in November, the grain is sown. Those who can fertilize their fields with manure do so, for artificial fertilizers are claimed to be "no good" and "too expensive."[16]

Work in the fields tapers off. The wooden flour bin is filled with fresh wheat flour, and there are barrels of wine in the cool *podrum*. Now, in the bright, chilly days of November, is the season of festivities. Most of the slavas occur at this time, when the harvest is in and traditional Serbian hospitality can be extended without stinting. And it is a time of weddings, when villagers are able to rest a bit from the ceaseless, arduous farm work and join their friends at merry feasts and dances. Marriages take place now for still another reason. For many weeks before Christmas food is restricted by religious fasting, and no feast would be complete without roast pig or lamb. It is necessary, then, that weddings occur before the period when no meat is permitted.

WINTER

Frost coats the ground each morning, and eventually the fields and slopes are blanketed with snow. From a high place the separate homesteads can be picked out in the wintry landscape, with their

---

[16] Commercial fertilizers cost 11 dinars a kilo, and peasants complain that that is almost as much as the price of corn (16 dinars a kilo).

haystacks and outbuildings frosted with snow, and with the rows
of bare plum trees making a pattern around each household cluster.
This is not a time of enforced idleness for the peasant, although he
jokingly calls winter his *godišnji odmor*, his annual vacation.[17] The
livestock must be watered and fed and the stalls cleaned every
day. Slop is heated for the pigs and corn shelled for the chickens.
Wood and water must be fetched, often from some distance through
snow drifts.

For the women, the cows still have to be milked and the cheese
made. Weekly supplies of bread are baked, and big pots of *pasulj*,
tasty bean gruel seasoned with paprika and dried meat, bubble on
the stove. Whenever her hands are not busy milking, kneading, or
stirring, the village woman picks up her distaff and spindle and
industriously spins fluffs of combed wool into yarn. Or she crochets,
knits, embroiders, or weaves—there is always something to be done.

Men repair tools and carve. The older men play the gusle and
sing. Very rarely do people read after the day's chores are done,
for literacy is limited and so are the number of books. Only a few
houses are electrified, and most villagers consider kerosene too expensive to waste on reading. Pleasures of the season include the
joyful Christmas customs and leisure time for visiting and gossiping, at home and at the kafana. But by February villagers anxiously
sniff the air for the first signs that winter is breaking up. Snow
turns to slush and then to mud, and the peasant anxiously examines
the fields for the first delicate blades of wheat. Then he makes his
plow ready and goes out to prepare the land for another year.

DIVISION OF LABOR

There are only a few jobs with which children do not help their
parents, or wives their husbands; conversely, there are a small
number of jobs labeled exclusively women's work, such as baking,
making cheese, weaving and spinning, cleaning the house, and
washing clothes. There are several factors preventing a sharper
division of labor. For one thing, sometimes the men are simply
not around to perform their regular daily chores, such as watering
the stock and chopping wood; they may be ill, at the market, ful-

[17] A reference to the annual two-week vacation allowed all government workers.

Examples of Labor Exchange

Work Performed	*Work Done in Return*
1. Dragoljub brings his seeding machine and helps seed Milosav's fields.	Milosav and his son are carpenters and make some repairs on Dragoljub's house.
2. Bogdan, his wife, and twin daughters (16 years); Tihomir, his wife, and son (21 years); and Milan's wife all pick grapes for one day in the vineyard of Djordje.	Djordje, his son, and daughter-in-law[a] work in Tihomir's vineyard for one day. The daughter-in-law works in Milan's vineyard for one day. Since Bogdan has no wagon, Djordje loans him his for several days.
3. Widow Ljubinka and her son (14 years) pick corn for Živomir one day.[b] Later they pick grapes there for two days, and in the spring they will help Živomir dig his vineyard for two days.	When it is time for plowing, Živomir will work for one and a half days with his plow and cows to plow Ljubinka's land.[c]
4. Radivoje's wife, Sreten's wife, Ilija, his wife, and daughter-in-law all work for one day hoeing in Velimir's cornfield.	Velimir's daughter-in-law hoes in Radivoje's cornfield for one day and in Sreten's for one day; Velimir hoes for two days and his daughter-in-law one day at Ilija's.

Paid Labor

5. Nenad, his wife, son (19 years) and daughter (17 years) pick corn at Milutin's for one day.	Milutin gives Nenad 1,000 dinars for the labor of four persons for the day.[d]

Labor Exchanged for Goods

6. Rajko, a miner, picks plums for Budimir for one and a half days.	Budimir gives Rajko 25 kilos of plums in return for his labor.

[a] Women usually return the labor of other women.

[b] Children under 16 years usually do not participate in labor exchange, but when they must, as in the case of widow Ljubinka's son, one day's work is equivalent to half a regular man-day.

[c] A man working for one day with his plow and yoke of cows is equivalent to five regular man-days.

[d] The men were paid at the rate of 300 dinars and the women 200.

filling work obligations at a neighbor's homestead, or away on military service—the women must then assume their work. The inverse does occur, although rarely, for the only ordinary reason for a woman's unavailability to perform her chores would be illness.[18] In such a situation, where there is no other adult female at

[18] This division of labor is not invariably true since there do occur cases of inversion of roles, as when a man who does not wish to assume the masculine role performs women's tasks such as spinning, weaving, and cooking. He is derisively called *predo*, from the verb *presti* (to spin). In Orašac there was one such case of an old man who lived alone and was hired by one of the families to watch sheep and spin.

home, the woman's husband would milk the cows and cook. In general, however, vestiges of the zadruga system remain, and the majority of Orašac households have adequate labor for all except the very biggest annual agricultural jobs.

The chart on page 72, "Daily and Seasonal Work Schedules for an Orašac Household," indicates the labor routine for each sex and generation on sample days. The picking of grapes in the fall illustrates how all members of the household work cooperatively, concentrating on one task and performing only the most necessary of the other chores, while on the other sample days each member of the family has his or her own specific duties. Examples of everyday labor exchange outside the family, which are in addition to the more formalized institutions of pozajmica, moba, and komišanje, are illustrated in the list given above, "Examples of Labor Exchange."

OCCUPATIONAL GROUPS AND LAND TENURE

A preliminary approach to the question of occupational groups in the village is presented in Table 4A, where the population is broken down into three groups of households: the pure agriculturalists, the mixed agriculturalists, and the landless residents. Households where agriculture and livestock raising are the sole means of livelihood compose the first group; these pure agriculturalists make up the largest group in the village, accounting for 59 percent of the total population in 1953.[19] The mixed agriculturalists, constituting 34 percent of the village population, are those households of which one member is a permanently employed wage-earner (it is rare for more than one member to have full-time employment).[20]

These two groups by no means represent absolute differences, since occasionally some of the pure agriculturalists assume part-time jobs when farming chores are not too pressing.[21] At the same

[19] Included in this group are households in which live the President of the Village Council (an elected position held for two years), six students at a high school or university, and two disabled war veterans.

[20] Those villagers who work full time on the state farm or for the cooperative are included in this category. According to present plans they will form no more than 10 percent of the total number of permanent wage-workers in Orašac, although a larger number of seasonal workers may be employed.

[21] Some have also lived and worked away from the village for varying periods.

Daily and Seasonal Work Schedules for an Orašac Household

	FALL (Saturday, October 24, 1953)	WINTER (Friday, January 15, 1954)	SPRING (Monday, April 5, 1954)	SUMMER (Monday, July 26, 1954)
Domaćin (Head of household) 55 years old	Feed, water stock; pick grapes; chop wood; feed, water stock	Feed, water stock; clean stable; mend boots, fence; carve distaff; chat and smoke with friends	Water stock; clean stable; sow corn	Water stock; thresh wheat at neighbor's; water stock
Žena (Wife) 56 years	Feed chickens; clean kitchen; prepare and take lunch to family in vineyard; pick grapes; help make supper	Make breakfast; spin; prepare lunch; spin and sing to grandchildren; prepare supper	Milk cows; prepare dough; bake bread; watch cows; spin	Feed chickens; milk cows; make cheese; wash clothes; make supper
Sin (Son) 34 years	Feed pigs; haul water; pick grapes; transport wagonloads of grapes home	Prepare slop for pigs; go to town for salt, kerosene; chop wood; feed, water stock	Feed pigs; dig vineyard; water stock	Clean stable; thresh wheat at neighbor's
Sna (Daughter-in-law) 32 years	Milk cows; haul water; pick grapes; help make supper	Feed chickens; haul water; weave; chat with visiting relative; milk cows	Feed chickens; haul water; make breakfast; make and carry lunch to father-in-law and husband; make supper	Haul water; work in vegetable garden
Unuk (Grandson) 12 years	Pick grapes; go to school; do homework	Carry and stack firewood; go to school; do homework; play flute	Gather kindling for bread oven; graze pigs; go to school; do homework	Herd pigs; watch cows; sing; play flute
Unuka (Granddaughter) 9 years	Help haul water; go to school; pick grapes	Go to school; learn to knit; sing	Help clean up kitchen; go to school; watch sheep; do homework	Watch sheep; eat with friends in meadows; play

Table 4. The Orašac Population by Occupational Groups, 1953

A. DISTRIBUTION OF OCCUPATIONAL GROUPS

	Number of Households	Number of People	Percent of Total Population
I. Pure Agriculturalists	276	1,286	58.9
II. Mixed Agriculturalists	147	748	34.3
III. Landless Residents	57	148	6.8
	480	2,182	100.0

B. GROUPS I AND II, BY LANDHOLDINGS

Landholdings in Hectares[a]	Number of Households	Number of People	Average Household Size	Percent of Group Population
GROUP I. PURE AGRICULTURALISTS				
under 1	6	23	3.8	1.8
1+	17	62	3.6	4.8
2+	36	120	3.3	9.3
3+	54	198	3.7	15.5
4+	16	84	5.3	6.5
5+	35	145	4.1	11.3
6+	22	134	6.1	10.4
7+	27	131	4.9	10.2
8+	13	66	5.1	5.1
9+	5	36	7.2	2.8
10+	8	48	6.0	3.7
11–15+	27	166	6.1	12.9
16–20+	5	36	7.2	2.8
21+	5	37	7.4	2.9
Total	276	1,286		100.0
GROUP II. MIXED AGRICULTURALISTS				
under 1	3	10	3.3	1.3
1+	31	113	3.6	15.1
2+	41	192	4.7	25.7
3+	32	145	4.5	19.4
4+	10	66	6.6	8.8
5+	9	65	7.2	8.7
6+	10	65	6.5	8.7
7+	5	25	5.0	3.3
8+	—	—	—	0.0
9+	2	19	9.5	2.5
10+	1	8	8.0	1.1
11–15+	1	11	11.0	1.5
16–20+	2	29	14.5	3.9
21+	—	—	—	0.0
Total	147	748		100.0

Source: Serbian Statistical Bureau.

[a] The entries 1+ in this column indicate one or more hectares but less than two hectares; 2+, two or more hectares but less than three; etc.

time in the mixed group most men who have full-time jobs outside of agriculture do farm chores after a day's work and utilize days off to work on their land. Both groups are properly called peasants; all the households own some land and all of the men, practically without exception, were born in Orašac. Further, in almost every case their families have lived in Orašac for a century or longer. There is little cultural or economic distinction between the two groups per se, although within the village as a whole there are considerable economic differences. The important thing is that these households share a common traditional way of life and set of values and tend to look upon the third group as outsiders.

Representing less than 7 percent of the total Orašac population, the third group, the landless residents, are difficult to define as a unit. They cannot be considered peasants. They are not native agriculturalists from Orašac or other villages; the majority of them were not born in Serbia. They are for the most part non-permanent residents and include mainly German miners and their families or single German men living at the mining kolonija. Also in this group are the priest and his family and the schoolteachers with their families, as well as some laborers from other parts of Yugoslavia who live temporarily in Orašac. None of these landless residents, with the important exception of the priest and teachers, plays a significant role in village affairs.[22]

To return to the pure and mixed agriculturalists, while it is true that there are no over-all economic differences between the two groups as far as standard of living is concerned, there are very definite variations in the pattern of landholdings. This is brought out in Table 4*B*, where among the mixed agriculturalists group there is a much greater concentration of small holdings (under five hectares), accounting for 70 percent of the Group II population; for the pure agriculturalists, Group I, only 38 percent of the households have small holdings.[23] One hundred forty-seven of the pure agricultural households have five or more hectares, compared

[22] Early in 1954 four agronomists and their families came to live in Orašac in connection with the establishment of the state farm in 1953.
[23] The very small pure peasant holdings belong to either old couples or widows with young children. There are practically no able-bodied men in this group.

to only thirty in the mixed group. Interestingly enough, those in Group II who do have holdings of five hectares or more have on the average more members in their households than do those of Group I. The same trend is true for the smaller holdings, although to a lesser extent, with an over-all average household size of 5.1 members in the mixed group, compared to 4.7 for the pure group. This situation is largely the result of overpopulation relative to the amount of arable land.

Before proceeding with a more detailed discussion of the significance of wage labor in the Orašac economy, we will further explore the primary cause for its development, namely, the pattern of land tenure. As in most European peasant communities there is fragmentation of holdings in Orašac, although not as extreme as in other areas. Cultivated land, vineyards, pastures, and woods may be scattered, but in Šumadija the orchard and vegetable patch are almost universally found near the homestead. Sometimes other types of land are also located adjacent to or near the homestead, while in many cases holdings are broken up into as many as ten different parcels. In Orašac it is rare for holdings to be located more than two kilometers from the owner's home. An exception is in the case of woods, for several Orašac households own small wooded tracts in upland villages, such as Garaši, and they make several trips a year there to obtain firewood.

A breakdown of landholdings in Orašac and selected nearby villages, in terms of total agricultural population rather than number of agricultural households, indicates that in four out of five villages the highest percentage of agriculturalists are in the 3.01- to 5-hectare category. With regard to relatively large and relatively small holdings, in all cases there is a greater percentage of the population on holdings of over 7 hectares than under 3 hectares. About 5 hectares, then, is a reasonable figure for the average-size holding in Orašac and in neighboring villages. This is closely related to the trend, seen in Table 4*B*, that the size of the household, in terms of number of members, increases with the increase in the size of the holding. Bearing in mind reservations such as the differences between the pure and mixed agriculturalists, it does not seem unreasonable to say that, taken as a whole, the land resources

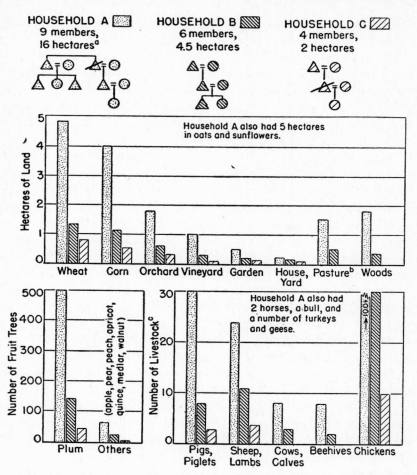

Figure 6. Three Contemporary Orašac Households, Compared, 1953

[a] Data is for early 1953, before government land reform limited all holdings to 10 hectares, exclusive of woods.

[b] Household *C*'s sheep are pastured on a neighbor's land, in exchange for labor.

[c] Numbers are for March, 1953, after newborn animals were counted.

of Orašac village and surrounding areas are shared by the inhabitants with some degree of equality; in any case, there is very definitely no true division into large and dwarf peasant holdings but rather a large middle group with a minority at both extremes, a slightly greater minority occurring on the side of the larger land-holders.

The differences in size and utilization of Orašac holdings are summarized graphically in Figure 6. Three households are compared with regard to number of members in the household, amount of land, land utilization, number of livestock, and variety of crops. Household *A* represents a relatively well-to-do household and Household *C* a poor one, although neither is an extreme example. In selecting them the intention was to represent the general range. Household *B* is average, and all three are actual households as they existed in the village in 1953. The differences between *A* and *B* are largely a matter of degree; significant is the fact that *B* has no horses[24] and no poultry other than chickens, with minor differences in the absence of sunflowers, oats, and certain fruit trees. On the other hand, the differences between Household *C* and the other two are very significant, in terms of quantity and variety all the way through the summary. Household *C* has no pasture or woods; it has only a very small orchard, and a tiny garden in which staple vegetables are raised. The poor household has neither wagon nor plow, and the only livestock are three pigs, four sheep, and a few chickens.

These resources must be considered in relation to the number of members in each household. We have seen that some of the large households contain full-time wage earners, because there is insufficient land relative to the number of people.[25] Figure 6 bears out the fact that the size of the household increases with the amount of land. Households *A*, *B*, and *C* have nine, six, and four members, respectively. *A* and *B* are pure agriculturalists, while the old man in Household *C* is a pensioned miner and consequently his household is in the mixed agriculturalist group.

[24] In 1951, 84.5 percent of the agricultural households in Serbia had no horses; in the prosperous Vojvodina 47.5 percent had none. See Tomić and Šević, "Poljoprivreda," in *Proizvodne Snage NR Srbije*, p. 138.

[25] The reverse situation occasionally exists—there are a few families in the village who have relatively large landholdings but insufficient labor to work them. In these cases a part of the land is rented *napola*: the peasant renting the land provides the seed and all the labor and gives the owner half of his crop. This system does not always work out to the advantage of the owner, for the peasant who works his land will rarely fertilize it, so that land farmed on this basis for several years gradually loses its fertility.

THE PEASANT AND A MONEY ECONOMY

Since the pure agriculturalists constitute almost three-fifths of the
Orašac population and the mixed group depends to a very great
extent upon agriculture, it is logical to consider the role of agriculture as a source of cash income before discussing supplementary
occupations. It should be emphasized here that no one in Orašac,
with the possible exception of a few miners, lives on a completely
cash economy—even the priest and the schoolteachers each have
a few chickens, one or two pigs, several fruit trees, and a small
garden. The economy of the pure and mixed agriculturalists is
still to a great extent a natural one; that is, the great majority of
Orašac peasants provide themselves with almost all their own food
and much of their clothing.

In spite of this general self-sufficiency all of them are involved in
some sort of cash economy. The exact extent of participation in
money economy varies considerably from household to household.
It is a difficult factor to assess, in large part because the keeping
of written accounts and budgets is not practiced in Orašac. Another
problem is concealment and distortion in any interviewing on this
subject. An approach to the question of peasant budgets is given
below under "Estimated Annual Expenses and Income in Two
Orašac Households, 1952–53," Households *A* and *B*.[26] These
summaries, are intended as approximations only, for although
based on interviews with two specific households they are founded
on recollections and estimates.[27]

The oldest and most constant expense of all Orašac households
is taxes. Until recently they were based on the estimated gross
income of the household; they are now determined by landholdings,
somewhat similarly to the system used in this area before the Second
World War. These taxes are based on a sliding scale corresponding
to the relative economic status of the household, so that Household *A*, with 16 hectares, pays 82,000 in regular state and local
taxes plus 20,000 dinars in special wine and rakija taxes, while

[26] Adequate data are not available for Household *C*.
[27] In certain instances supplementary or comparative data, where needed to present
a more typical picture, were obtained from other sources.

Estimated Annual Expenses and Cash Income
in Two Orašac Households, 1952–53

HOUSEHOLD A

Expenses	Cost in Dinars	Items Sold	Income in Dinars
State and local taxes	82,000	Wheat, oats[d]	70,000
		Corn[e]	18,000
Wine and rakija tax	20,000	Rakija[f]	80,000
Kerosene (50 liters)	4,500	Wine[g]	120,000
Salt (180 kilos)	5,400	Sheep with lamb	6,500
Sugar (36 kilos)	5,220	3 fattened pigs	14,000
Matches (30 boxes)	270	8 piglets	8,000
Soda (5 kilos)[a]	1,250	1 horse	80,000
		5 turkeys	2,500
Leather sandals (3 pr.)	6,000	20 chickens	4,400
Rubber sandals (6 pr.)	3,600	Eggs (about 1,000)	12,500
Men's shirts (5)	6,000	Kajmak	9,000
Men's britches (3 pr.)	6,000	Cheese (*sir*)	5,500
Men's caps (3)	1,500		———
Women's holiday clothes[b]	30,000		430,400
Household utensils	7,000		
Various farm implements	3,500	Total cash income	430,400
Shoeing horses, cows	3,000	Total expenditure	425,480
			———
Wagon repairs[c]	2,000	Cash on hand	4,920
Brick barn	200,000		
Doctor's fees, medicine	10,000	[a] For making laundry soap.	
Veterinarian	4,000	[b] Store-bought shoes, undergar-	
Electricity	2,000	ments, stockings; fabric and tailor, for	
Girl's school uniform	1,800	dresses, coats.	
Girl's school supplies	2,500	[c] For material and labor.	
School excursion	1,600	[d] Of 7,000 kilos produced, 3,000	
Church, priest's fees	800	were sold.	
Candles	500	[e] Of 10,000 kilos produced, 1,000	
Tavern	2,000	were sold.	
Soap, cosmetics	1,400	[f] Of 2,000 liters produced, 1,000	
Haircuts, shaves	500	were sold.	
Postage, paper	400	[g] Of 3,000 liters produced, 2,000	
Embroidery thread, string	3,500	were sold.	
Black pepper, ground	600		
Paprika, ground	700		
Rice (9 kilos)	3,600		
Coffee (1 kilo)	1,500		
Chocolate (6 bars)	840		
	———		
	425,480		

Estimated Annual Expenses and Cash Income in Two
Orašac Households, 1952–53 (Continued)

HOUSEHOLD B

Expenses	Cost in Dinars	Items Sold	Income in Dinars
State and local taxes	11,500	Rakija[e]	45,000
		Wine[f]	42,000
Wine and rakija tax	6,000	Grapes (200 kilos)	10,000
Kerosene (28 liters)	2,520	Apricots (150 kilos)	6,000
Salt (100 kilos)	3,000	2 fattened pigs	10,000
Sugar (30 kilos)	4,350	7 piglets	7,000
Cigarettes (30 packs)	9,000	1 pig	3,000
Matches (50 boxes)	450	2 lambs	5,000
Soda (3 kilos)	750	1 ram	4,500
		1 calf, 10-month old	10,000
Leather sandals (1 pr.)	2,000	Eggs (about 450)	5,500
Rubber sandals (2 pr.)	1,200	Kajmak	8,000
Men's britches (1 pr.)	3,000	Cheese	4,500
Boy's britches (1 pr.)	1,800		————
Women's holiday clothes[a]	8,000		160,500
Household utensils	2,700		
Various farm implements	2,000	Total cash income	160,500
Shoeing cows	2,000	Total expenditure	158,950
			————
House repairs	6,500	Cash on hand	1,550
Beehives	5,000		
Doctor's fees, medicine	15,000		
Veterinarian	2,000	[a] Fabric and tailor, for one skirt and
Calf, 18 months old	20,000	jacket and one girl's coat.
Corn (1 ton)[b]	18,000	[b] For pig feed.
Hay (1 ton)[c]	10,000	[c] For livestock.
Wood[d]	10,000	[d] Fuel.
Children's school uniforms	2,000	[e] Of 500 liters produced, 300 were
Children's school supplies	3,500	sold.
Priest's fees	300	[f] Of 800 liters produced, 600 were
Candles	300	sold.
Tavern	700	
Trip to Kragujevac	700	
Face soap	650	
Haircuts	100	
Postage, paper	300	
Black pepper, ground	300	
Paprika, ground	300	
Rice (3 kilos)	1,200	
Coffee substitute	210	
Chocolate (3 bars)	420	
Walnuts (10 kilos)	800	
Candy	400	
	————	
	158,950	

Household *B*, with 4.5 hectares, pays 11,500 and 6,000 dinars respectively.[28]

Another group of expenses incurred by all peasants includes the basic necessities—kerosene, salt, sugar, matches, tobacco, cigarettes, and soda for making soap. These are the so-called *monopolske stvari*, the items which have been the traditional government monopolies. All these items have been used by peasants since the latter part of the nineteenth century, and, in fact, salt and tobacco were purchased by peasants even at the time of the First Revolt. As we have seen earlier, peasants participated to a limited extent in a cash economy almost since the time of Orašac's settlement, and this participation has been increasing since then at a steady rate. The per capita consumption of these basic products does not vary too much with the economic status of the particular household. Household *A* requires more because it has nine members, compared to six for Household *B*. At the same time, the over-all expenditure for these items is less for Household *A*, where nobody in the family smokes. The 9,000 dinars spent for cigarettes in Household *B* is a significant expense.

Expenses of a third type are for items which might also be considered necessities in the sense that they appear in the budgets of almost all households, but the per capita cash outlay for them varies considerably. In this group are included shoes and clothing, household and cooking utensils, and farming equipment. Although most of the peasant's clothing is made at home, he still has to buy sandals, rubber boots, stout oxfords for holiday wear for his wife and daughter, and a variety of other expensive items, such as manufactured woolen goods for the holiday clothes of the women in the family. Most of the men's garments are made of woolen fabric hand-loomed at home, but a craftsman has to be paid to tailor the traditional three-piece outfit, and at another time special holiday garments with trimming must be ordered.[29] Bearing in mind the differences in household size, Household *A* spent considerably more for clothing in 1952–53 than did Household *B*. Many poorer households

[28] The system of taxation is viewed by the government not only as a means of raising the taxes but also as an instrument of government policy. These policies are discussed in more detail in Chapter 11.

[29] See Chapter 5 for a discussion of clothing and costume changes.

spent nothing at all. The price of manufactured clothing is relatively high compared to the price of agricultural products and wages. A man's cotton shirt, for example, costs about 1,200 dinars,[30] the equivalent of four days' wages for an ordinary laborer. Recently, however, there have been some price reductions.

Differences are less noticeable in items such as kitchen or household utensils and farming equipment. Since there is very little selection in Arandjelovac shops, quality is similar in all households; the factor that varies is quantity. For example, Household *A* might purchase enamel pots of two different sizes while Household *B* uses a pot of one size for a variety of cooking purposes. An exception to the matter of quality is illustrated by the fact that many poorer households continue to use earthenware crockery made by the potter in the town, for it is considerably cheaper than the manufactured enamel goods.

A final type of expenses, which might be called luxuries and miscellaneous, is the group in which the variations from household to household are the greatest. These include special additions to the diet, such as rice, coffee, ground black pepper, and chocolate. Household *A* spent 7,240 dinars for such things. Household *B* spent about half that amount, purchasing additional items, including walnuts (for holiday and ceremonial cakes), candy for the children, and a coffee substitute, in place of the very expensive coffee. Other luxuries include visits to the kafana in the village and in Arandjelovac, shaves and haircuts at the barber's instead of at home, facial soap and, occasionally, *kolonska voda* for younger women, trips to other towns, and excursions made by school groups.

As far as miscellaneous expenses are concerned, certain items are included here not necessarily because they are relatively unimportant or because they must be considered luxuries, but rather because variations are so extreme. First, it is important to mention that quite a few households purchase agricultural products from other peasants. Household *A* happens to be quite self-sufficient in this respect, but Household *B* spent a significant sum, 38,000

[30] The fabric costs 1,000 dinars, and an additional 200 dinars is paid to a tailor to make the shirt.

dinars, on firewood, corn for pig feed, and hay for the stock. Many households occasionally purchase vegetables from one another, if they have not raised certain types themselves that year. There is also much trading in livestock among peasants, and it is not uncommon for investments in cattle, swine, and, to a lesser extent, sheep, to form a significant part of a household's economy. Household *A* sold a horse, for part of the money needed for a brick barn. Household *B* sold a young calf and several other animals during the course of the year and also purchased an older calf.

Other important expenses are those for medical care. This is much less of a problem to the mixed agriculturalists, since all state employees (clerks, factory workers, miners) and their immediate nuclear families receive free treatment. On the other hand, pure agricultural households like Households *A* and *B* must pay for all medical services.[31]

The largest single expenditures during certain years are those for capital improvements, such as building a new house, a new barn, digging a well, having electricity installed, or buying a new wagon. Purchasing a radio or an accordion would also be in this category. In 1952–53 Household *A* spent the large sum of 200,000 dinars on a brick barn, considered to be among the best in the village and much admired by all. Such a project, or even a smaller one, is the result of years of planning and considerable thought, so arrange just how much livestock, wine, and brandy must be sold to raise the necessary funds. Frequently it takes several years to complete a project once it is under way. There are several half-built new-type houses in Orašac where construction has stopped until the next season, when the owner hopes somehow to sell a cow or a few hundred liters of rakija to get more money to go on with construction.

Then, there are a number of minor expenses. An important one, although very small in terms of cash outlay, is the contribution to the church and the priest's fees for special services. Many poorer households do not give any money to the church, and even the

[31] By no means do all the peasants use modern medical facilities. Cost is one problem, and then, too, there is still fairly widespread belief in traditional cures. This is particularly true among the older pure agriculturalists.

Prices of Selected Consumer Items in Arandjelovac, 1953

Item	Cost in Dinars	Item	Cost in Dinars
Cotton kerchief	400	Wooden mixing trough	1,500
Bride's dress	4,000[a]	Wooden mixing spoon	20
Rubber sandals	600	Kerosene lamp	280
Leather sandals	2,000	Oxen yoke	500[b]
High rubber boots	2,000	Wagon fork	1,000[b]
Straw hat	300–500	Pitchfork	100
Fur hat	2,000	Plow	4,500
Manufactured woolen		Radio	36,000
goods (1 meter)	1,000–3,000	Accordion	350,000[c]
Woman's fur vest	3,500	Books	600[d]
Second-hand sheet metal		Tombstone	100,000[e]
cook stove	4,000	Wood (1 cu. meter)	1,200
Second-hand stove for heating	2,500	Kerosene (1 liter)	90
Galvanized tin pail	600	Salt (1 kilo)	30
Small enamel mug	80	Sugar (1 kilo)	145
Large enamel pot	800	Lime (1 kilo)	15
Earthenware cooking dish	50	Soda (1 kilo)	250
Earthenware jug	200		

[a] Material cost 3,500 dinars and tailor's fee, 500.
[b] For materials and labor.   [c] Imported from Italy.
[d] For one semester for a child in seventh grade.
[e] For large, elaborately carved polished marble marker; porcelainized photograph inset costs an additional 5,000 dinars.

Costs of Some Services in Orašac, 1953

Service	Cost in Dinars	Comments
Having a haircut	25	Done by part-time peasant specialist.
Leading a kolo dance	50-100	The longer the dance, the more it costs.
Preparing rakije	—	Payment is in kind; two liters for each barrel distilled.
Threshing	—	80 kilos for each ton of wheat threshed.
Use of machine for separating grain	—	One kilo for each 100 kilos processed.
Having wedding feast cooked	1,200	Two days' and one night's work.
Rental of fiacre[a]	2,000	For carriage, horses, and driver for two days.
Electrification	70,000	To connect house two kilometers from line.
Electrification	6,000	Per outlet.
Hospitalization in Belgrade	500/day plus 10,000	Medical care and surgical fees for removal of tumor.

[a] To go to a relative's wedding in a village several miles away.

contribution from Household *A*, 1,600 dinars (including candles purchased at services), is relatively modest. School children must pay for all their textbooks, writing pads, pens, pencils, and ink, as well as the black cotton smocks worn by schoolgirls all over Yugoslavia and the special caps worn by the boys. Veterinarian's fees, repairs, occasional envelopes and postage, for writing to relatives in the city or in the army, all add up on the debit side.

Household *A* estimated 4,920 dinars as cash on hand at the end of the year, with a total income of 430,400 dinars and outlay of 425,480. This is definitely greater participation in a cash economy than is typical for Orašac as a whole. Household *B* represents a more characteristic picture, receiving 160,500 dinars and spending 158,950, just about breaking even and waiting until next year, or the year after that, to plan for something they had hoped to be able to buy this year.

Given above is a list, "Prices of Selected Consumer Items in Arandjelovac, 1953," including everyday objects the peasant has to purchase as well as more expensive items for particular occasions. Another type of expenses, "Costs of Some Services in Orašac, 1953," is also summarized. Examples of payment in kind are illustrated. Also included in the latter listing is the price of an operation and hospitalization in Belgrade, to give an idea of the cost for such services to pure agriculturalists.

AGRICULTURE AS A SOURCE OF CASH INCOME

There are very few agricultural or livestock products raised in Orašac which are not marketed at least to some extent. The most significant, as sources of cash, involve trading in wine and brandy and selling livestock, particularly horses, cattle, and swine. The two big grain crops, corn and wheat, are of distinctly secondary importance when it comes to marketing. Corn is used almost exclusively as a livestock feed and wheat for flour; only the very largest households have surplusses. This grain pattern is, as we have seen earlier, a relatively recent development.

It is hard to give any absolute ranking to the importance of the various products, chiefly because weather conditions are prone to affect severely the crop yields from one year to the next. However,

the "Items Sold" columns for Households *A* and *B* budgets give
a rough idea. A little less than half of *A*'s income and a little more
than half of *B*'s are provided by the sale of rakija and wine. Livestock trading accounts for about one quarter of both *A*'s and *B*'s
income. The remainder of the more prosperous household's income
is from the sale of wheat, a small amount of corn, and poultry and
dairy products. Household *B* rounded out its income with the sale
of fresh fruit and dairy products.

A relatively minor proportion of the peasants' produce is sold to
the local cooperative or directly to state agencies. The central
outlet, and for many households the only one, is the *pijac*, or
the peasant market, in Arandjelovac every Friday throughout the
year. Livestock and crafts are traded at a special *vašar* held periodi-
cally in Arandjelovac and other towns in the region. Most of the
produce is marketed in small quantities. Almost every village household has one and sometimes two members going to market each
week, to carry a few kilos of wine or brandy, a basket of eggs, a
crock of cheese, or a live, squawking hen. Since preserving fruits
and vegetables is not generally practiced, most of them are sold as
they appear in season. As would be expected there is a considerable range in prices during the course of the year, as shown in
Table 5.

Examples of actual livestock sales and the general range in price
for each type mentioned are cited in Table 6.

A picture of the differences among the peasants in terms of
agricultural income is partly given in the evaluation of gross annual
income compiled in 1952 for tax purposes. Conservative estimates,
they range from 2,000 dinars a year to 305,000. Actual peasant
incomes, including the value of the produce consumed at home,
are at least two or three times these amounts in terms of 1952–53
prices.[32]

From the examination of peasant budgets and other data several
points clearly emerge. The most important is that those households
with the largest landholdings produce the greatest surplus for sale.

---

[32] Taxes based on these assessments ranged from a low of 140 dinars, or about seven
percent of the total estimated household income, to a high of 104,000, about 35 percent.

Table 5. Agricultural Produce Sold in Arandjelovac Market, 1953
(In Dinars per Kilo)

Item	Average Price in Season	Annual Price Range[a]	Item	Average Price in Season	Annual Price Range[a]
Vegetables			**Fruits and Nuts**		
Beans	50	30–50	Apples	15	8–50
Cabbage	7	5–20	Apricots	50	30–55
Carrots	80	50–85	Cherries, sour	32	32
Cauliflower	50	50	Cherries, sweet	20	20
Garlic	50	50–80	Grapes, fresh	23	20–80
Onions	20	20–40	Grapes, dried	45	45–80
Peas	52	52	Lemons	100[e]	
Peppers	22	17–25	Medlars	20	20
Potatoes	20	15–30	Melons	12	10–30
Salad greens	30	30	Peaches	30	30
Snap beans	50	35–60	Pears	40	20–70
			Plums, fresh	6	6–10
Animal Products			Plums, dried	55	55
Beeswax	1,200	1,200	Quince	30	30
Cheese	85	80–120	Walnuts	80	80
Eggs	12[b]	10–20	Watermelon	12	5–20
Honey	250	250–300			
Kajmak	220	200–250	**Grains**		
Milk	30[c]	25–30	Corn	17	10–40[f]
Beef	75	60–85	Oats	10	10
Mutton	65	60–75	Wheat	22	20–50
Pork	150	150–170			
Veal	70	65–75	**Brandy and Wine**		
Chickens	80	80–200[d]	Rakija, ljuta	150[c]	140–160
Turkeys	100	100	Šljivovica	80[c]	70–100
Geese	100	100	Wine	60[c]	40–70

[a] Where no range is given, item is strictly seasonal.
[b] For one egg.   [c] Dinars per liter.
[d] Winter prices more than double.
[e] Very rarely, a peasant raises lemons and sells them by the piece.
[f] Much cheaper if purchased by the ton.

Table 6. Examples of Actual Livestock Sales by Orašac Villagers, 1953

Type of Livestock	Price in Dinars	Possible Price Range in Dinars
Cow, 3 years old	50,000	15,000–60,000
Calf, under one year old	15,000	10,000–20,000
Bull, one year old	41,000	38,000–45,000
Fattened pig	4,000	3,000– 5,000
Suckling pig	1,000	1,000– 1,200
Lamb, one year old	3,500	3,000– 4,500

This was true even before the First World War, when the Central Cooperative Society of Serbia made a survey showing that land-holdings of between five and ten hectares used 79 percent of their production in their own households, while those with fifteen to thirty hectares used 74 percent, and those with over fifty hectares of land used only 59 percent at home. The primary function of agriculture in Orašac is to provide subsistence, and producing for a market, while important, is definitely subsidiary.

Although practically all the households produce enough to feed themselves, many families are not able to market enough to pay their taxes and purchase even the basic necessities. Especially in larger families there exists more labor than is necessary to work the land, and as a result many peasants seek full or part-time employment outside of agriculture, in the local coal mine or the factories in Arandjelovac.

There has also been a marked shift in marketing patterns. The decrease in the significance of wheat as a cash crop has already been mentioned. After the First World War the marketing of farm products increased, or began where none existed earlier. This is true of poultry, milk products, and fresh fruits and vegetables and is a development brought about by the growth of the town population, including the position of Arandjelovac as a small-scale industrial and tourist center. The whole region of Šumadija has been affected by increasing demands of the Belgrade market and, with some improvements in transportation, by the growth of the export market. This last development seems destined to grow in importance. In fact, the intention of the agronomists in the Orašac County area is to step up production of specialty crops associated with orchards and vineyards and to de-emphasize the subsistence aspects of the economy such as sheep raising. Regardless of how these plans ultimately turn out, one thing is certain: if the industrialization of the region continues the pure agriculturalists will be drawn increasingly into a cash economy. This is a trend which has continued in spite of wars and changes in government and which is clearly shown in the slow but steady rise in the peasant's standard of living.

SOURCES OF INCOME OUTSIDE PRIVATE AGRICULTURE

The earliest information available on sources of income outside private agriculture in Orašac is in the census of 1895, when sixty-one persons out of a total of 1,514 people in residence at the time were listed as belonging to households which did not derive their main income from working their own land. This number undoubtedly included the priest and schoolteacher as well as one or two clerks and officials connected with village government. The others were local merchants and artisans. At that time they amounted to only 4 percent of the population; by 1953 the proportion of mixed agriculturalists and landless residents had increased tenfold, accounting for 41 percent of the population of 2,182.

The situation began to change early in the twentieth century, particularly with the establishment of the coal (lignite) mine in Orašac. A few of the early peasant workers at the mine are now on pension, after thirty-five years of labor, and there are more than a dozen Orašac villagers with over twenty years of service at the mine.

Between the wars approximately 13 percent of the population of the county was not dependent primarily on agriculture. By 1948 the figure had increased to 19 percent. The region is without question still overwhelmingly agricultural, however. Non-private agriculture (state farms and cooperatives) represented over 55 percent of the total county income from economic enterprises in 1952. In the whole of Orašac County that year there were only about 1,600 factory workers and miners (in lignite mines, quartz quarry, sand and clay pits, glass and refractory materials factories).

Orašac village, then, is atypical of the villages in the county with regard to the number of inhabitants having sources of income outside private agriculture. These sources may be broken down into several categories: agricultural work on land other than one's own, part-time nonagricultural work, usually in Arandjelovac and occasionally in Orašac, full-time occupations (at the mine, factories, and village offices), special crafts, pensions, and, finally, income from relatives residing outside the village. Within this break-down, both the permanently employed and the part-time workers fall into two classifications: there are mixed agriculturalists (Group II) who live in households with an adequate amount of land and a surplus of able-bodied working members, so that the labor of one can be spared sufficiently to allow him to have an outside job, and there are those who are forced to work to subsist, pay taxes, and purchase necessities, including mixed agriculturalists with insufficient land and landless residents (Group III).

Earning money as an agricultural laborer is less common now than was formerly the case. Most peasants do their own work or exchange labor through pozajmica. Yet before the war wealthier peasants often employed others to help with the farm work. There was adequate labor available, for jobs in the town or in industry were either nonexistent or difficult to obtain. With the establishment of the state farm in Orašac in 1953,[33] the state may take the place of the large peasant landholder as an employer of paid agricultural labor, both full- and part-time. According to the head agronomist for the Orašac state farm, in the spring of 1954 there were to be about one hundred workers employed on the farm during the coming peak season, but at present there were only twenty full-time laborers, half of them from Orašac and half from neighboring Stojnik.[34]

There are also wages earned for part-time labor. Many villagers, including members of pure and mixed agriculturalist groups and landless residents, are employed at present or have worked at some time in the past on temporary projects. Construction work in and around Arandjelovac has been of increasing importance since the war. Many peasants participated in road gangs, railroad work, and construction projects, such as the building of workers' flats and the new factories.

People in the next three categories, including full-time workers, full-time specialists, and pensioners, total 278 Orašani in 1953. Table 7 lists the various occupations for males and females, with 202 people in the mixed agriculturalist group and 76 in the landless resident group. Of the total number, 104 men are miners,

[33] The state farm is made up of land confiscated from peasant holdings exceeding 10 hectares (exclusive of woods), in accordance with a land reform act which went into effect in this area in the summer of 1953.

[34] The farm occupies land in both villages.

Table 7. Full-Time Occupations of Mixed Agriculturalists and Landless Residents, 1953

Mixed Agriculturalists (Group II)
  Total: 202

Males		Females	
Miners	64	Widows on pension[e]	12
Pensioners[a]	35	Agricultural laborers[c]	8
Skilled industrial workers	30	Seamstresses	2
Unskilled laborers	19		
Masons[b]	8		
Carpenters[b]	6		
Clerks	5		
Railroad workers	4		
Agricultural workers[c]	3		
Landlords[d]	3		
Officials	2		
Waiter at kafana	1		

Landless Residents (Group III)
  Total: 76

Males		Females	
Miners	40	Workers at the mine[i]	6
Other workers at the mine[f]	8	Teachers	3
Miscellaneous workers[g]	6	Agricultural laborers	2
Pensioners[h]	6		
Teachers	4		
Priest	1		

Source: Serbian Statistical Bureau.

[a] Includes 31 former miners, 2 former railroad workers, 1 former clerk, and 1 former road worker.

[b] There are a variety of craftsmen in the village, but only these are full-time specialists.

[c] Work almost full time on other people's land.

[d] Old people who rent out small amounts of land.

[e] Includes 10 miners' widows.

[f] Includes 2 machinists, 2 unskilled workers, 1 electrician, 1 carpenter, 1 first-aid attendant, and 1 apprentice.

[g] Includes 3 masons, 1 agricultural laborer, and 1 bookkeeper.

[h] All former mineworkers.

[i] Includes 2 cooks, 2 janitresses, and 2 helpers.

about two-thirds of whom come from mixed agricultural households.[35] The list includes additional skilled industrial workers,

[35] These numbers do not include, of course, all those Orašac peasants who have ever worked at the mine. It is considered by many to be unpleasant work, and consequently there has been a fairly large turnover. Many peasants in the present pure agriculturalist group have worked at the mine for several months or even several years at some former time.

unskilled laborers, and others in the village. Pensions provide a source of income for fifty-three people, most of them retired miners or widows of miners.

Mining is the most important full-time occupation aside from private agriculture in Orašac. Those working at the Orašac mine are numerically insignificant to the county population as a whole,[36] but peasant miners throughout Serbia as a whole present an interesting fact: of all the miners in Serbia, in 1950, more than half were members of land-owning agricultural households and an additional quarter owned homes and practiced limited horticulture and livestock raising. This means that more than three-quarters of the Serbian miners were closely connected with village life.[37] Thus, although Orašac is an atypical village in the county because of the mine, the miners in the village are representative of the economic pattern of Serbian miners in general.

The Orašac mine is among the smaller lignite mines in Serbia, but its production is by no means insignificant. Since its peak year of 1948, output has been gradually declining. Certain of the veins appear to have been exhausted, but it is not certain that the Orašac mine will have to be abandoned. The mine was closed for repairs for several months in 1953–54, during which years about 150 people were working there. When in full production some 250 people are said to be employed, and it was expected that after repairs the mine would again employ a full force. Many of those working at the mine are from the adjacent villages of Stojnik and Misača.

After the war the new government gave considerable attention to the mine and built a mining colony of seventeen concrete block buildings, including a two-story barracks for single workers, an office, and duplex dwelling units. All construction was completed in 1948, but by 1953, when employment was at a low ebb, only a few of the dwellings were still occupied. The two rows of barren, low buildings, unrelieved by flowers or by trees, are not considered part of the village by the Orašac peasants. They frequently

[36] Mining is, however, the second most important economic enterprise in Orašac County in terms of both gross annual income and number of workers employed.
[37] *Proizvodne Snage NR Srbije*, p. 315.

praise their own homestead sites, the fresh air, attractive foliage, and lack of immediate neighbors, and if one villager builds a home too close to another, they will scoff disdainfully, "Hummmf— why don't you go live *u koloniji?*"

Since the war a new type of full-time workers has emerged. This is the group of men, both skilled and unskilled, who hike in to Arandjelovac every day to work in the factories. A factory producing bottles and other glass products and a plant for the production of refractory materials, using local clay deposits, have actually been in existence since the late 1920s, but they have been expanded, and in 1952–53 a new factory, for electro-porcelain insulators, was built. Despite the fact that many peasants, from Orašac as well as the other villages, have become machine operators or "experts" in other ways they still continue to "commute," returning home in the evening and remaining firmly attached to the traditional way of life. At present there are about forty such men from Orašac, and their numbers will no doubt increase as the factories go into fuller production.

A final type of full-time occupation includes those peasants employed by the local village council, the cooperative, and the state farm's office. They are two elected officials, various clerks and bookkeepers, and the waiter at the kafana, in addition to a few watchmen and janitors, included in Table 7 as unskilled laborers.

For all these workers who receive regular wages, the pay is fairly standardized. Permanent employees of the state earn, on the average, about 7,000 dinars a month for unskilled labor and 10,000 for skilled work. In addition to the monthly salary each employee is entitled to pensions and medical care already mentioned. A relatively high monthly allotment, based on number of children and amount of land owned, substantially increases each man's salary. "Examples of Orašac Salaries, 1953," which are listed below, show that an unskilled worker, the janitor at the Village Council, gets a total monthly salary considerably higher than wages received by the President, Secretary, or clerk of the Village Council, due to his very small landholdings and his children's allotments.

Examples of Orašac Salaries, 1953

Job	Salary in Dinars	Comments
Common laborer	250–300/day	500/day for reaping.
Skilled laborer or artisan	500/day	
President of Village Council	8,000/mo.	
Secretary of Village Council	7,400/mo.	Including 700-dinar allotment for each of two children.
Clerk at Village Council	5,400/mo.	
Janitor at Village Council	8,300/mo.	Including 1,800-dinar allotment for each of two children.
Miner	10,000/mo.	Including allotments for children.
Skilled factory worker	10,000/mo.	Including allotments for children.
Church sexton	8,000/yr.	An honorary position.

Returning to the various sources of income outside of private agriculture, another category is the specialists or village craftsmen. They have the oldest tradition of all. In addition to the masons, carpenters, and seamstresses who work full-time there are about the same number of specialists in the village who work seasonally, when there is a letup in farming chores. Income from specialists' goods or services is very variable and rather irregular. Sometimes they are paid in cash, but as often as not they receive a prearranged amount of produce or goods or even labor of some sort.

Aside from the usual crafts,[38] there are at present in Orašac several accordion players who perform at village and family festivities, a slaughterer, and a few practitioners of folk medicine. Certain specialists, such as bagpipe players and men who made woven corncribs and other outbuildings, have entirely disappeared in the village. Several new types have developed—for example, well-diggers and the men who own the brandy stills and threshing machines.

Pensions are still another type of income. Of all the Orašac pensioners in 1953, the average length of time worked was seventeen years. The value of individual pensions ranges from 4,400 dinars a month to 8,800. The average monthly sum for all fifty-three recipients is 4,900 dinars. Pensioners are almost entirely former

[38] In the village, brickmaker, carpenter, barrelmaker, wagonmaker, stovemaker, housebuilder, and tailors for male and female garments; in town, barber, wooldyer, coppersmith, tombstone-cutter, tanner and furrier, potter, miller, ropemaker, candlemaker, boot- and sandal-maker, smiths for farm tools and shoeing animals, and saddle- and harness-maker.

miners or miners' widows. The retired miners are now for the most part in the mixed agriculturalist group, and the monthly pension they receive is a significant addition to the economy of their individual households.

Lastly, and least significant as a source of income, are the cases of peasants who leave Orašac more or less permanently to live in Arandjelovac, another town, or even Belgrade. This has occurred not infrequently, and those who leave usually cease to contribute to their family's income although they maintain strong kin ties and often return to the village to visit. Nevertheless, there are a few cases of men living and working in other places and supporting their wives and children who remain in the village to work the land.

Today, when a man whose only job is to work his land is asked how he earns his living, he will reply assertively that he is a *pravi* or *čist seljak*, a true or pure peasant, thereby distinguishing himself from those who receive all or part of their income from sources other than private agriculture. His household is in a relatively unfavorable situation compared to that of the mixed agriculturalist. He has no assured steady livelihood but is dependent on luck and the weather, while members of mixed peasant households who are state employees have regular salaries and other benefits. In addition, until recently the tax structure did not favor the pure peasant who tried to produce higher yields in order to market the surplus; those who produced chiefly for their own needs, and perhaps were not as good farmers, paid much smaller taxes. These developments have tended to create understandable dissatisfaction among the pure agriculturalists.

A good illustration of the significance of nonagricultural sources of income is the household of Velimir Petrović, which includes his wife, son, daughter-in-law, and grandchild. They have only two hectares of land, one cow, a few pigs and chickens, and no sheep. Their house is sturdy and neat, built of concrete, and they have sufficient food and clothing and even a luxury, a sewing machine. The relative prosperity here is explained by the fact that Velimir is a craftsman when he is not attending to farm work. He repairs fences, carves distaffs, and weaves straw hats. Duško, his son, is a skilled worker, a glass cutter, in Arandjelovac, who saved enough money to buy an accordion and now supplements the household's income by playing at weddings and dances.

Another case is the household of Budimir Stojanović. Budimir himself spends all his time working the land and caring for the livestock, but his household is classified as mixed agriculturalist because his son Radovan is a clerk at the village Cooperative. There are seven members in the household, three of them children, living on less than four hectares of land. Yet they were able to complete a new brick and concrete house one year and to have a well dug four years later with money earned from agriculture supplemented by Radovan's salary and allotments for the children.

In contrast, many households with twice as much land but no outside source of income have a difficult time making ends meet because of the burden of taxes and necessity of buying a few essentials.[39]

These two examples also illustrate a change in the use of money. Formerly the primary function of cash was to purchase land, for the more land a peasant had, the greater was his economic status in the eyes of the other villagers. The peasant budgets for two pure agriculturalist households and these illustrations for two mixed agriculturalist households show how a different money-spending pattern prevails today. True, some peasants, especially those with very small holdings, may wish to acquire a little additional land, but the emphasis today is definitely on capital improvements to the homestead and more spending on goods for personal consumption.

[39] Formerly peasants frequently found themselves in debt, a major socio-economic problem of pre-war governments. With the coming of the Communist government and the nationalization of all financial institutions, almost all peasant debts were canceled.

CHAPTER 5

SHELTER, CLOTHING, AND FOOD

CHANGES in Serbian rural culture are perhaps most clearly
defined in observations of homes, house furnishings, and clothing.
Considerable variations in diet have occurred too, but they have
not been as marked.

HOMES AND HOUSE FURNISHINGS

To the Serbian peasant a home represents a good deal more than
simply a place to eat and sleep. His homestead, enclosed by a
fence he has made with his own hands and surrounded by his
plum orchard, is literally the center of his universe. This is especially true in Orašac where, because of geography and historical
traditions discussed earlier, homesteads are scattered. Figure 7 is a
diagrammatic representation of a prosperous homestead at about
the turn of the century. It can be seen immediately that it is a
compact, self-contained unit, with the central main house, the
sleeping quarters for young couples, various storehouses, and other
small outbuildings within the *avlija*, or courtyard. Outside are the
hutches and stalls for each different kind of livestock, the haystacks, manure pile, garden, and orchard. A composite diagram of
the homesteads of Households *A*, *B*, and *C* in 1954 (Figure 8)
shows that the wealthiest still retains the traditional homestead
cluster. It has innovations of a well and an outdoor toilet within
the courtyard, and certain of the traditional outbuildings have lost
their function. For example, the vajat formerly used for sleeping is

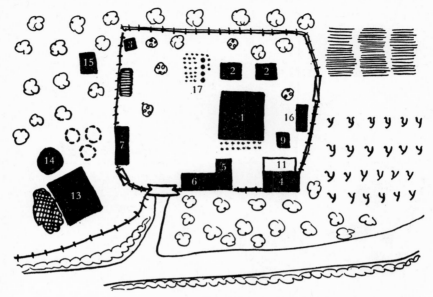

Figure 7. Prosperous Šumadijan Homestead, 1900

Key for Figures 7 and 8

═══	village path	🝆🝆🝆	plum orchard
┼┼┼┼	sturdy fence	🝆🝆🝆	other fruit trees
┬┬┬┬	makeshift fence	⌇⌇⌇	acacia trees
⊃⊂	covered gateway	ɣ ɣ ɣ	vineyard
⊂⊃	gate	○ ○	haystacks
⦙⦙⦙	flower garden	▩	manure pile
▬▬	vegetable patch	▥	woodpile

1. House, *kuća*
1a. Old house, *stara kuća**
1b. New house, *nova kuća**
2. Sleeping quarters, *vajat*
2a. Formerly sleeping quarters, now used for storage*
3. Bread oven, *peć*
4. Grain storehouse, *ambar*
5. Stone cellar, *podrum*
6. Shed, *kačara*
7. Corncrib, *koš*

8. Smokehouse, *sušnica**
9. Dairy shed, *mlekar*
10. Well, *bunar**
11. Summer kitchen, *letnja kuhinja*
12. Toilet, *nužnik**
13. Stall, *štala*
14. Sheep hutch, *ovčarnik*
15. Pigsty, *svinjac*
16. Chicken coop, *kokošarnik*
17. Beehives, *pčelarnik*

* Found only in Figure 8.

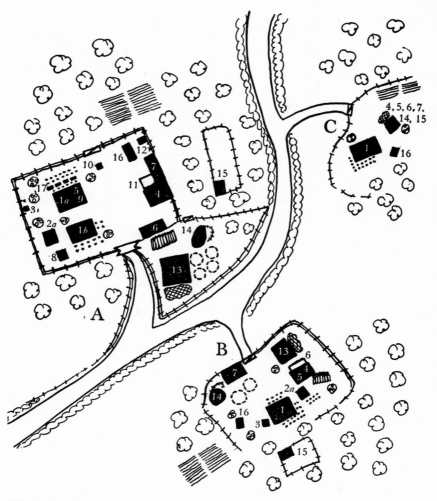

Figure 8. Composite Diagram of Three Contemporary Orašac Homesteads
(*A*) Wealthy household. (*B*) Average household. (*C*) Poor household.

now an additional storage house; the podrum and *mlekar*, or dairy shed, have been moved into the main house. The homestead of *B* is contained in a less sharply defined enclosure, with animal stalls on one side of the courtyard, although the pigsty is in the traditional location in the orchard. Household *C* uses one small shack to serve as stall for the few animals and storehouse for the small amount of produce. It has no outdoor bread oven and must use a neighbor's. The homestead unit itself is barely delineated.

In general, then, the *average* Orašac homestead has more or less the complete complex of outbuildings, except for a well and an outdoor toilet—these are relatively recent even in wealthier households. Formerly water was obtained from springs, and today several households may share a well. As for toilets, those few that do exist are crude lean-tos over a hole in the ground. But general opinion is that "the open air is much healthier." Livestock stalls, with the exception of the few brick cow barns in the village, are constructed as they have been in the past—wattle and daub huts, straw or thatch structures, or woven twig enclosures. Old-fashioned conical mud beehives have been largely discarded in favor of modern wooden ones.

Even the rudest homestead is entered through a gate of some sort, and richer ones have wide covered gateways through which wagons may pass. Both the old and newer types of fences and gates are in use in Orašac today. If a new *kapija* (covered gateway) is built, however, it is in the modern style, with brick posts and a roof of tile.

Another feature of every homestead, no matter how poor or small, is the flower garden. According to a local saying it is possible to tell if there is a young girl in the household by the condition of the garden. Many are carefully tended, bordered with whitewashed stones, and colorful blossoms are the pride of all the girls and women. The most important plant is sweet basil (*bosiljak*), considered a sacred herb and used in many religious ceremonies. Irises, lilacs, tulips, carnations, and roses figure prominently in the folk songs, although the most common flowers at present are hyacinths in the spring, peonies and giant dahlias in the summer, and varicolored chrysanthemums until the first frost. Geraniums are cultivated in old cooking pots. They add a touch of color to every window sill or doorstep.

Despite the standardization of outbuildings and the general layout resulting in a basic pattern, each "average" household is different. This is due first to economic positions, the amount of land owned, the terrain, and individual predilections of the owners. Perhaps another reason for variation within the general courtyard pattern is that the actual arrangement of the courtyard has less social significance to the peasant than does the arrangement of the interior of the house. Further, the courtyard provides considerably more room for maneuvering than does the relatively crowded interior.

As for the house itself, Figure 9 illustrates the well-defined series of house types which have succeeded one another since the late eighteenth century. The developmental sequence shown is generally characteristic of all Šumadija and specifically true for Orašac. The earliest type of Orašac house, first described in 1784, was the *brvnara*, or log cabin. Locally it was known as the *osačanka* (9a), named for a region in Bosnia from which the craftsmen who built these homes originated. It was still seen in Šumadija until well into the mid-nineteenth century and closely resembles peasant homes in the wooded regions of Bosnia today.[1] The basic log construction was similar to that of the cabins built by American frontiersmen in the same period. Here likeness ended, for the roof of the Serbian log cabin was high and steeply sloping and made of overlapping wood shingles. The chimney was also of wood, a tall smoke vent in the center of the roof above the hearth. Interiors were simple, usually consisting of one main room and sometimes one smaller one, with a floor of packed earth. Simple as these homes were, they were at first used only by the more prosperous, permanently settled peasants. Constant migrations and wars were going on, and many rural inhabitants lived in small huts or temporary shelters.

After about 1820 a new type of house appeared in the village. This was the *polubrvnara* (9b), or half-log cabin, a few examples of which still exist in Orašac today. It had two or more small rooms,

[1] Kojić, *Stara Gradska i Seoska Arhitektura u Srbiji*, pp. 125–26.

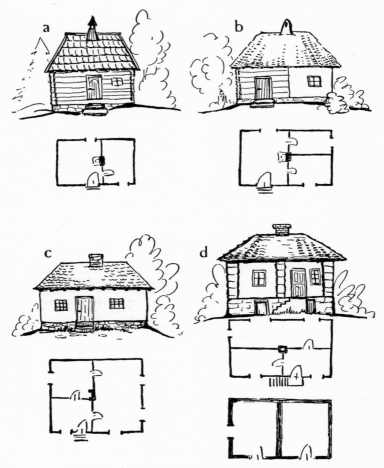

Figure 9. Development of Šumadijan House Types

(a) *Osačanka*, early-nineteenth-century, small log cabin with wood-shingle roof. (b) *Polubrvnara*, mid-nineteenth-century transitional type, half log, half mud plaster, with tile roof. (c) *Bondručara*, late-nineteenth-century to present, wattle and daub construction, whitewashed walls and tile roof. (d) *Zidana*, post-First World War to present, brick and concrete with kitchen and storage on lower level, traditional tile roof. (After Kojić, *Stara Gradska i Seoska Arhitektura u Srbiji*, p. 125.)

and the general layout was larger than that of the earlier log cabin. Wood was becoming a little less plentiful, and half the exterior was plastered with whitewashed mud over a wattle framework. The wood-shingle roof was replaced by a tile roof, with considerably less of a slant than the older type, and the wooden smoke vent by a mud chimney.

The *bondručara* (9c) began to be built in Orašac in the latter half of the nineteenth century. By this time the oak forests were fast disappearing and consequently wood was no longer the main construction material. Of wattle and daub construction, supported on wooden posts, the bondručara type had a lower tile roof and whitewashed interior and exterior walls. The size of the house and the size and number of rooms increased, many having two or three sleeping rooms. Despite this enlargement, the pattern of one larger main room has never altered. The vajati came to be used less frequently.

This type of house is still used by the majority of Orašac households in all classes. None has less than two rooms and many are larger. They are substantially the same as those built in the late 1800s—in fact, most of them are the same houses. All have dirt floors, although newer ones tend to have larger rooms and a few more windows.

Early in the twentieth century a new type of house was seen occasionally in rural Šumadija. It first appeared in the more prosperous valley regions and was not built in the neighborhood of Orašac until after the First World War. Representing the greatest advance in Serbian peasant architecture, the *zidana* (9d) house is a sturdy two-story dwelling of fired brick and concrete construction, with outdoor steps leading to the upper level. In 1954 only about ten percent of Orašac village households had such homes, although the percentage was higher in richer villages and those nearer Belgrade. This is as would be expected, for the design represents an adaptation of urban style and method to rural conditions.

Better protection, comfort, health, and prestige are enjoyed by the households living in the most modern type of house. Windows are more numerous and larger, usually opening out from the center like French windows. In addition, the zidana house replaces several formerly necessary outbuildings, such as the podrum, mlekar, and outdoor kitchen, by incorporating them into the lower level. Frequently when a new house is constructed the older one previously occupied by the household remains facing it or adjacent to it; in Figure 8*A*, for instance, the former dwelling takes on the function of a vajat, serving as supplementary sleeping quarters.

So much for the development of the basic house structure. The interior and furnishings, too, have also undergone a series of changes. One characteristic that has remained constant, however, is the kitchen as the heart of the house. It is the place where the family gathers when not sleeping or in the fields, the only heated room, and, under ordinary circumstances, the only place illuminated by kerosene lamp or electric light.[2] The term *kuća*, generally used by city people and peasants alike to designate "house" in general, was originally the word for kitchen or, more specifically, hearth. Today villagers use the literary Serbian word *kuhinja* for kitchen. Until houses began to be enlarged, with the introduction of the half-log cabin, the hearth was, in essence, the house. There was very little furniture, and the earliest dwellings were dominated by a copper or iron kettle suspended by a chain from the ceiling beam over an open fire on the dirt floor. Strips of meat and bacon were hung to smoke on the rafters. People sat on low three-legged stools and ate from small round wooden tables barely raised off the ground.[3] A crude cabinet held household utensils, and flour was stored in a divided wooden chest. Another large carved chest held clothing and blankets. At night the family slept on straw pallets around the hearth. For illumination hand-dipped candles were placed on small wooden stands. Windows were covered with stretched animal intestines or oiled paper. Most utensils were of wood—brandy flasks, bowls, plates, and spoons. One important piece of equipment was the *crepulja*, a large earthenware disk under which bread was baked on the open hearth, covered with hot ashes from the fire.

[2] An electrified home usually has an outlet in each room, but it is considered wasteful to have more than one light burning.
[3] The design of the *sofra*, or *sovra*, as the villagers call it, is directly related to Turkish tables.

This type of kitchen, which persisted in Orašac until early in the twentieth century, is illustrated in Figure 10.[4] While changes cannot be dated absolutely, it appears that most innovations occurred within the memory of the older Orašani. Villagers in their fifties and sixties all described conditions which existed in the first twenty years or so of their lives as similar to those summarized above. It seems fairly certain that by 1920 kerosene lamps, sheet-metal stoves, beds, and glass windows were used by most of the households and that in the period between the wars they became increasingly common. A typical contemporary kitchen is shown in Figure 11 with many of the earlier furnishings still in use. For example, the low tables and stools (Figure 12d, f) are important kitchen accessories today, but they are supplementary to sturdy handmade tables and benches of standard size. Another feature of most kitchens today is the crude bed with wooden slats (12e) in one corner, where the very old and/or very young of the household may sleep all year round or at least during the cold months. In the zidana type house the kitchen floor is of concrete; the storage cellar, which cannot be entered through the adjacent kitchen but only from outside (9d), frequently has a stone floor.

Present-day kitchen utensils are shown in Figure 13; they are of three types—those handmade at home, those made by peasant or town specialists, and manufactured items purchased at state stores. Among the items made at home are gourds for siphoning brandy and for holding water (13g, m) and the hollowed tree stump mortar, with pestle, for grinding lump salt (13j), the latter no longer in general use today. Utensils made by special craftsmen include the crocks and jugs (13d, e) turned on the potter's wheel in Arandjelovac as well as metal and wooden objects fashioned by Gypsies and other craftsmen. A variety of kettles (13i), pans, shearing scissors, wooden buckets and casks, measuring containers, mixing troughs, breadboards and ladles are sold at county fairs several times a year. Most of these objects have not altered in form in the past century and a half, especially the round *merica*, or grain measure (13b), hanging *slanica*, or salt box (13f), and the traditional

[4] Kitchens of this type can still be seen in many parts of southern Serbia and Macedonia.

Figure 10. Nineteenth-Century Šumadijan Kitchen

Figure 11. Contemporary Orašac Kitchen

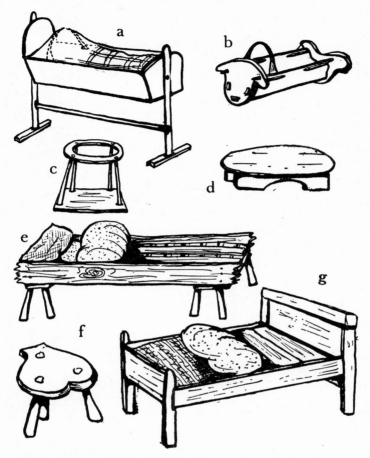

Figure 12. Household Furniture

(*a*) *Ljuljka*, mounted cradle showing how blanket is draped over sleeping baby. (*b*) *Kolevka*, low cradle on rockers. (*c*) *Dubak*, baby stand.
(*d*) *Sofra*, traditional low wooden table. (*e*) Bed with wooden slats.
(*f*) *Stoličıca*, heart-shaped, three-legged stool. (*g*) Modern bed.

Figure 13. Common Household Utensils

(*a*) *Čabar*, storage bucket for cheese. (*b*) *Merica*, container for measuring grain and flour. (*c*) *Bakvica*, bucket for drinking water. (*d*) *Ćup*, large earthenware storage crock. (*e*) *Testija*, jug with drinking spout on handle. (*f*) *Slanica*, salt box. (*g*) *Nategača*, gourd for siphoning. (*h*) *Naćve*, mixing trough. (*i*) *Bakrač*, copper cauldron. (*j*) *Tučak i stupa*, pestle and hollowed stump mortar, for grinding salt. (*k*) *Ložara*, basket woven from dried grapevines. (*l*) *Čutura*, wooden brandy flask. (*m*) *Tikva*, gourd water holder. (*n*) *Lopar*, board for removing bread from oven.

čutura, the wooden brandy flask (13*l*).[5] Manufactured utensils
found in most village kitchens include some enamel cooking ware,
enamel mugs and plates, a knife or two, a kerosene lamp, and
perhaps an iron heated by hot coals.

More prosperous households tend to have some "silverware,"
china dishes, glasses, and cotton tablecloths. These are put to use
only on holidays and other special occasions. With the growing
emphasis on a cash economy, more and more average households
are beginning to acquire such items. Concerning the relative
wealth of households, the impression that only the richer family
can have a zidana house has not been intended. In Chapter IV
we saw how Budimir Stojanović's household, comparatively poor
in terms of land, was able to build a modern house. At the same
time, many prosperous households live in older bondručara houses,
finding them adequate for their needs.

The house type itself, then, is not necessarily a symbol of the
wealth of the household. Nor can the fairly standardized kitchen
be considered indicative of financial status. It is only by an observation of the other room, or rooms, that the relative wealth of
an owner can be assessed. This is especially true if the house boasts
a *gostinska soba*, or "good room." The actual year-round function
of such a room is as storage space for dowry furniture, clothing,
and linens and as a display place for the household's best blankets
and embroideries. In this room the slava feast takes place, and it
is rarely used otherwise except when a relative or friend spends
the night.

Everyday furnishings include makeshift slat beds or carefully
constructed more modern ones (12*e*). The standard mattress is
flax sacking stuffed with dried corn husks, covered with a coarse,
hand-loomed linen sheet or a mat of braided rag strips. Cradles
are of two types (12*a*, *b*), and baby-stands (12*c*), "so that the baby's
legs will grow straight," are also standard equipment. Every household has at least one old wooden clothes chest similar to the kind
used by their ancestors. A relatively new addition to the bedroom

[5] Since the Second World War, however, metal army canteens are more commonly
used.

is the local version of the standard European clothes closet, called a *šifonjer* in Serbian. It is considered a desirable and very impressive piece of furniture to own but is invariably half-empty and looms incongruously large and bulky in the low-ceilinged dirt-floored cottage room. Nevertheless, almost every household has one, and one of its advantages seems to be its upper surface, on which apples, pears, and slatko are stored out of reach of mice and children. Other features of an Orašac sleeping room are the wall decorations. Most important is the *ikona*, an inexpensive lithographed picture of the family's patron saint. Sprigs of dried basil are tucked into the frame. A house may have a small shrine below its holy picture. Hanging in a place of honor is a photograph of the family's patriarch or deceased elder, usually embellished with a fine handwoven, embroidered towel draped over the frame. Other small photographs of relatives, many of them in military uniform, adorn the whitewashed walls.

On the day of the household's slava, the one good bed is covered with the family's best linens, blankets, and pillow covers (Figure 14) and the other beds are disassembled. Otherwise, the average sleeping room may contain as many as three beds, depending on the size of the household and the number of sleeping rooms available. Each bed, in which two or more people usually sleep, is shorter and about as wide as an American single bed. Common sleeping patterns are: husband, wife, youngest child; two, three, or four children, not necessarily all of the same sex; adult and young grandchild, not necessarily of the same sex.[6]

A completed zidana house always has wooden plank floors in the sleeping rooms on the upper level, and some even have garishly stenciled designs on the walls. The inhabitants of one older-type house, in their desire to be modern, had a relative with artistic inclinations decorate a wall with an idyllic dream mural, copied from an old advertisement.

Electricity is at present considered the most wonderful furnishing

[6] During the summer many people sleep out of doors, either in an old vajat or sheltered by the overhanging roof of one of the outbuildings. Cooking is also usually done outside in the summertime.

a house can have, but electrification is not primarily dependent on the wealth of the household, for only the five percent of Orašac houses located near the road are electrified (in 1954). The number of electrified homes is, however, slowly increasing. A 25-watt bulb is commonly used, and some of the houses have a slightly stronger one outside. Of these homes, six have radios (the kafana and school

Figure 14. Typical Orašac Sleeping Room

director's office also have one radio each).[7] Two houses have radios obtained as war booty from the Germans; neither house is electrified, but the radios sit in places of honor in each—above the šifonjer, draped with an embroidered towel.

Next to "marrying off" a son or daughter, one of the most important events in the life of a peasant is making the decision to build a house. This may be done when he splits off from his

[7] About a dozen houses possess old-fashioned crystal sets powered by batteries.

family zadruga, in which case he almost always builds his house nearby. In former days, however, new homes were built on virgin ground, the exact spot determined by a variety of folk methods which have since been abandoned. One of the most popular methods in Šumadija was to drive several sheep into a cleared field. The spot where they chose to lie down was considered lucky.[8] Since the Second World War it has been the goal of everyone planning to build a new house to have it zidana and constructed "according to a plan." Aside from the basic materials, an additional large financial outlay is required for iron reinforcing rods, window and door frames, and machined lumber.

Despite this goal many people end up constructing a bondručara house, for dried mud bricks, roughly hewn planks, wattle, and mud plaster can be secured much more cheaply and easily. Or a compromise may be worked out, in the construction of a dwelling that is transitional between the bondručara and zidana. Costs can be cut down by using certain second-hand materials or by substituting mud bricks for fired ones or mud plaster for cement in building a zidana-style house. A compromise house cost a little under 100,000 dinars in 1953 (about $350), using both new and second-hand materials; a modern zidana house, built in 1948, when materials were cheaper, cost 283,000 dinars (about $900). Discounting labor costs and fluctuating prices, these examples give a rough idea of the relative cash outlay for materials. Government loans are available, especially for those people employed in factories, but loans do not appear to play a significant role in peasant housing. Since the average annual income is something over 150,000 dinars, once taxes are paid and necessities purchased, there is very little cash to plan on. Nevertheless, once a household has made the decision to build a new home, it goes ahead with what it can do at the moment, proceeding year after year until the house is finally completed.

And when that day finally arrives, there is a *gozba na kuću*, a big house-warming celebration. Relatives and friends are invited, and each guest brings a small gift—a towel, glass, enamel mug, or cooking pot. The host roasts a pig and often hires an accordionist

[8] Mijatović, *Servia of the Servians*, p. 52.

for dancing after the feast. However, a household head may not call a party, claiming his budget cannot stand the strain of additional expense at this time. One thing almost everyone does is summon the village priest, who blesses the new home with prayers and holy water.

CLOTHING

In clothing more than in any other aspect of Orašac culture, the influence of almost five hundred years under the Turks is most evident.[9] In the nineteenth century Serbian urban and military clothing were the chief determinants of the change in village costumes, but after the First World War, Western influence was the strongest factor. One observer, writing in 1894, said that if a peasant maiden were to go to a dance or fair dressed in the folk costume of thirty or forty years earlier she would be regarded as a curiosity.[10] This statement is equally true today.

In evaluating a description of changes in the Orašac folk costume, the situation is more complex than it is for house types. There is a fairly clear sequence of changes, but dress is one of the most variable aspects of material culture, differing according to sex, age, wealth, the seasons, everyday and holiday wear, and to a lesser extent individual preferences. This is particularly true for the women's folk costumes of Šumadija, which vary from region to region and even between villages, although they conform to the same general pattern. On the other hand, men's costumes have been fairly uniform, not only in Šumadija but in all of Serbia. What follows is a summary of the costume changes experienced by the majority of the people of Orašac. One should bear in mind that variations did not affect all the villagers at the same time and that several different types of costumes could and did exist simultaneously.

The first in the series of changes began early in the nineteenth century, when the leaders of the First and Second Revolts and the more prosperous peasants began to dress in exact imitation of their

[9] Many Serbian words referring to costume parts are of Turkish origin—e.g., *jelek, džoka.*
[10] Miličević, *Život Srba Seljaka,* p. 35.

Turkish opponents. This was significant, for during the entire period of Turkish rule the Serbian rayah were forced to dress in the plainest garb as a sign of their subjection. Yet even the simple outfits worn by most of the men showed some Turkish influence. They consisted of fitted white woolen leggings and a loose jacket

Figure 15. Nineteenth-Century Šumadijan Folk Costumes

(*a, b*) Everyday dress for men and women, early nineteenth century. (*c*) Šumadijan bride with *smiljevac* headdress, about 1850. (*d*) Prosperous men's dress, latter part of nineteenth century. (*e*) Women's dress, late nineteenth century. (Figs. *a* and *b* after Vasić, "Srpska Nošnja za Vreme Prvog Ustanka," in *Istoriski Glasnik;* figs. *c* and *e* after mannequins in the Ethnographic Museum, Belgrade; fig. *d* after Erdeljanović, *Etnološka Gradja o Šumadincima*.)

worn over a linen shirt. Hair was worn in a long braid and caps were of red felt, similar to the Turkish fez. Another item derived from the Turks was the wide woven sash wrapped around the waist, formerly used for carrying tools and arms. Women wore long white linen shirts under coarse woven aprons and loose white wool jackets. Every married woman covered her head with a large kerchief. Men and women alike wore leather sandals which they made at home, the forerunners of the characteristic *opanke* of Šumadija (Figure 15a, b).

By about the middle of the nineteenth century most villagers were able to adopt the Turkish outfits worn earlier by their more prosperous countrymen. The change reached the village via contact with urban Serbs who had assimilated Turkish dress, particularly the men's costume. This was basically a three-piece outfit of baggy Turkish-type trousers, full in the seat and tapering below the knees, a short jacket (*anterija*), and a vest (*jelek*) worn on top of the jacket. Richer men had outfits made of fine imported woolen goods, and they wore great silk sashes instead of the more common woven woolen type. Their jackets and vests were trimmed with black braid, and they had high spats to match. Toward the end of the century the fez became more and more unpopular, although it was worn by some men until well into the 1900s. A brimless hat of black lamb's fur was worn instead, and the *šubara* is still the traditional Šumadijan headgear (15d). For the average peasants the costume change represented a liberation from the drabness of their former white wool garments.[11]

The basic garment of the women's outfit remained a long hand-woven linen shirt extending to the ankles. It was usually embroidered at the hem and had wide full sleeves. Two woven wool aprons were worn over it, one hanging in the back, usually of darker tones, with a front apron of bright geometric designs. Next came a Turkish-type vest (*prsluk*), of fine striped or solid-colored material trimmed with gold braid. Over all this was worn a *zubun*, the knee-length sleeveless coat of white wool, elaborately trimmed with red half-moons and spirals appliquéd according to

[11] P. Petrović, *Život i Običaji Narodni u Gruži*, p. 142.

characteristic Šumadijan designs, black silk tassels, and gold and silver sequins. The maidens' costume included strings of coins worn around the neck and a red fez on a coronet of braids (15*e*). Married women, following a fashion established in Belgrade and other cities, wore, secured on the back of the head, an oval wooden frame over which a large silk kerchief was draped. The most distinctive female headdress of the period, however, was the *smiljevac*, or bridal headdress. Of natural and artificial flowers, rows of coins, silver balls and sequins, and waving peacock feathers, it was more than a foot high and was anchored on the head by a chin strap strung with coins (15*c*). The bride wore this on her marriage day and on all special occasions after that until she bore her first child. It was such an elaborate and expensive item that it was frequently borrowed or rented.

Toward the end of the nineteenth century, especially by the time of the war between Serbia and Turkey (1876–78), parts of the folk costume underwent another series of changes. Men discarded the fez, the elaborate sash, the spats, and the very baggy pants. Women no longer wore the smiljevac or fez, and there was a gradual adoption of a long woolen skirt, which was worn over the linen shirt and replaced the dark rear apron and the zubun. The overskirt, of dark brown-, black-, or wine-colored wool, was knife-pleated. It usually had a broad band of stripes near the hem-line; the hem rose in accordance with the dictates of fashion, with the cue coming from urban styles. Geometric designs on the front aprons began to be replaced by striped ones and eventually by floral patterns.

In the hot summer months the peasants traditionally removed the outer woolen garments (Figure 16). The men, their heads protected by wide-brimmed straw hats, took off their jackets and trousers and worked in knee-length shirts and long linen underdrawers. They still wore the vest, woolen sash, and high colorful knitted stockings, as well as leather sandals with turned up "noses" in front, bound to the legs with shiny leather straps.[12] Women worked in their ankle-length shirts, wearing vest and apron but

[12] The opanci, of tanned pigskin, were now made by special craftsmen.

Figure 16. Everyday Summer Dress in Orašac, about 1900

not the wool overskirt. They wore high black knitted stockings all year round, and opanci similar to those of the men.

After the First World War the peasants of Šumadija patterned their pants after army riding britches, and many adopted the *šajkača*, similar to the American overseas cap. At present the sajkača is usually worn for everyday work while the fur šubara is saved for holidays and winter. The *čakšire*, or britches, are worn by all men; the younger men especially prefer the so-called "French cut," tightly fitted to the knee and flaring out above. At the same time, the present-day folk costume of the men retains very important elements of Turkish origin—the anterija and jelek. Most men actually have two complete suits of clothing. For holiday wear many have the outfit made of *čoha*, a fine woolen fabric imported from England before the war. The jelek and anterija are trimmed with silk cording and braid, in handsome designs against the rich dark-blue cloth. The amount of trim on this vest was felt to be indicative of a man's social position. These fine outfits are carefully saved, and in many cases the sons of the original owners now wear them. In addition, almost every man has a similar outfit made of *sukno*, brown homespun woolen goods. Rough and durable, it is much less lavishly trimmed, usually with black wool braid instead of silk. The jacket is a little longer and is called a *gunj;* the over-vest, or *džoka*, is worn in the same manner as the holiday jelek. Completing the costume are the šubara or šajkača, black knitted socks, not as high as those worn ten years ago, which are trimmed at the cuffs with gay floral needlepoint embroidery, and the inevitable turned-up sandals. Today most men wear shirts of store-bought cotton, made up at home or at the tailor's. As for underwear, they all wear long linen or cotton drawers (*gaće*), which also serve as lining for the scratchy woolen britches and as sleeping garments.

The men's costume, then, has not altered considerably. In the last few years, however, there have been certain innovations on the part of the younger men. Instead of the traditional three-piece homespun outfit there is a suit of manufactured cloth, consisting of standard Western double-breasted jacket and sharply flaring peasant britches, often with cap to match, considered most fashionable. Most young bridegrooms in 1953–54 got married in this outfit. Regular Western-type trousers, which the peasants call *civilne pantalone*, are worn by two or three villagers who work in the factory. Almost without exception, all Orašac males, including the miners, wear the peasant britches. The biggest recent change has been in footwear. Opanci are still worn by men of all ages, for both everyday and holiday wear, but high rubber boots and *curule*, rubber sandals introduced in the 1930s, are very common as work shoes. On Easter Sunday, 1954, when everyone was dressed in his best clothes, a number of the village youths sported high polished leather boots and freshly whitened sneakers. To be really modern some wore manufactured cotton socks of a cheap quality.

Young men tend to wear their hair longer than do the older men and combed back off the forehead. They are generally clean-shaven, and if a village youth succeeds in raising a mustache he is teased by his friends. Formerly all males wore a large handle-bar or walrus mustache, but only the older ones retain this style. A small neatly clipped mustache, copied from urban styles, is preferred by most middle-aged men.

As for the female version of the traditional regional costume, it now resides folded in newspaper and laurel leaves in the wooden clothing chests. Unlike the male costume, the women's folk dress has almost completely disappeared in this region, to the extent that it is a rare household today which can provide a complete female outfit. The women of Orašac say they stopped wearing it in the 1930s. After that came a long period of war and deprivation, and at present they have all become accustomed to urban dress and would not dream of going back to wearing the folk costume, not even on an important holiday. The only surviving features are the high woolen stockings, the opanci, and the traditional covered head for the married woman. She usually wears a gay red or blue kerchief everyday and a starched white one for holidays, in the house as well as outdoors. Maidens generally have retained the traditional *kike* hairdo, with long braids crisscrossed at the nape of the neck and pinned up on each side of the head. The costume, seen only when high-school students borrow their mother's or aunt's old outfits for performances dealing with folklore, is illustrated in Figure 17. The traditional linen shirt, shortened to blouse-length, is trimmed with embroidery or wide cuffs of crocheted string lace, and the full sleeves are caught up at the elbow with bright red ribbons. The pleated skirt is of modern length, with a striped or floral apron and a narrow, hand-woven sash. Over the blouse goes the prsluk, which originated in Turkish times —it is invariably deep blue, maroon, or purple velvet, trimmed with intricate borders and sprays of gold or silver embroidery and hooked up over the bosom to form a fitted vest.

Today women of all ages wear modified urban clothes. Older women tend to wear longer skirts and would never wear anything without long sleeves and a high neck. The standard clothing is a

Figure 17. Orašac Youth and Maiden in Holiday Dress

somber-toned skirt, several sweaters, the high black stockings, and
a kerchief. Many women in Arandjelovac wear kerchiefs, too, but
they can always be distinguished from village women in that they
arrange theirs well back on their heads, while the peasants fold
their kerchiefs forward over their forehead, forming a frame around
the face. Most women wear the shapeless, sleeveless *combinezon*, or
slip, usually their only undergarment. In the summer younger
women frequently go about barefoot or work in the fields and
around the house without the high black stockings. In the past
five years or so many older women have begun to shed their stockings when it gets too warm.

For colder weather women have their sleeveless fleece-lined
jacket, or *kožuh*, made by the same craftsmen in Arandjelovac who
fashion men's fur hats. It is illustrated in Figure 18, which shows

Figure 18. Everyday Dress in Orašac Today

an Orašac man and woman in standard everyday dress. Recently purchased jackets may be embellished with garish symbols of modernity—strips of colored plastic trim and ties with black and white rabbit fur pom-poms. A heavy knitted sweater is worn underneath it, and two skirts may be worn for extra warmth. Older women of more prosperous households envelop themselves in huge black knitted shawls, made of quality pre-war manufactured yarn.

The holiday clothing of girls of marriageable age most closely resembles that of their peers in the towns. Many have a pink rayon combinezon and a pair of perlon (similar to nylon) stockings to wear under a long-sleeved, loosely fitting wool dress, conservative brown or gray coat, and stout *antelop* (suede) or leather oxfords. The other currently popular outfit is the *kostim*, or suit, with man-tailored, broad-shouldered jacket and short, severe skirt to match. In fact, these garments are similar to those worn in

America in the 1930s. Styles are adopted by the villagers within a few years of their introduction into the provincial town. The small towns, in turn, take their fashion cues from Belgrade and other cities of central Europe, again several years behind style changes in the West. Manufactured woolen goods are very expensive, and it is generally the youths of the household who are the best-dressed. When an Orašac girl wears her holiday finery, it is likely that the only garment made at home is her sweater, often knitted in gaudy color combinations, such as chartreuse and bright pink, in sharp contrast to the rest of her outfit and made possible by the availability of commercial dyes.

Children's clothing is almost entirely hand-me-downs from older brothers, sisters, and cousins. The standard summer dress for preschool-age children is a short smock. Children commonly go barefoot and are not dressed in underpants until they are four or five years old. For the colder months mothers knit socks, mittens, and sweaters for their children, these items generally being the only ones made expressly for them. Little boys ready to start school receive a pair of čakšire, usually a size or two too large. When the seat and knees wear out they are patched: they must serve for a few more seasons. Each schoolboy wears a šajkača, and in the winter a knitted scarf is wrapped under his chin and tied on top of the cap to keep his ears warm. High-school boys wear special class caps. Starting in the fifth grade all girls wear black cotton smocks over their dresses.

It is difficult to explain why the men's traditional dress has been retained in Šumadija while the women's costume is no longer worn. It would be easy to say that the men are more conservative or that the materials for the women's costume are now difficult or impossible to obtain. The fact that in other parts of Yugoslavia, in Macedonia especially, the women have retained the folk costume and the men have adopted Western dress would seem at least partially to invalidate these explanations. Purely economic factors can be ruled out, since in many poorer areas the women still wear costumes more expensive and complicated than those of Orašac. A possible reason for the situation of the women's folk costume in Šumadija is the decline of women's crafts in general. This may be due to the gradual breakup of the zadruga and the trend toward nuclear families having their own separate households. The woman must participate to a greater extent in the household's agricultural activities and has less time to devote to handicrafts. The male costume is also more economical; the woven woolen fabric lasts longer than manufactured cloth, while the women's folk dress was less utilitarian.

Another issue of interest is the relationship between clothing and physical comfort. Wool is the basic material from which most clothing is made. It can be hot, scratchy, and uncomfortable in warm weather. As was pointed out earlier, women wore high knitted stockings all year round, and until relatively recently it was considered immodest and even indecent if they appeared without them. At the same time, most men wear their rough woolen britches even on the hottest summer days. Some observers have ascribed this to peasant conservatism and have also stated that villagers become accustomed to wearing such garments. The element of conservatism is surely at work—almost every older man has saved a long linen shirt from his younger days, but he would no more remove his britches and go out to reap wheat in long shirt and drawers than a New Yorker would go to Jones Beach in a gay nineties bathing suit. As to accustoming oneself to the clothing and becoming impervious to weather changes, judging by the comments of most of the Orašac men themselves, the matter is mainly an economic one. They cannot afford to buy lighter fabrics to be made up into summer work clothes.

When it comes to burial clothing, however, most people revert to tradition. Older women as well as men save in clothes chests folk outfits which they are to be dressed in when they die. It was said that folded away in her *sanduk* old Baba Milojka had the sole remaining ankle-length pleated wool skirt in Orašac. When we visited her and asked to see the skirt, she reluctantly opened the lid of the chest only after making it clear that the skirt was not for sale or barter and that come what may she was going to greet her ancestors dressed in proper attire.

HOUSEHOLD CRAFTS

Household handicrafts are mostly women's work, related to the preparation of clothing, blankets, and other cloth items. When more elaborate folk costumes were worn many parts were purchased from special craftsmen in town. These included the suits of imported fabric trimmed with silk braid and the women's velvet vests embellished with gold thread. Another purchased item was

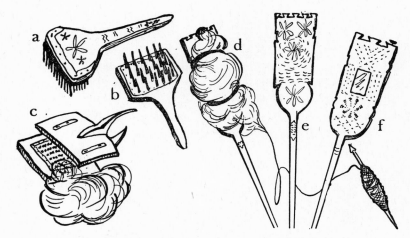

Figure 19. Tools for Cleaning and Spinning Wool

(a–c) *Grebeni*, types of wool combers. (d) *Preslica sa vretenom*, distaff and spindle. (e–f) Contemporary distaff designs.

the fine colored yarn for embroidering men's socks. All other woolen goods were made from the household's own wool, by the same process in use today.

After the sheep are shorn the wool is carded and carefully combed into clean swirls (Figures 19a-c). Spinning it is an arduous, never-ending task. A girl learns to spin when she is about thirteen years old; from that time on, it is rare to see her hands idle, for whether walking to market, tending the sheep, or waiting for the pot to boil, a Šumadijan woman's hands are always busy spinning. She straps a fluff of wool onto her distaff (19d-f) and tucks the long

handle into her left waistband. Crooking her left hand around the
head of the distaff she pulls out a tuft of wool, deftly twisting it
into yarn with the thumb and forefinger of her left hand. At the
same time she holds the top of a slender spindle in her right hand,
rotating it by a flicking wrist movement and continuously winding
the yarn onto it (Figure 17). The ambidexterous action is constant

Figure 20. Details of Costumes and Designs

(*a*) Sleeve of *anterija*, men's jacket, showing black silk braid trim.
(*b*) *Pojas*, men's sash woven of varicolored wool. (*c*) *Jelek*, men's
holiday vest, with intricate patterns in silk braid on back. (*d*) *Torba*,
woven wool carrying sack. (*e*) Old-type knitted stocking with geometric design. (*f*) *Tkanica*, women's woven sash. (*g*) Contemporary
men's sock of black wool trimmed with needle-point flowers on cuff
and instep. (*h*) *Nazuvica*, knitted toe-warmer worn over socks. (*i–k*)
Woven blanket designs.

and amazingly nimble, especially considering the blunt, work-worn fingers of most of the women.

Once the yarn has been prepared it is wound in skeins on a *motovilo*, or notched stick, and then rolled up into balls. Home-prepared yarn is used for all knitted goods but is most important for weaving. This is done on a simple single-harness horizontal loom, made by a village craftsman. The yarn is woven into colorful blankets, carrying sacks, and the sukno suiting. Previously, wool was dyed with linden and walnut bark, pepper leaves, and certain minerals, but today a variety of commercially prepared colors can be obtained, and village women prefer bright cabbage-rose and violet designs rather than the older striped and geometric patterns (Figures 20*i-k*). The carrying sacks in general retain more conservative patterns although they are woven in the new, gay colors (20*d*). Another item prepared on the looms is the variety of traditional sashes and belts (20*b, f*). Since they are no longer worn many younger women do not know how to weave them.

Cotton cloth as well as linen for shirts, sheets, and towels and hemp sacking for bags and mattresses were all woven at home, but as manufactured goods gradually become available the trend is more and more away from the home crafts. Peasant women pride themselves on their knitting, and although manufactured knitwear can be bought in Arandjelovac the villagers claim that theirs is of purer quality wool, more durable, and more attractive—all this despite the fact that every village girl longs to own a factory-made sweater. The characteristic Šumadijan men's socks (20*e, g, h*), still worn on holidays, are losing favor to more simple solid-color socks, and, again, many younger women have not learned the needlework skill necessary for the floral trim. Another declining art is embroidery, for silk thread of pre-war quality is no longer available. Crocheting has become more popular, and balls of cotton string are purchased and worked into trimmings for dowry sheets and pillowcases. Many women make doilies and runners patterned after urban styles but rarely use them in their cottages. "Lace" or net curtains, hung over the windows on holidays, are made of store-bought string or home-produced flax thread.

Every woman in Orašac sews clothing for her immediate family. When store-bought goods are used, however, a tailor is usually given the work. For female holiday garments this is usually a local woman skilled at operating an old-model sewing machine.[13] Fabric for men's clothing, whether homemade sukno or manufactured goods, is brought to the *abadžija* in town. There the garments are custom-tailored and trimmed with traditional black braid (20a, c).

Wood carving has always been a male craft. Small carved items, such as wooden spoons and spindles, are made by local Gypsies and sold in town, and large, important items, such as clothing

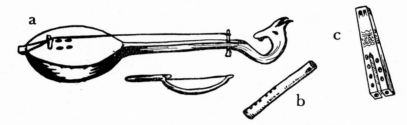

Figure 21. Musical Instruments

(a) Traditional-style *gusle* with bow. (b) *Svirala*, shepherd's flute.
(c) *Dvojnice*, double flute.

chests, looms, and tables and benches are made exclusively by recognized *majstori*, or master craftsmen. But many of the Orašac men spend their winter days carving distaffs, picture frames, and occasionally musical instruments. The flat top surface of the distaff gives plenty of room for the expression of individual tastes and imagination; one pre-war distaff had a portrait of King Alexander carved into it. Another peasant made a special distaff for his granddaughter with a pocket mirror glued into the surface, "so that she can push the wool aside," he said, "and smooth her hair and make herself pretty if a bachelor passes by."

There are two types of shepherd's flutes used in Šumadija, the *svirala*, or the simple single flute, and the double *dvojnice* (Figure 21b, c). Both are made by village craftsmen and by artisans from

[13] In the village she is called a *singerica*, after the Singer sewing machine.

other regions who sell them to Orašani at the county fairs. The traditional folk instrument of Serbia, the gusle, is usually made by the individual who will play it or else by a close acquaintance, for the gusle is a cherished personal object. The instrument's single string is a strand of horse-hair which is played with a bow. Its plaintive strains have one purpose only—to accompany the chanting of the heroic epic poems for which the Serbs have become famous. Until about thirty years ago the traditional gusle was always very simple, with a short bow and no ornamental carving except for a stylized ram's head on the neck of the instrument (21a). In Orašac, however, the gusle became longer and considerably more elaborate, with ornate carving on the base, dragons forming the neck and snakes entwined around the bow. The villager derives great pleasure from carving this instrument and even more enjoyment from playing it while chanting before an admiring audience of grandchildren. Another folk instrument is the *gajde*, or bagpipe, no longer made in Orašac.

THE ORAŠAC DIET

An idea of village food was presented in Chapter Five, in the sections on crops and the annual agricultural cycle. The accompanying chart, "Daily and Seasonal Menus for Households *A*, *B*, and *C*," is included to round out the picture. In the summer, breakfast is an hour to an hour and a half earlier than in the winter, and the other meals follow about five and a half hours apart. Not shown on the chart is an additional summer meal eaten at about 10 o'clock in the morning, when a lunch is carried to the men working in the fields. In the daily menu supper usually consists of the same food as lunch, generally in the form of leftovers. In the winter and spring, when food is scarcest, many households eat the same basic food three times a day for weeks and even months. The seasonal pattern, then, most strongly controls Orašac eating habits. Summer provides the most varied and well-balanced diet, with plenty of fresh fruits and vegetables. Certain vegetables, such as potatoes, carrots, and cabbage, are sometimes stored in the ground or in the cellar, to be used sparingly in the lean months. Other than drying small amounts of meat and fruit, the villagers lack effective methods of

Daily and Seasonal Menus for Households A, B, and C

	Spring 6:30–7 A.M.	Summer 6 A.M.	Autumn 6:30–7 A.M.	Winter 7–7:30 A.M.
Breakfast (*Doručak*)				
A	Fried eggs with onions, garlic, bread, cheese, dried meat, jam, brandy	Eggs, bread, cheese, potato soup with milk, fresh tomatoes, cucumbers, scallions	Fried eggs, potatoes and onions, bread, cheese, prunes, brandy	Eggs and garlic, bread, cheese, pancakes with prune jam, brandy
B	Dried meat or bacon, bread, onions, garlic, brandy	Eggs, bread, potato soup with milk, fresh tomatoes, scallions, cucumbers	Fried eggs, potatoes and onions, bread, cheese, brandy	Bean gruel, garlic, bread, cheese, brandy
C	Bread, garlic	Fried eggs and onions, fresh cucumbers, bread, cheese	Potato soup or bean gruel, bread	Bean gruel, garlic, bread
Lunch (*Ručak*)	11:30 A.M.–12 noon	2 P.M.	11:30 A.M.–12 noon	12 NOON
A	Bean gruel with dried meat, fried potatoes, onions, bread, cheese	Chicken paprikaš, fried potatoes, snap beans, fresh tomatoes, bread, fresh fruit	Potato paprikaš, peppers, onions, bread, cheese	Bean gruel with dried meat, stuffed cabbage, bread, onions, cheese
B	Bean gruel, dried meat, bread, cheese	Potato paprikaš, snap beans and bacon, bread, fresh fruit	Potato paprikaš, peppers, bread, cheese	Bean gruel with dried meat, onions, bread, cheese
C	Bean gruel, bread	Potato paprikaš, bread, cucumbers, fresh fruit	Same as breakfast, plus onions, cheese	Bread, bean gruel, fried onions
Supper (*Večera*)	6 P.M.	7:30 P.M.	6 P.M.	5:30–6 P.M.
A	Same as lunch	Potato paprikaš, snap beans, fresh tomatoes, cucumbers, onions, brandy	Same as lunch, plus wine	Same as lunch, plus gibanica, brandy
B	Same as lunch	Snap beans with bacon and onions, fresh tomatoes, cucumbers, onions, bread	Same as lunch, plus wine	Same as lunch, plus cabbage and bacon, brandy
C	Same as lunch	Same as lunch	Same as lunch	Same as lunch

preserving. The harvest months of July through October actually
represent something of an orgy to the typical Orašac peasant—
be he a young schoolboy or a grandfather. Regardless of what
he may be doing at the time, he constantly stuffs himself with
plums, hacks watermelons into segments and devours them, gnaws
at an apple or pear, or pops grapes into his mouth. Perhaps this
compensates for the many months of monotonous diet; he can
savor the memory until next year.

Of much less significance than the seasonal variations are those
related to the size and wealth of the household. Household *A* has
more eggs, enough brandy and wine to serve at most meals, more
variety, and even a few special treats, but the basic pattern of
food staples continues to be fairly constant for all households of
Orašac.

Without a doubt the most basic food is bread. The change from
corn to wheat flour was discussed earlier. Most households today
use a dark, coarsely milled wheat flour. Corn flour is used for certain meals and is considered especially fine when served with
cooked cabbage and pork. Once a week the *domaćica*, or woman of
the household,[14] bakes the bread for the coming week. She makes
about one and one-third pounds per day for each member of the
household. For a family of six, for example, she must bake twenty-
five kilos of bread, in the form of eight or ten large loaves. She
measures out about fourteen kilos of flour in her large mixing
trough and stirs in ten liters of water, a pinch of yeast, saved from
the last bread-making, and a handful of salt. All this is kneaded
by hand until it is of gummy, fairly uniform consistency. The
dough must then be left to rise for an hour or so—the more im-
maculate housewives cover the trough with a cloth to keep the
flies off. When ready, it is poured into soot-blackened baking pans
and carried out to the yard, where a fire of twigs and corn stalks
has been made in the outdoor bread oven. The fire must be tended
constantly, and when the loaves are ready they are set on the
ground to cool and are then carried inside to be used as needed.
A very few Orašac households use a whiter, more finely milled

---

[14] When there are several mature women in the household, as is often the case, the
task is rotated on a weekly or bimonthly basis.

flour for everyday baking. This is a definite economic distinction, as most households use their white flour only for holidays.

Although a few households are able to enjoy dishes made with chicken and dried meat with some regularity, a characteristic of the Orašac diet is the scarcity of meat. Meat is usually eaten only on holidays and special occasions, such as weddings and graveyard feasts. An exception is made when a moba is called to work; in this case the host sees to it that the women of his house prepare a hearty feast, including a stew or meat in some other form. Meat gristle and fat are relished, and lard is used in abundance for all cooking purposes. Along with the extensive use of lard, the villagers like their food highly seasoned. Salt and ground paprika go into the preparation of almost all dishes, and those who can afford to buy ground black pepper use it generously, especially in soups. The main seasoning agents, spicy peppers and garlic, are grown in every household garden. Garlic is sometimes even consumed as just another vegetable in the stew.

After bread, the main staple is *pasulj*, the thick bean gruel made of beans boiled in water until pulpy and then added to a spicy paste of flour, salt, and paprika cooked in lard. Sometimes bits of dried meat or bacon are added for extra flavor. As the chart brings out, pasulj and bread form the basic winter and spring meals in all households.

Traditional Serbian dishes prepared to vary the menu, if the larder permits, include a stew or paprikaš in which potatoes and hot peppers are the chief ingredients. Another favorite meatless dish is *gibanica*, a heavy pastry filled with kajmak and baked in lard. It is prepared in a round pan and cut in wedges or else shaped in rolls similar to strudel.

According to some of the women, stuffed peppers and stuffed cabbage were not made in the village until twenty or thirty years ago. They require more time and effort to prepare than do gruel or stews, and they also call for meat and rice, two items not found in the peasant pantry except for special events. Nevertheless, they are now as much a part of peasant cooking as of urban tradition, and no Orašac villager asked to describe *Srpska hrana*—Serbian cooking—failed to mention them. Peppers are stuffed with a mix-

ture of highly seasoned chopped pork and rice and are placed in a
covered pot for several hours, to simmer in their own gravy and
lard. The aroma is delicious, but the results are, like so much of
the village cookery, heavy and greasy for Western tastes. For the
sarma, or stuffed caggage, cabbage leaves are marinated in brine
in wooden casks for several days. Each leaf is filled with a meat
and rice mixture similar to that of the peppers, folded over securely, and cooked in a large covered pot. A special treat is sarma
made with tender grapevine leaves instead of cabbage, enjoyed
only in July, before the vine leaves get too fibrous. All of these
stuffed dishes are traditionally served with a helping of sour milk
on top.

There have been a number of other innovations in the peasant
diet, most of which the men disparagingly refer to as "women's
food." These are foods copied from town habits and reflect the
increasing participation in a cash economy. Most of them require
sugar, an item older Orašani say they never had in their youth.
Slatko as well as a variety of sponge cakes, tortes, and cookies
prepared for special occasions were all introduced from the towns
within the last forty years. As a result, most villagers attribute their
exceedingly poor teeth to the increased consumption of sugar—
and they are probably right, although no effort is made to do anything about it. A treat requiring no sugar and enjoyed by all villagers is *palačinke*, thin pancakes made of a batter of eggs, milk,
and flour, fried in lard and rolled up with some prune jam.

Dairy products consumed are mostly in the form of kajmak and
sir, the white loaf cheese prepared in every household. Butter is
never made, for the butterfat content of the milk is very low, and
lard fulfills all purposes for which butter would normally be used.
Each cow is milked twice a day, and the milk is strained through
cheesecloth or some other clean rag. It is used in cooking or made
into kajmak and cheese. The villagers recognize milk as a very
healthy food, but during our entire year in Orašac not one person
was seen drinking it, although there may be some who do.

In this chapter various aspects of the material culture of Orašac
have been examined. Changes which have occurred are in most

cases traceable to various forms of urban influences. Certain of the changes, such as the use of a standard-size plank table, instead of the low Turkish-style table, and the weaving of blankets with floral patterns, in place of striped or geometric designs, have been related only indirectly to economic conditions. Other changes, such as the introduction of the zidana-type house, have been closely tied to the extent of the villagers' participation in a money economy.

Some areas of culture appear to have changed more quickly than others. In the past century and a half there has been a sequence of costume types closely influenced by urban trends. On the other hand, most agricultural implements and many household utensils either have changed relatively little or have been replaced by modern manufactured items.

These occurrences are symptomatic of very basic developments taking place in other areas of Orašac culture, but none of the innovations in and of themselves seems to have caused any real dislocations. Rather, they have been accepted, many of them eagerly, and incorporated into the over-all pattern. The present-day material culture of Orašac in many ways lags significantly behind that of much of rural Europe; in a sense it may be called traditional, but it is nevertheless ever changing.

CHAPTER 6

SOCIAL ORGANIZATION

In Chapter 4 we considered some forms of social interaction in Orašac, in relation to the question of earning a living. This chapter will discuss the more basic units of social organization, to show how the villagers live out their lives together. In Orašac no man can live for himself alone, or completely by himself, because his immediate family, household group, clan, and neighbors are all essential to his survival, and he to theirs. Possibly the most fundamental reason for this is that the people of Orašac are agriculturalists. In order to raise crops successfully with the technology they have at their command, individuals or even small nuclear families cannot do the job alone. An additional explanation is their historic traditions of mutual help and interdependence, dating back to the time of Turkish rule.

The social groups, and how they influence Orašac activities, will be examined—starting with the most intimate group, the nuclear family, and considering in turn the household unit, zadruga, clan, neighborhood, and finally the village itself.

NUCLEAR FAMILY, HOUSEHOLD GROUP, AND ZADRUGA

The household group—*domaćinstvo* or *kuća*—may comprise either the members of the nuclear family or the zadruga, but these terms are not synonymous. The *porodica*, or nuclear family, consists of a man and his wife and children, while the household group is made up of people—closely related except in rare cases—who live together and participate in a common economy. The zadruga always consists of two or more nuclear families sharing a common homestead and economy.

In Orašac and surrounding areas the large household group, composed of two or more nuclear families and usually two or more generations, is for all practical purposes synonymous with the zadruga, that is, all zadrugas, with very few deviations, are limited to one homestead. In Orašac there was only one instance of exception to this generalization. This was in the case of the Dimitrijević zadruga, the largest in the village (in fact the largest in the entire county). In 1953 it consisted of twenty-two members occupying two separate homesteads about a half a mile apart and sharing all land, livestock, and equipment and operating on a common budget.

Earlier, when larger zadrugas were more common, the distinction between zadruga and household group was a more meaningful one (as it still is in some parts of Yugoslavia). It apparently was never of great significance in this part of Šumadija, where large zadrugas were not too common, at least as far back as the records go. In 1890, the earliest year for which we have detailed records on this subject, there was only one zadruga with more than thirty members out of a total of 4,980 households in Jasenica County. In Orašac itself there were only three with more than sixteen members, almost half of the households having six to ten members. The various household sizes for all the villages in the county in 1890, summarized in Table 8, are listed according to the percentage of households in each size category. With the exception of Arandjelovac and Topola, both small market towns at the time, overwhelmingly the most significant category in every village is that of six to ten members, comprising about half the total households in the county. About a quarter have from four to five members, and only about one-eighth have more than ten members.

Table 9 gives data on household size in Orašac for 1890, 1928, 1948, and 1953. The two most recent years are further broken down into Groups I–II (pure and mixed agriculturalist households) and Group III (landless households). The salient point is the very noticeable shift toward smaller households. In 1953 almost 5 percent of the Groups I–II households were peasants living alone,

Table 8. *Household Size of Villages in Jasenica County in 1890, by Percentage of Households in Each Category*

VILLAGE	NUMBER OF MEMBERS IN HOUSEHOLD									NUMBER OF HOUSEHOLDS
	1	*2-3*	*4-5*	*6-10*	*11-15*	*16-20*	*21-25*	*26-30*	*31+*	
Arandjelovac	8.3	27.7	34.5	26.6	2.6	.3	—	—	—	383
Banja	1.1	6.5	22.9	52.7	13.7	2.7	.4	—	—	262
Belosavci	2.6	18.1	20.7	44.1	11.9	2.6	—	.7	—	193
Blaznava	2.2	12.4	26.3	49.6	8.8	—	—	—	—	137
Božurnja	—	17.8	30.1	42.3	6.8	2.4	.6	—	—	163
Brezovac	—	10.3	27.9	52.2	7.4	2.2	—	—	—	136
Bukovik	3.1	16.2	33.0	43.0	2.6	1.1	.5	.5	—	191
G. Trešnjevica	.6	10.6	30.6	51.3	5.7	.6	.6	—	—	160
Jagnjilo	.6	11.2	28.5	46.8	8.6	2.9	1.1	—	.3	348
Jelovik	2.0	15.0	21.0	52.5	6.5	2.5	.5	—	—	200
Kopljare	3.2	14.1	23.7	48.1	7.7	3.2	—	—	—	156
Maslošsevo	.9	15.2	23.7	50.2	9.5	.5	—	—	—	211
ORAŠAC	.5	13.1	24.8	47.6	12.6	1.4	—	—	—	214
Ovšiste	1.5	14.3	21.1	54.1	6.8	.7	1.5	—	—	133
Stojnik	1.1	11.3	26.7	47.4	10.1	2.6	.4	.4	—	266
Stragari	.9	20.5	20.9	46.6	10.7	.4	—	—	—	234
Šatornja	1.7	9.7	24.1	50.6	13.1	.4	.4	—	—	237
Topola	2.5	17.9	27.6	45.8	5.5	.5	.2	—	—	435
Vinča	2.2	11.2	23.9	41.8	18.7	.7	1.5	—	—	134
Vlakča	.8	8.4	20.8	55.2	10.0	3.2	1.2	.4	—	250
Vrbica	2.0	13.1	24.7	45.7	10.9	2.0	1.6	—	—	304
Vukosavci	.9	11.6	21.4	57.2	8.9	—	—	—	—	112
Zagorica	.8	10.7	17.4	54.6	14.1	1.6	.8	—	—	121
Average[a]	1.4	12.9	24.5	49.2	9.8	1.6	.5	.09	.01	Total 4,980

Source: *Population Census of the Kingdom of Serbia as of December 31, 1890*, I, 246.
[a] Excluding the small market towns of Arandjelovac and Topola.

Table 9. Household Size in Orašac Village, 1890, 1928, 1948, 1953

	1890		1928[a]		1948[b]				1953[b]			
					GROUPS I-II		GROUP III		GROUPS I-II		GROUP III	
NUMBER OF MEMBERS	No.	Percent	No.	Percent	No.	Percent	No.	Percent	No.	Percent	No.	Percent
1	1	0.5	8	4.6	20	5.3	39	35.8	19	4.6	15	26.3
2–3	28	13.1	35	19.8	78	20.6	40	36.7	90	21.8	27	47.4
4–5	53	24.8	47	26.7	153	40.5	23	21.1	144	34.9	12	21.0
6–10	102	47.6	71	40.3	115	30.4	6	5.5	152	36.8	3	5.3
11–15	27	12.6	11	6.3	11	2.9	1	0.9	7	1.7	—	0.0
16–20	3	1.4	4	2.3	1	0.3	—	0.0	—	0.0	—	0.0
21–25	—	0.0	—	0.0	—	0.0	—	0.0	—	0.0	—	0.0
Total	214		176		378		109		413		57	

Sources: Records of the Orašac Village Council and unpublished material provided by the Serbian Statistical Bureau.

[a] Statistics provided by the Village Council are incomplete for several large clan groups; 176 households, representing an accurate and complete listing, are used as a sample.

[b] For 1948 and 1953 the total number of households listed in the local records are slightly lower than the official government census records.

compared to only .5 percent in 1890.[1] Even more outstanding is
the almost complete disappearance of the larger zadrugas, i.e.,
those with more than ten members. In 1890 they composed 14 percent of the population; this figure shrank to less than 2 percent
by 1953. The ratio of Groups I–II households in the six- to ten-
member category declined by about 10 percent, to just under
37 percent in 1953. This decrease in household size can also be

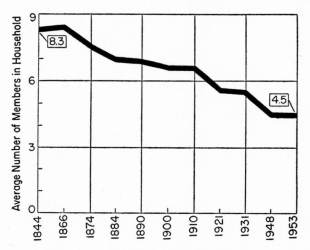

Figure 22. Average Household Size in Orašac, 1844–1953

Source: Serbian Statistical Bureau.

approached in terms of the average household size for the whole
village. Here data for the village of Orašac are available for a much
longer period. Figure 22 shows that the average household was
almost twice as large one hundred years ago, with a drop from
over 8 members in 1844 to 4.5 in 1953. This decline seems to have
been a gradual one, although it is difficult to analyze the change
precisely because of the irregularity of the census years.

Closely linked to the sharp decline in household size has been
the smaller number of children borne by individual mothers.
These differences show up very clearly in Tables 10 and 11. The

[1] This does not mean that these people are completely isolated since more often than
not they have fellow kinsmen as close neighbors.

Table 10. Number of Children Borne by All Orašac Mothers as of 1953, by Ages of Women

AGES OF WOMEN IN 1953	NUMBER OF CHILDREN												TOTAL IN EACH AGE GROUP
	0	1	2	3	4	5	6	7	8	9	10	11	
17–20	50	9	2	—	—	—	—	—	—	—	—	—	61
21–25	44	32	29	6	—	—	—	—	—	—	—	—	111
26–30	15	21	48	25	6	2	1	—	—	—	—	—	118
31–35	7	10	27	32	11	7	4	1	1	—	—	—	100
36–40	6	5	14	20	16	5	1	1	—	—	—	—	68
41–45	7	4	21	15	13	7	5	1	—	1	1	—	75
46–50	5	5	8	23	15	8	1	1	—	—	—	—	66
51–55	5	6	13	10	11	14	6	2	—	—	—	—	67
56–60	3	6	11	10	7	7	2	2	—	2	1	—	51
61–65	3	1	5	10	5	5	3	3	—	1	1	1	38
66–70	1	—	3	7	2	7	3	2	—	—	—	—	25
70 and over	1	3	2	6	4	5	7	1	1	1	—	—	30
Totals	147	102	183	164	90	67	33	14	1	5	3	1	810

Source: Records of the Orašac Village Council.

Table 11. Births in 1881 and 1951, Compared, by Number of Child Borne by Each Mother

YEAR	NUMBER OF CHILD BORNE												TOTAL BIRTHS
	1st	2d	3d	4th	5th	6th	7th	8th	9th	10th	11th	12th	
1881	11	9	6	3	4	5	6	5	7	—	1	1	58
1951	17	18	11	5	—	1	—	—	—	—	—	—	52

Source: Records of the Orašac Village Council.

first table gives an analysis of the female population of Orašac over seventeen years of age, by age groups and number of children by each. The second gives a comparison of number of births according to which child borne, e.g., first, second, third, by all mothers giving birth in 1881 and in 1951. Both tables show the same pattern of a marked decrease in the number of children borne by Orašac mothers. From a total of fifty-eight births in 1881, twenty-seven occurred to mothers who had five or more children; in 1951 there was only one birth in that category. For the five-year period 1949–53, there were only 2 percent of a total of three hundred births in this category. Those mothers who were having their fourth children or up account for only 7 percent of the births, while 16 percent bore their third children, 29 percent their second, and 36 percent their first. A complex of causes has undoubtedly brought about this development, in large measure because of conscious birth control, albeit of a very primitive nature, mainly by abortion. Of considerable importance, too, is the declining death rate necessitating fewer births to maintain the population. Also basic is the fragmentation of landholdings associated with the decline of the size of the zadruga: while an additional child is of no economic burden to a large household with adequate land, it can impose a real problem on a small farmer with a very limited amount of land. It does not seem to be completely coincidental that the greatest decline in the zadruga occurred when free land for settlement became exhausted.

Although there may have been a few exceptions, the medium-sized zadruga of from ten to fifteen members was the most important historically in Orašac and its surrounding region, and probably in most of the other areas of Šumadija as well.[2] As we have seen, even zadrugas of this size began to break up late in the nineteenth century. Yet they did have very definite advantages, some of which can be found in the larger households existing in Orašac today. Chief among these advantages is division of labor, for in these households the individual members do not have to work nearly as hard as those who belong to smaller ones. Conse-

[2] Nuclear family households were never common in Orašac in the nineteenth century and were, in fact, looked down upon.

quently they have more time for other occupations, and often some of the finest handicraft work and woven goods are found in the homes of these larger zadrugas. The men had more time to engage in local politics (pre-war), and it was from among their ranks that the leaders of the village were usually drawn. Even if the zadruga today is not relatively richer than two or three smaller households which combined approximate it in size, the fact that its wealth is concentrated makes it seem more important.

We have defined the formal structure of the zadruga and have seen how its size has changed, but little has been said about the fundamental concepts on which the zadruga is based. One of the most important of these is the role of the starešina. The data from Orašac do not seem to support the view of the zadruga system being of an extreme patriarchal type, with its emphasis on male supremacy and the starešina as an absolute ruler.[3] There is little doubt, however, that the authority of the starešina was one of the cornerstones upon which the zadruga system was built.

The Orašac zadrugas were formally patriarchal, in the sense that one of the older males, although not necessarily the eldest, was starešina, and that he in effect made most of the important decisions for the household. However, the zadruga was democratic, in an informal way, since the head almost always sought the advice of all the mature men before making his decisions. Also, his power was by no means absolute but was subject to the wishes of the other members, and, if necessary, he could be removed. This applies particularly to those zadrugas where the ties of kinship between members were at times artificial or remote and therefore not primarily the links which held the group together.

On the other hand, the smaller zadrugas, most common in Orašac, were based primarily on close kinship ties. They usually consisted of two brothers and their families, with their father as the starešina. In such cases the power of the starešina was obviously much greater since it was that of a father over his sons, rather than an individual selected by general agreement largely by personal qualifications. The position of the father was based on one

---

[3] This is the type proposed for Serbia by Tomasić (*Personality and Culture in Eastern European Politics*).

of the cardinal principles for behavior in traditional Serbian society, i.e., obedience toward one's elders, particularly male elders and especially the father. The head of the household was expected to (and usually did) consult with his sons on important matters. Even here the son could replace the father if the latter became incapacitated for one reason or another.

Formal respect for the head of the household and older males in general was shown in many ways. For example, when a young boy or even a young adult met an older man he would take off his hat and say, "Good day." A new daughter-in-law had to wash the feet of the male elders at the end of each day's work. When a starešina entered the home of a neighbor or a friend, all the children and young adults of the household kissed his hand as a sign of greeting and respect. All of these acts a head of a household regarded as his due, and if anyone failed in his obligations toward him there were often likely to be serious consequences. One grandmother related the story of how, as a young woman, it was her duty to prepare the meals for her father-in-law since his wife had died. One evening she had been unable to do this because her youngest child was ill. When her father-in-law returned home and found that his supper was not awaiting him, he was so infuriated he flung all the cooking pots out into the fields. This is obviously an extreme example, and undoubtedly there were even some household heads who were dominated by their wives. Nevertheless, cultural norms favored dominance by and respect toward all elder males.

Yet women, too, played significant roles, especially if they were wives of heads of households. They planned and coordinated all women's work within the home. A local folk saying declares, "*Žena je domaćin kuće a čovek je gost*" (In the house the woman is the head and the man is the guest). Although the wife always formally deferred to her husband, this does not mean that she was never consulted, or that her influence on her husband was negligible. In an informal way her influence could be and often was considerable. In fact marriage was in a sense regarded as a partnership, although with a formal inequality. One old man close to ninety reflected this attitude when, in describing how he rose from a poor peasant to become the head of a large and fairly prosperous household, he concluded by saying, "and all this I have done together with my *baba*."

Today the traditional patriarchal structure has been greatly altered. This is not to say that older people no longer occupy a position of respect in Orašac society, for they still definitely do. The social distance between older and younger groups has, however, decreased, and many of the formal signs of respect have either largely disappeared or been basically changed. There are still a few homes where the children kiss the hands of their elders and stand up when they enter the room, but they are a small and decreasing minority. Formal acts of respect are followed, however, when greeting an elder whom one does not see more than a few times a year. For the everyday course of action hand-kissing has been replaced by a nodded greeting and simply the words "*ljubim ruku*" (I kiss your hand).

One villager, today the head of a household of eight members, including a son and several grandchildren, humorously—or was it cynically—described the changes which have come about. He related how, when his father was starešina, everyone stood up respectfully when the household head entered the house and returned his greeting of "*Dobro veče*" (good evening). But today, when *he* returns home from the fields after a day's work and says good evening, his son replies "*Čuti, bre*" (shut up, man)!

This attitude is also shown in other ways. When we were interviewing the heads[4] of zadrugas, in a few cases the old man did all the talking while his mature sons and sometimes even grandsons listened respectfully. There were many more cases where sons did not hesitate to interrupt their fathers, and in one or two instances grandsons corrected or contradicted their grandfathers.

Another sign of the decline of patriarchal authority is that in some instances the strict rules concerning the division of labor are beginning to break down. It is now not unusual for a man to help his wife around the house with what was formerly considered to be exclusively women's tasks, especially if she is temporarily dis-

---

[4] Today the head of the household is no longer called *starešina* but simply *domaćin*. This in itself may be considered a symptom of decline of the zadruga structure.

abled. This development is, of course, closely linked to the decline
of the zadruga itself, for in the traditional household there was
always another woman to step in and do the work. In any case it
is now a rare starešina who would throw the cooking pots out of
the house.

Despite the fact that today households are smaller, and that
women have achieved a greater degree of equality, there is no
question but that the male is still supreme in the Serbian household. The patriarchal concept has been greatly modified but by
no means destroyed.

The present pattern emphasizes the cooperative character of
managing the household. The official census records always list a
starešina for each household. However, being usually the eldest
male, he may be in his eighties or older and obviously incapable
of taking an active part in affairs. When he becomes incompetent
or too old, matters are placed in the hands of a son or sons, but in
most cases it no longer appears necessary to formally replace the
head of the household.

Several additional influences, all emanating from urban centers,
are combining to bring about the decline of patriarchal authority.
These include government institutions, military service, suffrage,
new government policies, and economic factors. Certainly the
agencies of the government in the village, namely the school and
the Village Council with their associated organizations, have
played a large role. Perhaps most important is that with the increase in both the number of children going to school and the
length of time they spend there, a situation is developing whereby
the children feel they know more about the world outside the
village than do their parents.

Compulsory military service, in effect for more than eighty
years, has added another pressure. When a young man spends a
period of two or more years absorbing aspects of other ways of
life it is sometimes difficult for him to readjust to a subordinate
role. The right of all adult males to vote, granted in 1869, has
also tended to undercut the role of the starešina as the only one
who dealt with the government. Then too, since the end of the

Second World War a woman with the ability and qualifications can get a job and earn as much as a man. Of course most peasants do not or cannot take advantage of this situation, but they are at least aware of it through their relatives in the army or in the towns.

It is no secret that the peasants staunchly oppose many of the basic precepts of Communism such as collectivization of agriculture. On the other hand, there can be little doubt that some points of Communist philosophy, such as emphasis on the equality of women and the opportunities for youth, have found receptive ears in the village. This is especially true since these attitudes have been accompanied by concrete acts—changes in marriage laws, female suffrage, and the organization of special youth groups, for instance.

Most of the other factors influencing the decline of patriarchal authority may be subsumed under the heading "economic." With the villagers' increasing participation in a money economy and the growth of personal property the strains on the zadruga increased. Beginning in the latter part of the nineteenth century and especially in the twentieth century the use to which the zadruga's cash income should be put became a problem. One partial solution was found in that women were permitted to market certain quantities of garden and dairy products. They used the money gained by selling flax, poultry, and cheese to supply their personal needs in clothing and other items. Sometimes this system did not work out too well, as when the men or the starešina himself wanted the money for other purposes, such as to buy land. In one peasant autobiography a man recounts that when he was a child his grandfather, who was head of the zadruga, acted in such a tyrannical way that the women were forced to steal cheese and eggs from the family larder in order to buy what they considered essential. Such situations may occur in smaller households, but here the pressures holding the group together are much greater than are those of the larger zadrugas. The growth of the dowry system, which involves among other things land, has also played a part in the dissolution of the zadruga, notably in the period since the First World War.

Very difficult to assess is the role of the full-time wage earner as a factor in the break-up of the zadruga.[5] Orašac men have been permanently employed at the local mine for over fifty years, but the average household size of Orašac has declined at about the same rate as that of neighboring villages where there are no mines In Table 4B we learned that in most cases the mixed agricultural households are larger than those of the pure peasants. This is particularly true of the largest zadrugas in the village. In the Dimitrijević zadruga, for example, four of the men are at present or have at one time been permanently employed at the mine.

In most social science literature industrialization seems to be closely linked to family breakdown. For the case of large-scale industry entering into a previously agricultural area, this description is undoubtedly valid, and this may be the main referent of Mosely's statement. There are, however, many instances of relatively small-scale industrial operations which have a stabilizing effect. This would seem to be the case of the coal mine in Orašac. Orašac has had an almost constant increase in population while some of the nearby villages have suffered decreases; it seems entirely possible that many people who have remained in Orašac and worked at the coal mine might otherwise have been forced to go elsewhere to seek a livelihood.

This theory is not to minimize the effect of economic changes on the zadruga. The crux of the problem is that no one factor can be considered paramount—it is the combination of forces working together which has been most important. One Serbian scholar, writing in 1876, attributes the breakup of the zadruga at that period to the "influences of the laws and new ideas concerning the position of the individual in the group," existing even between the closest relatives.[6] Another writer ascribes the decline to the ending of Turkish rule and the fact that life was no longer insecure

[5] Philip E. Mosely takes the position that "When outside wages are an exception, they are readily turned into the common fund, but when working for hire becomes an essential element in the household economy, the zadruga is almost certain to dissolve into its component small families." ("The Peasant Family: The *Zadruga*, or Communal Joint-Family in the Balkans," in Ware, ed., *The Cultural Approach to History*, p. 107.) This may very well be true for other areas, but Orašac data do not seem to bear out this point of view.

[6] Miličević, *Kneževina Srbija*, p. 299.

in Serbia. He also assigns an important part to the women who became impatient working under the orders of the wives of headmen, then dividing the results of their own and their husbands' work on equal terms with other members of the zadruga who did not work as hard as they.[7] This last factor is significant because if one member of the zadruga insisted on dividing the others usually agreed.

More recently Mosely pointed out that a desire to be "modern" is more effective in destroying the zadruga than any economically determined motive.[8] This seems to be a very valid point, for it appears that the most basic factor in the decline of the zadruga is the increasing contact of the peasant with the town, both in an economic and psychological sense. Since this wish to be modern crystallizes all of these other factors in the peasant mind, it can be safely considered more important than any of its component factors.

But, just as patriarchal authority is not extinct in Orašac today, there are many elements of the traditional zadruga system which have survived. An idea of these remnants can be gathered from Table 12, where the Orašac population in 1948 is broken down into different kinship categories according to the relation of each to the head of the household.[9] Since the most basic unit of the household is the nuclear family, sons, wives, and daughters are the highest on the list. That the zadruga in its most limited sense— as a unit of two nuclear families—is still important is shown by the fact that next in importance are daughters-in-law and grandchildren. There are thirty households where women are listed as heads. They are all widows with the exception of two rare cases where the women have husbands. On the other hand, almost three times as many mothers of household heads are recorded, implying that in most cases where the father has died, the son replaces him as head. There are even six instances of the son being the recognized head when the father is still alive.

[7] Mijatović, *Servia of the Servians*, p. 176.

[8] Mosely, review of *La Zadruga sud-slave dans l'évolution du groupe domestique*, by Sicard, *American Slavic and East European Review*, VIII, No. 1 (February, 1949), 71–73.

[9] The term starešina is used because it is the one most commonly encountered in the literature and because the official census records still employ it, even though in the village domaćin is the word generally used to designate the household head.

Table 12. Orašac Population by Relationship to Head of Household, 1948

	NUMBER OF POPULATION	
RELATION	*Groups I–II*	*Group III*
Starešina (head of household)	348	117
1. *Sin* (son)	347	39
2. *Žena* (wife)	286	51
3. *Kći* (daughter)	230	40
4. *Sna za sinom* (daughter-in-law)	150	2
5. *Unuk* (grandson)	144	1
6. *Unuka* (granddaughter)	127	2
7. *Majka* (mother)	86	18
8. *Starešina* (female head of household)[a]	30	3
9. *Brat* (brother)	21	12
10. *Sinovica* (niece, brother's daughter)	22	—
11. *Sestra* (sister)	14	15
12. *Sinovac* (nephew, brother's son)	17	2
13. *Sna za bratom* (sister-in-law)	11	—
14. *Vanbračna žena* (common-law wife)	10	3
15. *Sna za unukom* (granddaughter-in-law)	9	—
16. *Zet* (son-in-law)	8	—
17. *Praunuka* (great-granddaughter)	8	—
18. *Praunuk* (great-grandson)	7	—
19. *Otac* (father)	6	5
20. *Tašta* (mother-in-law)	5	2
21. *Tast* (father-in-law)	1	1
22. *Baba* (grandmother)	4	4
23. *Sna za sinovcem* (nephew's wife)	2	—
24. *Muž* (husband)[a]	2	—
25. *Pastorak* (stepson)	2	1
26. *Pastorka* (stepdaughter)	4	—
27. *Deda* (grandfather)	1	—
28. *Svastika* (wife's sister)	1	1
29. *Jetrva* (brother's wife)[a]	1	—
30. *Dever* (husband's brother)[a]	1	—
31. *Vanbračan muž* (common-law husband)[a]	1	—
32. *Maćeha* (step-mother)	1	—
33. *Posvojica* (adopted child)	3	—
34. *Vanbračno dete* (illegitimate child)	—	1
35. *Poočim* (stepfather)	—	1
36. *Rodjaka* (female relative)	—	1
37. *Pomoćnik* (household helper)	1	—
38. *Pomoćnica* (household helper, female)	1	—
39. *Pomoćnikovo dete* (helper's child)	1	—
	1,911	323
Total population	2,234	

Source: Records of the Orašac Village Council.
[a] When a female is starešina.

The classic-type zadruga, consisting of two or more brothers and their families, is today uncommon in Orašac. Only twenty-one brothers of household heads are listed; in a few cases the brother is a young unmarried man, and in two instances more than two brothers compose the household. There are about twelve households which have four generations. A final point is that matrilocal residence is extremely rare—only eight sons-in-law are listed, compared to one hundred and fifty daughters-in-law.

Table 13. Percentage Distribution of Population by Relation to Head of Household—Farm and Nonfarm Households in Rural United States, Château-Gérard, and Orašac Compared[a]

	United States Farm	Château-Gérard Farm	Orašac Farm[b]	United States Nonfarm	Château-Gérard Nonfarm	Orašac Nonfarm[b]
Head of household	27.8	27.2	19.8	27.2	30.0	37.2
Wife	21.4	23.6	15.5	20.7	21.8	16.7
Child	40.8	37.7	30.7	39.9	30.4	24.8
Grandchild	1.8	3.7	14.2	1.9	3.1	0.9
Parent	1.5	2.0	5.1	1.7	1.6	8.0
Other relative	3.5	4.7	14.6	4.3	8.1	12.4
Lodger	2.6	0.7	0.0	3.5	2.0	0.0
Servant	0.6	0.3	0.1	0.8	1.0	0.0

Sources: Turney-High, *Château-Gérard*, p. 75 (including U.S. data from *Statistical Abstract of the U.S.*, 1949, p. 24) and records of the Orašac Village Council.

[a] The figures for the United States and Château-Gérard are for 1949; those for Orašac are for 1948.

[b] Farm represents Orašac Groups I–II (pure and mixed agriculturalists) and Nonfarm represents Group III (landless residents); these terms are used here to be consistent with Turney-High's table.

By contrast, the nonpeasant inhabitants of Orašac in 1948 were almost entirely single workers living alone or with simple nuclear families.

Thus very definite traces remain, although the zadruga has lost much of its former significance. The typical Orašac household is still larger and more complex than that of areas in western Europe and America. This is brought out in Table 13, where the farm and nonfarm populations of Orašac, Château-Gérard,[10] and rural

[10] Turney-High, *Château-Gérard*, p. 75.

United States are compared. A chart like this has certain limita-
tions, of course, since Belgian and Yugoslav villages are not strictly
comparable to the rural population of the United States. There
are nevertheless specific gross differences brought out here. The
nuclear family is overwhelmingly the most important part of the
household in each case, but it makes up 90 percent of the United
States farm households, 88.5 percent of Château-Gérard, and only
66 percent of Orašac. In Orašac a full third of the household members are other relatives, including parents and grandchildren. Even
if much of the traditional zadruga organization has broken down,
its influence is still strongly felt in Orašac social organization today.
Underlying the question is the fact that in Orašac, and Yugoslavia
in general, unlike Belgium and America, there has been relatively
much less opportunity for employment in the cities, forcing most
of the population to remain on the farm.

What we have seen in this discussion, then, is not the disappearance of the zadruga or of patriarchal authority but rather a modifi-
cation of the social structure which existed at the time of the
settlement of Orašac. Changes have been taking place, or the
zadruga has been "declining," ever since liberation from the
Turks. The question is not of the concept of traditional or modern
social structure but of differences in degree and rate of change.
What has been described here is the zadruga or household, like
an amoeba, constantly growing, changing, and dividing but never
standing still.

CLAN GROUPS

After the actual household unit the social unit most important to
the peasant is his *vamilija* (*familija* in literary Serbian)—his lineage
or clan. Each is composed of groups of households which trace
their origin from the same ancestor, share a common name, and
have the same patron saint. The common ancestor is usually a
male, and descent is always traced in the male line.

Two Orašac genealogies, for the Stojanović and Andrić clans,
are given in Figure 23. Stojan and Andrija, the clans' founders, are
said to have settled in Orašac in the late eighteenth century, and
both participated in the First Revolt. The chart shows the growth

and development of the two clans, resulting today in sixteen
Stojanović and only four Andrić households. Clan groups such as
these comprise most of the Orašac population, ranging in size from
that of the largest clan, Nedić, with forty-five households and 208
members, to that of several where but a few households remain
today. These very small clans may have been in the village just

Table 14. Traditional Orašac Clan Groups[a] in Order of Size, 1953

Clan Name	Number of People	Number of Households	Clan Name	Number of People	Number of Households
1. Nedić	208	45	22. Simić	35	4
2. Joksimović	129	30	23. Dimitrijević	32	4
3. Stojanović[b]	114	16	24. Lukić	31	6
4. Anić	98	16	25. Jokić	31	6
5. Maričević	98	25	26. Stevanović	28	6
6. Jakovljević	97	19	27. Jovanović	22	5
7. Matijašević	93	17	28. Aničić	21	4
8. Vasiljević	83	18	29. Rajčić	21	3
9. Pejović	81	14	30. Milovanović	18	4
10. Starčević	77	19	31. Radovanović	17	5
11. Petrović[c]	64	13	32. Andrić	17	4
12. Milojević	55	9	33. Vasović	17	2
13. Gajić	53	10	34. Ilić	14	3
14. Lazarević	50	13	35. Janić	13	2
15. Stanić	49	13	36. Miloradović	12	4
16. Pavlović	49	10	37. Todorović	8	4
17. Minić	47	8	38. Sekulić	7	1
18. Vasilić	42	8	39. Radojević	6	2
19. Lučić	38	8	40. Djordjević	5	1
20. Obradović	35	7	41. Filipović	1	1
21. Pajević	35	7	Totals	1,931	396

Source: Records of the Orašac Village Council.
[a] Those living in Orašac since 1928 or longer.
[b] Three more Stojanović households, not descended from Stojan, also live in the
village.
[c] There are two other Petrović households in Orašac, unrelated to each other or to
the traditional Petrović clan in the village.

as long as the larger ones, but they have decreased in size because
of fewer sons and greater emigration. The so-called traditional
Orašac clans, those who have been in the village twenty-five years
or longer, are listed according to size in Table 14. In addition,
there are a few new peasant families, of one or two households
each, who arrived in Orašac after 1928 and who are not included

A. STOJANOVIĆ CLAN

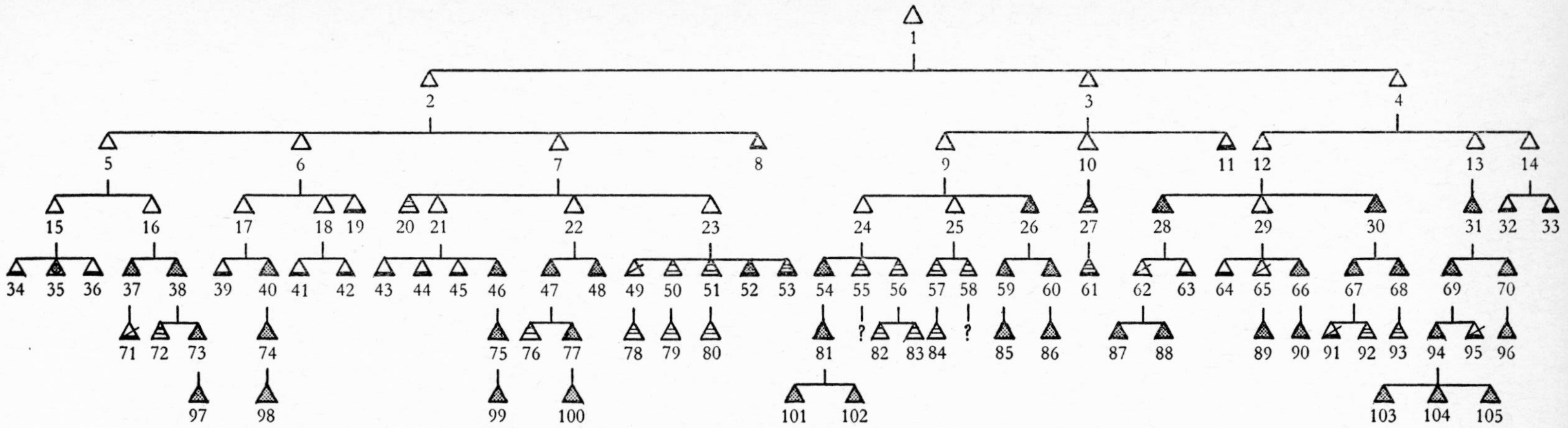

B. ANDRIĆ CLAN

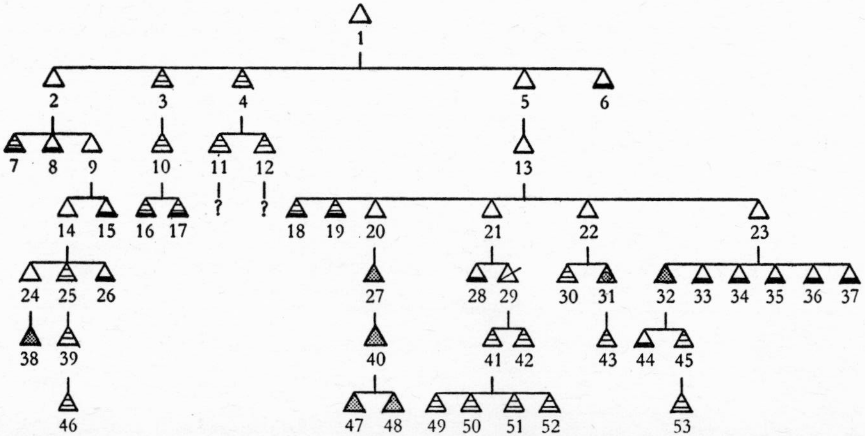

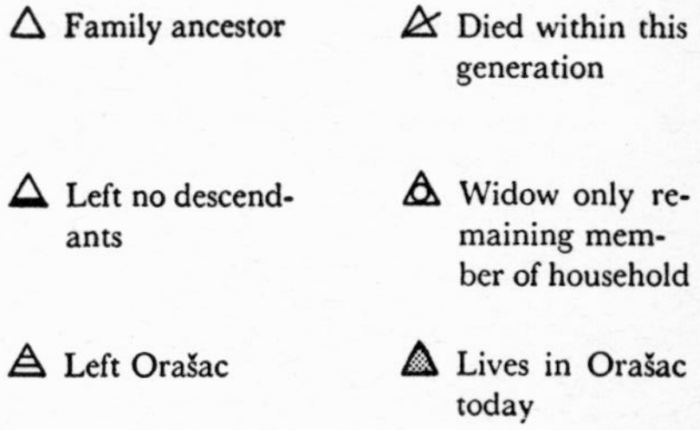

Legend:

△ Family ancestor

◮ Died within this generation

◭ Left no descendants

◭ Widow only remaining member of household

◀ Left Orašac

▲ Lives in Orašac today

STOJANOVIĆ CLAN

1 Stojan
2 Petar
3 Miloje
4 Mihailo
5 Miloš
6 Uroš
7 Nikola
8 Stevan
9 Vučić
10 Matija
11 Lazar
12 Radovan
13 Radoje
14 Radivoje
15 Milutin
16 Andrija
17 Djordje
18 Tanasija
19 Vladimir
20 Antonija
21 Svetozar
22 Ljubomir
23 Miloš
24 Radojica
25 Andrija
26 Ljubomir
27 Blagoje
28 Petar
29 Miloje
30 Radomir
31 Dragomir
32 Velimir
33 Branko
34 Živomir
35 Pavle
36 Velimir
37 Svetozar
38 Velislav
39 Dragoljub
40 Veljko
41 Svetislav
42 Dragoslav
43 Živomir
44 Miloš
45 Vitomir
46 Dragiša
47 Mileta
48 Milosav
49 Dragoslav
50 Radislav
51 Radosav
52 Kronislav
53 Branislav
54 Velimir
55 Radomir
56 Dragomir
57 Dragoljub
58 Kosta
59 Milivoje
60 Živomir
61 *
62 Velimir
63 Svetislav
64 Budimir
65 Čedomir
66 Periša
67 Vitomir
68 Tihomir
69 Momčilo
70 Milorad
71 Radomir
72 Miodrag
73 Milovan
74 Miodrag
75 Radiša
76 Dragoljub
77 Žarko
78 Dušan
79 Radomir
80 Radovan
81 Dragoljub
82 *
83 *
84 Andrija
85 Dušan
86 Dragan
87 Svetislav
88 Vojislav
89 Dragić
90 Dobrivoje
91 Miodrag
92 Radovan
93 Dragoljub
94 Milić
95 Dobrivoje
96 Branibar
97 *
98 Djordje
99 Slobodan
100 Milan
101 Radovan
102 Dragovan
103 Miomir
104 Miodrag
105 Malibor

ANDRIĆ CLAN

1 Andrija
2 Milovan
3 Proka
4 Dimitrije
5 Marko
6 Gavrilo
7 Miloš
8 Mojsilo
9 Ilija
10 Lazar
11 *
12 *
13 Teodor
14 Andrija
15 Elisija
16 Milan
17 Andrija
18 Gliša
19 Luka
20 Marko
21 Obrad
22 Matija
23 Grujica
24 Milan
25 Branislav
26 Radisav
27 Milutin
28 Miloš
29 Milovan
30 Milan
31 Jovan
32 Živomir
33 *
34 *
35 *
36 *
37 *
38 Radomir
39 Andrija
40 Dragoljub
41 Aleksandar
42 Živomir
43 Dušan
44 *
45 Miloje
46 *
47 Dragoslav
48 Marko
49 *
50 *
51 *
52 *
53 *

* Name not known.

Stojanović men who left Orašac

20, Belgrade, became a tailor; 27, Arandjelovac, merchant; 50, 51, 53, Belgrade, rubber factory workers; 55, Czechoslovakia, POW, did not return; 56, Novi Sad, tax collector; 57, Arandjelovac, merchant; 58, Belgrade, clerk; 61, son of 27; 72, Kostolac, border official; 76, Major, Yugoslav army; 78, moved to Velika Ivanča village; 79, 80, Belgrade; 82, 83, sons of 56; 84, Belgrade, student; 92, Smederevo, veterinarian; 93, Belgrade, student.

Andrić men who left Orašac

3, Arandjelovac, merchant; 4, Belgrade, army officer; 7, Kragujevac, worker in munitions plant; 10, Arandjelovac, artisan; 11, 12, sons of 4, army officer, engineer; 16, Prizren, lawyer; 17, Arandjelovac, tailor; 18, 19, Belgrade, merchants; 25, Belgrade, florist; 30, Belgrade, engineer; 39, Belgrade, factory worker; 41, (?); 42, moved to Bukovik village; 43, Belgrade, engineer; 45, Belgrade, agronomist; 46, son of 39; 49–52, sons of 41; 53, son of 45.

Figure 23. Two Orašac Genealogies

A. Stojanović Clan. Informant: Mileta Stojanović (47).   B. Andrić Clan. Informant: Živomir Andrić (32).

in the listing. Minor fluctuations in size did not affect the fact that these clans always represented the great majority of the village population; they accounted for almost 99 percent of all the Orašac households in 1928 and 82.5 percent in 1953.

Within the traditional clans there are fifteen which have ten or more households each. These larger clans alone are made up of 278 households and include 1,348 people, or about three-fifths of both the total number of households (480) and the total population (2,182) in 1953. Over the years the larger clans have generally continued to increase, at a rate slightly higher than that of the smaller clans.

The most important ties binding the members of the vamilija are, of course, those resulting from their common ancestry. In the smaller clans the term *rodbina*, or close relatives, is usually synonymous with clan members. In larger clans differences between those who might normally be members of the household group and those who usually would not are reflected in the use of *rodjeni*, literally meaning "born" relatives. When added to the broadly classificatory kinship terms, this word makes them apply specifically only to born relatives. For example, *rodjeni brat* or *rodjena sestra* can only mean brother and sister, while brat or sestra alone may refer to any of the children of a mother's or father's brothers and sisters.[11] The terms for cousin may be further extended to specify whether they are father's brother's son, for instance (*brat od strica*), or mother's sister's daughter (*sestra od tetke*).

The Serbian kinship system identifies specifically five ascending and five descending generations in a direct line from ego.[12] There is special terminology for collateral relatives for one ascending and one descending generation. The system, for three generations ascending from ego and three descending, is presented in Figure 24.

A very real kinship is felt by all members of the clan, varying

[11] Rodjeni is also used with reference to "born" grandparents and grandchildren (rodjeni deda, rodjena baba, rodjeni unuk, rodjena unuka); if omitted, the basic terms can apply to grandparents' siblings and their spouses and the grandchildren of ego's brother and sister. In everyday conversation, however, the expression rodjeni is rarely used.

[12] Great-great-great grandfather is *čukundeda*, and great-great-great grandchild is *bela pčela*.

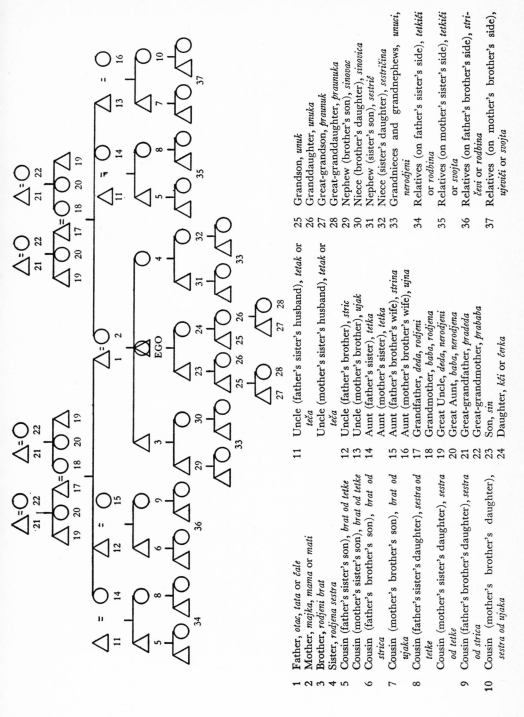

1. Father, *otac, tata* or *ćale*
2. Mother, *majka, mama* or *mati*
3. Brother, *rodjeni brat*
4. Sister, *rodjena sestra*
5. Cousin (father's sister's son), *brat od tetke*
6. Cousin (mother's sister's son), *brat od tetke*
7. Cousin (father's brother's son), *brat od strica*
8. Cousin (mother's brother's son), *brat od ujaka*
9. Cousin (father's sister's daughter), *sestra od tetke*
10. Cousin (mother's sister's daughter), *sestra od tetke*
11. Cousin (father's brother's daughter), *sestra od strica*
12. Cousin (mother's brother's daughter), *sestra od ujaka*

11. Uncle (father's sister's husband), *tetak* or *teča*
12. Uncle (mother's sister's husband), *tetak* or *teča*
13. Uncle (father's brother), *stric*
14. Uncle (mother's brother), *ujak*
15. Aunt (father's sister), *tetka*
16. Aunt (mother's sister), *tetka*
17. Aunt (father's brother's wife), *strina*
18. Aunt (mother's brother's wife), *ujna*
19. Grandfather, *deda, rodjeni*
20. Grandmother, *baba, rodjena*
21. Great Uncle, *deda, nerodjeni*
22. Great Aunt, *baba, nerodjena*
23. Great-grandfather, *pradeda*
24. Great-grandmother, *prababa*
25. Son, *sin*
26. Daughter, *kći* or *ćerka*

25. Grandson, *unuk*
26. Granddaughter, *unuka*
27. Great-grandson, *praunuk*
28. Great-granddaughter, *praunuka*
29. Nephew (brother's son), *sinovac*
30. Niece (brother's daughter), *sinovica*
31. Nephew (sister's son), *sestrić*
32. Niece (sister's daughter), *sestričina*
33. Grandnieces and grandnephews, *unuci, nerodjeni*
34. Relatives (on father's sister's side), *tetkići* or *rodbina*
35. Relatives (on mother's sister's side), *tetkići* or *svojta*
36. Relatives (on father's brother's side), *stričevi* or *rodbina*
37. Relatives (on mother's brother's side), *ujevići* or *svojta*

Figure 24. Serb Kinship System

in intensity, of course, according to the distance of the relationship. Every Orašac peasant can identify all of the households belonging to his clan, chiefly by the name of the domaćin of each house. In most cases he is able to name the members of the households and tell something about them, even though they may be located in another section of the village. The average villager can also trace his ancestry back six to eight generations, without the benefit of any written record. Many can reconstruct their complete clan genealogy by memory (in terms of male ancestors) back to the founder of the clan. It was in this manner that the genealogies for the Stojanović and Andrić clans were recounted.

Several of the older men in the village are renowned for their knowledge in these matters, not only with regard to the genealogy of their own clan but to those of other related clans as well. The most remarkable case of this ability was demonstrated by a peasant belonging to the Nedić vamilija. Without any notes, and with few uncertainties, he traced his origin to the widow Neda who came to Orašac in the late eighteenth century. Proceeding through the male line he identified all of her descendants, including the more than two hundred members of the Nedić clan living in the village today, as well as many who had left Orašac two or even three generations ago. In addition he was able to tell the native village and in many cases the original clan names of the brides of the various Nedić men. His knowledge was most complete on those of his male ancestors from whom he was directly descended. For them he gave approximate birth and death dates and specific biographical data. In all, over five hundred people within the Nedić clan were identified in one way or another. He also recited approximate genealogies for several other Orašac clan groups, particularly those which had intermarried with his own. Although it would be something of an exaggeration to say that he could precisely identify his own relationship to all 2,000-odd villagers and to trace the ancestry of all the clans in Orašac, nevertheless he was able to give an approximate idea of the degree of relationship among a significant portion of the village population.

The prevailing ability to trace kinship bonds both diachronically and synchronically is naturally symptomatic of the meaning of the clan in everyday life. Unlike the zadruga the consciousness of clan ties do not seem to be lessening, for the ability to trace these relationships is by no means restricted to older people. Young men in their twenties are sometimes able to identify as many as several hundred kinsfolk.

CLAN AND NEIGHBORHOOD

A member's awareness as to his clan is reinforced in many ways. These include a common slava, reciprocal attendance at each other's weddings and funerals, and also clan exogamy.[13] Most important of all is that households of the same clan more often than not are centralized in one neighborhood, forming both a kinship and a geographic unit.

The village is divided into a number of these neighborhoods. Since the Orašac homesteads are spread out over a large area of the village the *komšiluk*, or neighborhood, forms a definable geographic unit as is shown by the clusters of houses in Map 3. The geographic names of the various regions of the general area are known and used by the peasants when speaking of the village as a whole, but when reference is being made to a specific part of the village the name of the main clan group inhabiting it is more commonly used. Within the village, for example, if a peasant says he is going *u Joksimoviće* you know he is heading for the Gajevi section. Of course once he is in Gajevi and is asked where he is going he will answer with the name of the head of the specific household, such as *kod Radisava*, to Radisav's; the last name is not necessary, for everyone will know whom he means.

When the residence areas of different clans are broken down in terms of the geographical sections of Orašac, it is found that only about twenty percent of all the households live in regions where there are fewer than four households of the same clan, and many of these twenty percent are among the smallest clans in the village.

The coincidence of neighbor and kinsman is a direct outgrowth of the original settlement pattern, whereby each clan founded a homestead in a particular part of the general area which is now

[13] Sex affairs between members of the same clan are strongly prohibited no matter how distant the kinship.

Orašac. Through time, as the zadrugas enlarged and divided, the new households continued living in close proximity to their parent zadrugas. The same pattern has continued up to the present day. In fact, the only reason why a more perfect division of the village into neighborhoods based exclusively on clan groupings does not exist is that over the years some sections have become relatively crowded. This forced newly formed households to move to less densely settled neighborhoods or nearer the land they inherited.[14] In time these households divide, and in the course of a few generations the neighborhood is composed of several households of the newer clans. Two generations ago, the Mecenac section had households of only the Nedić, Petrović, and Starčević clans. Today a few households of eight other clans now live there.

The peasant likes to consider his own clan as composed of the best and the finest people in the village. On a narrower scale he enjoys thinking of himself as a little smarter than the next fellow or of his own household as a little better than that of his neighbor. This feeling is often intensified when a small number of one clan's households are in a komšiluk inhabited predominantly by members of another clan. In one particular instance two brothers were "alone" in a neighborhood to which they had moved as children, when their father divided from his zadruga. When the brothers grew up they too divided but lived in adjacent houses. Because of conflicting personalities a great deal of enmity developed between them, yet they continued helping each other and exchanging visits and favors. When one of the brother's daughters-in-law was asked why they behaved in this way despite the intense animosity, she replied that it would be *sramota*, a disgrace, if they did otherwise. It was certainly true that neither household had much use for the other, she explained, but they were the sole Stojanovići in the midst of the Starčević neighborhood and therefore had to put up a good front for the sake of the name of the vamilija.

Although members of a villager's own clan group are usually treated more intimately, the *komšija*, or neighbor, is very highly

[14] The parent household, consisting of the head and most of the members, remains on the old homestead. The one who goes to another neighborhood is usually a younger brother, a son, or grandson with his nuclear family, splitting off and becoming the domaćin of his own home.

regarded in Orašac. As one villager defined it: "If you are in trouble or need anything you go to your komšija . . . sugar, kerosene for your lamp, a hoe or a sickle, even a little money . . ." It is understood that if necessary these items may be borrowed without permission as long as they are returned in their original condition. The importance of this concept was learned by us soon after we took up residence in the village. We had to leave for a few days and upon our return to Orašac found members of the village family with whom we lived wearing our clothes and using our combs. The bed we had been given was occupied by the fully clothed, loudly snoring figure of a visiting relative. When asked why these liberties had been taken without permission the domaćica replied that no wrong was done, for was it not true that the Amerikanci were welcome to borrow anything of *theirs* if the occasion arose?

Social activities are also important in neighborhood relationships. Only the "best" neighbors are invited to the slava of a household of another vamilija. Frequently these are the closest neighbors. On the other hand, all the neighboring households who participate together in labor pools are invited to weddings and other festivities. Larger weddings may include relatives and friends from all parts of the village, but inclusion of one's neighbors is mandatory.

The informal aspect of neighborhood relations is worth considering. Frequent visiting back and forth, which occurs between women and, to a lesser extent, between men, is of great importance in further strengthening ties. Casual visiting takes place throughout the year and is more common during the winter, when there is less work to be done. The significance of these relationships is particularly relevant because the homesteads are scattered over a wide area. This dispersion especially affects the women, since their other chances for social contacts outside the immediate neighborhood are only occasional visits to relatives and friends for slavas or weddings and brief encounters with fellow villagers in town on market day. The church is not particularly important in this respect because the average peasant attends only a few times a year. Men enjoy a greater degree of freedom. They make more trips to the market, and the local kafana and Village Council provide meeting places, both of which are not accessible to women for the same purpose. These are all minor factors, however, for the social life of both the men and the women is definitely centered in the komšiluk. As the villagers themselves say, *Komšija bliži od košulje*—A neighbor is closer than one's shirt.

There are two factors characterizing differences between neighbors and relatives living in an area. One is the variance in the intensity of the relationships, and the other is their degree of durability. First, as might be expected, there is a greater degree of visiting and exchanging of labor and favors among relatives living in the same area than among neighbors—although this does not invariably hold true. Second, underlying the reciprocal relationships between neighbors is the idea of mutual help. When this concept becomes less important, because of personality differences or other causes, then the degree of neighborliness also begins to diminish correspondingly. This is not the case when clansmen are neighbors.

The interplay of these relationships was brought out in a situation involving three households. Two of them were headed by Mihailo and Miloje, cousins who had originally been members of one zadruga. They were of moderate circumstances, and neither household had a well. Both obtained water from a third household, located about an equal distance from each of them, which belonged to another clan. Lazar, the domaćin of the third house, was regarded by each cousin as his best neighbor. When Mihailo and Miloje had their slavas, Lazar was invited as the honorary best neighbor at each and had to go from one house to the other on that day. Mihailo had a slightly larger family than his cousin, and one of his sons worked at the mine. This enabled his household to save enough money to have a well dug. After it was completed Mihailo's relationship with Lazar began to cool noticeably. Miloje scoffed at his cousin's well as a needless luxury. After several months Mihailo's household started declaring that although it was good to be on friendly terms with one's neighbors it was not necessary to overdo things and, after all, those folks *kod Lazara* were really quite lazy and shiftless. Meanwhile Miloje started to use Mihailo's new well, located more conveniently to his house than was Lazar's, and within a month he was making plans to build a well of his own.

SECONDARY RELATIONSHIPS

There are several other types of social relationships operating in Orašac. These include *kumstvo*, or godfatherhood, and *pobratimstvo*, or blood-brotherhood. Most important, however, are the secondary relationships determined by affinal kin, as diagrammed in Figure 25. The degree of contact is closely related to the distance from Orašac to the village of the wife's family. Since approximately one third of the brides come from Orašac itself and most of the others are from villages in the vicinity, this is not usually a problem. Physical distance is not the chief limiting factor, however, because the prevailing patriarchal ethos and almost universal patrilocality are the strongest determinants of the relationship. Illustrative of this attitude is that paternal kin are reckoned "by blood" as far back as six or eight generations, while maternal kin are "by milk" and are never calculated back more than three generations. Besides the wife's visiting her parent's home from time to time, in-laws are frequently honored guests at family slavas.

In Serbian society godfatherhood is an extremely important position of respect. The common pattern is for the godfather to live in another village, and on the few occasions when he sees his godchild he is treated with the utmost esteem. Godfatherhood is inherited in the male line, and if a godfather should have only daughters then the family to whom he is *kum* must choose another. Similarly, if his godchildren should be only girls then he ceases to function as kum. A godfather is usually selected on the basis of a deep friendship formed by the household's starešina. In many families the relationship has existed through so many generations that it cannot be recalled how or how long ago it began.[15]

The chief function of the kum is selecting a name for his godchild and bestowing it at the christening ceremony. When a celebration is held on the occasion of the child's first birthday[16] the god-

---

[15] There does not seem to be any economic or political consideration attached to this relationship.

[16] This custom, not practiced universally, is the only time a birthday is celebrated.

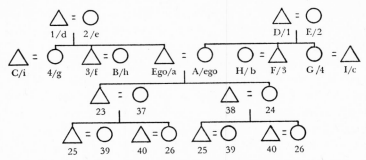

Relationship to *Ego* (male) represented by character left of
oblique bar, that to *ego* (female) by character right of bar.

1	Father, *otac, tata* or *ćale*		26	Granddaughter, *unuka*
2	Mother, *majka, mama* or *mati*		37	Daughter-in-law, *sna, snaha, snaja* or
3	Brother, *rodjeni brat*			*snajka*
4	Sister, *rodjena sestra*		38	Son-in-law, *zet*
23	Son, *sin*		39	Granddaughter-in-law, *sna za unukom*
24	Daughter, *kći* or *ćerka*		40	Grandson-in-law, *zet za unukom*
25	Grandson, *unuk*			

	Male Affinal			*Female Affinal*
A	Wife, *žena*		a	Husband, *muž*
B	Brother's wife, *sna*		b	Brother's wife, *sna*
C	Sister's husband, *zet*		c	Sister's husband, *zet*
D	Wife's father, *tast*		d	Husband's father, *svekar*
E	Wife's mother, *tašta*		e	Husband's mother, *svekrva*
F	Wife's brother, *šurak*		f	Husband's brother, *dever*
G	Wife's sister, *svastika*		g	Husband's sister, *zaova*
H	Wife's brother's wife, *šurnjaja*		h	Husband's brother's wife, *jetrva*
I	Wife's sister's husband, *pašenog*		i	Husband's sister's husband, *zet*

Figure 25. Affinal Relations

father is an honored guest, and later, when his godson is married,
he participates in the ceremony as the young man's sponsor and
presides over the wedding feast from the seat of honor. Outside of
these few important events there is relatively little contact.

Blood-brotherhood, like godfatherhood, is a means of artificially
extending kin ties. A blood-brother is most often sought when a
person feels himself to be seriously ill and in danger of dying. Sometimes the relation is not even between the parties directly concerned, for a mother will occasionally seek a blood-brother when
her child is ill. Two people are united in blood-brotherhood in a
ceremony performed by them over the grave of a close relative

of the person seeking a *pobratim*. The latter says, "*Otkupim roba od groba, pred Bogom i Svetim Jovanom*" (I redeem the slave from the grave, before God and St. John). While this is stated the former binds a metal chain around the sick person's legs and the wooden cross at the grave, locks it, and then unlocks it replying, "*Pred Bogom i Svetim Jovanom, otkupljujem roba od groba*" (Before God and St. John, I have redeemed the slave from the grave). This ritual is repeated twice more, and the two parties kiss solemnly, now bound in pobratimstvo. The graveyard is the site used for this ceremony to literally symbolize preventing the death of the "slave," or sick person, and also so that the family ancestors can spiritually witness the act. After the ceremony the two are supposed to remain brothers for life and observe all the obligations that come with this close relationship. For example, their children are not supposed to intermarry. Occasionally these precepts are carried out, but more often, after the crisis has passed, the two tend to drift apart, particularly if they live in different villages. As might be expected this relationship is usually most significant when the blood-brothers are also close neighbors.

Today the practice appears to be dying out. As one man expressed it, "Now when a person is sick he goes to a doctor instead of seeking a blood-brother." There are, however, a few people, especially youths, who seek a pobratim merely on the basis of friendship. In these cases the ceremony is considerably modified; sickness plays no role and most of the ritual is omitted, so that they simply kiss over the grave.

A final type of synthetic kinship is in the assumption of a clan name not inherited. In Orašac this is illustrated by the Stojanović vamilija. The official records list nineteen households by that name, but only sixteen of these are descended from Stojan. The other three households are headed by brothers who acquired the name by adoption. According to them their parents were from Lipovac, where their mother was left widowed. Later a Stojanović from Orašac married her and brought her and her young sons to Orašac. No children resulted from this marriage, and when the sons by the first marriage came of age they took the name of their stepfather. This was done formally in the church and, according to their story, in the county court as well. The explanation offered by a "true" Stojanović was: "Hummmf! That's easy! They came here and saw that we Stojanovići were the finest and most industrious vamilija in Orašac, and that's why they took our name." Whatever the case may be, the households of the three brothers cannot intermarry with other Stojanovići, and they have graveyard plots next to those of the traditional clan households. "Even so, they are not the same as we are," one Stojanović elder summarized stubbornly.

THE VILLAGE AS A SOCIAL UNIT

In a limited sense the village itself is something of a social unit, and persons from the same village refer to one another as *moj seljak*—my villager.

When talking to or about other villagers there is a tendency to de-emphasize the vamilija and deal with individuals. This is shown by the extensive use of nicknames, in place of personal or family names, employed when discussing a particular person with others. They are never used in direct address because they are usually unflattering, pointing up the unfavorable aspects of an individual's physical features or personality. No one seems overtly resentful of a nickname because every adult male and many of the women have them. They are well known by everyone throughout the village. A certain man with a long narrow face is called *Konjska glava* (Horse-face), and a woman with a wide mouth and toothy grin is known as *Krokodil*. Some nicknames call attention to physical defects: a man who carries his head to one side, as must be done when playing the Serbian bagpipes, is called *Gajdaš* (Bagpipe-player), another is *Ćora* (Turkish for One-eyed), and *Ćelavac* means Baldy. *Mućak* (Rotten egg) is the name of a village good-for-nothing, and a woman whose sloppy housekeeping habits are known past her own courtyard fence is called *Djundra* (from the word for manure). In other cases people are nicknamed after various nationality groups: a miserly man is called *Cincarin* (Tsintsar),[17] and a certain dark-skinned woman is Ciganka (Gypsy).

[17] The Tsintsars were a distinctive nationality group, closely related to the nomadic Vlachs, who were important in urban commerce in Serbia in the nineteenth century.

In addition to a sort of all-village unity via the use of these most personal nicknames, there is the fact that most of the forty-one traditional clans are descended from about ten earlier ones.[18] These ten in turn were said to have been founded by brothers or other relatives who originally settled in Orašac. Furthermore, about thirty percent of the village youths choose brides from within Orašac (intermarriage is permitted after five generations, except among clan members). The awareness of the village as a social unit is at least in part a reflection of these ties.

[18] A similar pattern prevails throughout much of Šumadija.

CHAPTER 7

THE QUESTION OF CLASS

SERBIAN RURAL SOCIETY is remarkable for its homogeneity and lack of an aristocracy or gentry. This absence of a formal class structure is a heritage of the many hundreds of years of Turkish rule during which the old feudal nobility was eliminated. The Serbian state was founded by men of peasant stock, but certain differences were evident even in the beginning, for both Karadjordje and Miloš Obrenović were well-to-do peasant traders before becoming national leaders. During the nineteenth century a commercial and business class began to develop with the growth of urban centers. More prosperous merchant classes did not evolve until the late nineteenth and twentieth centuries.

These changes were slowly reflected in the villages. Toward the end of the nineteenth century the *gazda*, or wealthy peasant, became significant. He was distinguished from his fellow villagers by his greater material wealth—larger landholdings, more livestock, and in some cases better house and outbuildings. These individual differences, then, were gradations of status based primarily on economic factors. The essence of these differences seems to lie in the term gazda and the connotations it has for the Orašac peasant. Above all, it is a relative term. Within the memory of some of the older villagers, a gazda was considered to be "a man who had a yield of 500 kilos of wheat from his land." Today even the poorest peasant gets that much. Prior to the time of these recollections the gazda was evidently of very small importance or was nonexistent.

Without doubt the most significant factor in the prestige of a gazda was the amount of land he possessed. Toward this end the ambitious starešina often drove himself and all the members of his household to work as hard as they could. Several factors aided the head of the household. Chief among them was the amount of labor in his zadruga, usually by the number of able-bodied sons, brothers, and nephews. All other factors being equal, a man who had only daughters could not expect to progress very far. Livestock trading was very significant as a means of raising funds, and in the larger zadrugas one man often devoted himself exclusively to this pursuit. Additional assets were provided if the brides marrying into the household brought dowries of land. Just as necessary as all these possessions was the ability of the starešina to wisely coordinate the joint efforts of the household members.

A case in point, illustrating some of the factors in the rise of a gazda, is that of Luka Lučić. Before the war he was the richest man in Orašac. He owned over one hundred hectares of land, large amounts of livestock, a kafana, and three houses in Arandjelovac. His grandfather, however, had been a very poor peasant with only three or four hectares. The grandfather had four sons, all strong and very industrious, but three of them died before they reached middle age. Because of this there was no division through inheritance, and when Luka's grandfather died the one remaining son, his father, received all. Luka's father supplemented his livestock and agricultural income by serving as a *jatak*, sheltering the highwaymen who were still common in this area until the latter part of the nineteenth century. With the money they paid him he purchased land from other peasants. Later he started loaning them money,[1] and gradually he was able to make investments in the town, continue to add to his growing landholding, and achieve the position of the "biggest gazda" in Orašac.

There were other factors influencing an individual's status. Schooling, particularly the ability to read and write, was important. A gazda rarely was illiterate even though he may have had but two or three years of education.

---

[1] This activity was not typical of a gazda, however, for most money lending was done either by small merchants in Orašac or by professionals in Arandjelovac. In fact, many gazdas acted as patrons of the poorer peasants, loaning them money at no interest in times of need and sometimes going bankrupt in the process.

The status of a gazda was heritable only to a limited extent. Most of the sons remained on the land and, in accordance with existing social and economic pressures, many zadrugas divided after the starešina's death. If a man happened to be an only son, or sole surviving son, and inherited all his father's land, he was not recognized as a gazda in the eyes of his fellow villagers until he was past forty years old. There were certain moral qualifications, too—a sense of social responsibility and the ability to manage the affairs of the household. In short, he was supposed to be a shining example of a *dobar domaćin*, a good, solid householder. A man of modest means could also be regarded as a dobar domaćin although he would not be considered a gazda. This is not to say that every gazda was of sterling character but, rather, that his status in the community was very much dependent on factors other than economic power. All this helps to explain why clearly defined class distinctions have no tradition in Orašac.

Most peasants interviewed in 1953–54 felt that although there exists the term *stara gazdinska kuća*, or prosperous household established and maintained through several generations, the affluence of most wealthy households did not last more than fifty years. Nor did it always take two or more generations to achieve the status of gazda. A few former Orašac gazde spoke of poverty and even privation in their youth.

In Orašac in the late 1930s a man was regarded as a gazda if he had economic qualifications, including over ten hectares of good-quality land, at least two horses, several head of cattle, and proportionate amounts of other livestock. Most likely he employed some seasonal labor to help him work his land. His house was well constructed, with many outbuildings and a formal covered entrance gate. He also had a carriage in which to make trips to town. His equipment was not necessarily the most modern. In fact, many of the more prosperous households clung to traditional styles longer. Just who in Orašac was a gazda at that time was, of course, a relative concept—poorer households estimated a higher number than did more comfortable households.

The status of the gazda could be manifested in several ways. For one thing, since many of them were self-made men of dynamic personality, they frequently dominated local politics. The richest among them acted as patrons of the school, awarding prizes to the best pupils and donating small articles of equipment. There were also some differences in dress, limited for the most part to the quality of the fabric and such things as the amount of embroidery on a man's vest. Their fellow-villagers, especially the poorer peasants, deferred to them socially, since the gazda was a potential employer. On this point there was also the question of genuine respect for accomplishment. During what the peasants regarded as their golden era, the first decade of the reign of their beloved King Peter I (1903–21), it was felt that any man who worked hard enough could become a gazda. There was, therefore, a great deal of admiration for those who made the grade. Among some, however, there was an attitude of bitterness and resentment. Many Orašac men questioned on this subject remarked that some of the richer peasants abused their social position and treated poorer people harshly.

All these differences were quantitative and not qualitative. Even the richest peasant in the village worked the land with his own hands. At the same time, landless laborers were and still are virtually unknown in the region of Šumadija, as compared to other areas such as the Vojvodina, where there were large landowners and a sizeable landless class. In Orašac, located in the heart of an area where people won their land from the forests and successfully revolted against the Turks, a strong egalitarian tradition has prevailed. This has been an element preventing the development of class.

From this brief discussion we may conclude that class, in the sense of clearly defined groups based on a complex of social and economic criteria, did not exist in Orašac.[2] What did exist were varying degrees of prosperity reflected in gradations of social status. The term gazda was strictly relative, based largely on an individual's achievements.

[2] The village priest and a few school teachers constituted a special group, of course, but they are not considered here because they were all temporary residents.

CHAPTER 8

LIFE CYCLE I

In this and the following chapter we shall see how the Orašani live out their lives as individuals. Variations on the culturally approved patterns will be discussed in terms of day to day and year to year occurrences as well as special events and rituals. These are brought out in autobiographies written by the villagers, in anecdotes and interviews, and in the selections of folk songs included here.

INFANCY

Children are universally desired in the village, for their own sake and as potential additions to the household's labor force. Boys are especially hoped for, because it is they who will carry on the family tradition. A man who has only daughters is looked upon as being very unfortunate. The standard explanation for the sour disposition of one particular villager was, "*Oj*, what can you expect? He has no sons."

A day or two after a child is born the father must register the birth at the Village Council. This is required by law, and all villagers comply although a few may delay for several days. At the Council the new father is congratulated by those present and he usually invites them to a drink at the kafana next door. If the father is a state employee, at the mine, state farm, local offices, or at a factory in town, he receives a subsidy of 8,000 dinars for the infant's layette. It is usually spent on flannel cloth, facial soap, and perhaps some nursing bottles.

Before 1947 the village priest kept a record of all vital statistics, so that when a birth was registered at the church it was recorded for the state at the same time. Today, however, if you want a birth listed in the church records it must be registered with the priest separately, prior to the infant's christening. Almost without exception this is done by all of the peasants. At this time the priest gives the baby a temporary name and blesses some water brought from home by the father. The infant is bathed in it every day for forty days or until he is christened.[1]

In most cases the christening ceremony takes place a week to ten days after the child is born. The kum is the most important participant, and traditionally he selects and confers the name without consultation with the child's parents. He also provides the infant's christening shirt. Formerly it was of hand-woven cotton trimmed with lace edging, but today it is more apt to be fashioned from store-bought flannel. In recognition of his position as the honored godfather, he is presented with a pair of knitted stocks, hand-loomed underdrawers and a shirt which the mother has prepared for him. More prosperous households sometimes include a hand-woven blanket in their gift.

Sometimes the grandparents accompany the child's father and the kum to the priest's rectory, where the ceremony is performed. The priest pours water over the naked infant, and the kum pronounces the name he has chosen. A bit of the baby's hair is snipped off and rolled into a ball with some wax from one of the burning candles, and it is placed in the candlestick along with similar balls. Then incense is lit in a burner and the kum, priest, and father walk three times around the ceremonial table, swinging a censer and chanting. The sign of the cross is made over the infant, and a crucifix is touched to various parts of his body. As a final token of good luck the kum spits lightly over his godchild, "to get rid of the devil."

Upon returning to the parents' and grandparents' home, the kum is seated as the guest of honor at a special feast. The infant is

---

[1] At this time the infant was often placed, tightly swaddled, in his cradle with his head between a pair of spiked wool combers. This was a barricade against evil spirits. A further precaution was to put a clove of garlic on the baby's forehead. Today only a very few households still practice this custom.

displayed on a bed, and relatives and neighbors come in, slap money or small gifts on his blanket and loudly proclaim their good wishes. The proud grandfather acts as host, urging everyone to drink from his flowered flask.

Babies are swaddled, "so their legs will grow straight." They are bound tightly, round and round, with thin braids of yarn, and wrapped in two or three layers of flannel and blankets, even in warm weather. More conservative households swaddle infants for about three months. In one home in which the young mother's mother-in-law was dead, tradition was defied and the infant was never swaddled. Had there been a mature matron in the household there would have been objections and warnings.

All mothers nurse their babies, sometimes for as long as three years if another child does not come along in the meantime. The usual period for weaning is from twelve to fourteen months. Some households have nursing bottles with rubber nipples and start feeding the baby cow's milk diluted with warm water at one and a half months. At three months a mush of bread and milk is introduced, and at six to eight months coddled eggs with bread crumbs are given. This diet is continued until the baby's first teeth appear. After this he is fed standard food except for extremely greasy, spicy, or salty dishes. Nursing continues on a demand basis.

Toilet training is a casual affair. The baby is cleaned and changed at least twice a day. If he happens to urinate while someone is holding him, it is disregarded or laughed off. Bed-wetting, too, is not considered a serious matter. It is felt that as the baby develops he will eventually be able to imitate his older brothers and sisters without any formal instruction. If a small child has to urinate at night he is held over the dirt floor or an enamel pot, depending on the standards of the household. The villagers see no need for, or significance in, toilet training and are embarrassed to discuss it.[2]

During his first year the infant spends most of his life securely bundled in his cradle. The mother is as attentive to his needs as

[2] One peasant dismissed the subject with a shrug of his shoulders—"What do you want to know all this for? It has absolutely nothing to do with the history of Orašac!"

possible, but she has many household chores as well as work in the fields. Sometimes she carries him to the fields with her, but more often he is left home under the care of another female member of the household. Because of constant pressures of work, it is considered a virtue if the infant is *miran,* or quiet, and pacifiers are frequently used. He is often picked up and fondled by various members of the family, men as well as women, especially his grandparents.

The paternal grandmother and even the grandfather play an important role in caring for the child. Their strength may be relatively limited compared to that of the young parents, who consequently spend a greater amount of time away from the house working at harder chores. This is especially the case now that large zadrugas have become uncommon. The baby and its parents frequently sleep in different rooms, particularly in the winter. The cradle is left near the stove, and it is usually the grandparents who sleep in the warm kitchen while the more hearty young couple sleeps in a cold room. Still another factor making for an intimate relationship between children and their grandparents is that it is the parents who do most of the reprimanding and punishing.

There are many lullabies and nonsense tunes sung by mothers and doting grandmothers, as they rock the baby in his cradle. This one is typical:

> Ljulju, ljulju, ljulju, podajte ga Dulu.
> Nini, nini, nini, podajte ga strini.
> Ljulju, ljulju, ljuške, na Moravi kruške.
> Dole sedi teta, kolačiće pljeska,
> I meni bi dala, ali ne da tetak.
> Izeo ga mačak na veliki petak!

> Rock-a-bye, rock-a-bye, rock-a-bye, give him to Dule.
> Nini, nini, nini, give him to Auntie.
> Rock-a-bye, rock-a-bye, rock-a-bye, pears on the Morava.
> Auntie is sitting down there making little cakes,
> And she would give me some, but Uncle doesn't let her.
> May the tomcat eat him up on Good Friday!

CHILDHOOD

Serbian children begin to crawl and utter recognizable sounds at the age of seven to nine months and frequently walk before they are a year old. At this point a baby emerges from the category of *beba*, or infant, and is considered a *dete*, a child. He is permitted to crawl around on the dirt floor, and in many households he spends considerable time in his wooden stand, out of reach of the fire, general mischief, and anything he might put in his mouth. From the time he begins to talk and walk with ease until he enters school, at the age of seven, he is often left in the care of older children and sometimes to himself, to explore the homestead within the confines of the fence.[3]

This period is a pleasant one, for harsh discipline is alien to the culture. The child grows up in an emotionally warm atmosphere and learns to freely expect and return love. There is always someone around to fondle him, sing to him, or tell him a story. Whoever it is, however, it is least likely to be the child's father. Open displays of affection are encouraged, and demonstrative expressions may occur even on solemn occasions. At a graveyard feast a three-year-old climbed up on his grandfather's lap and began to stroke his face and hug him. If the old man was mildly annoyed, since he was eating and talking at the time, he did not show it. He simply returned the caress and gently asked the child to leave.

Despite the warm relationship between children and elders and regardless of the lessening of patriarchal authority, respect and obedience are still expected. Children do not eat with adults, and they learn to be content with what they are given. Growing up in a friendly and fairly large household, the child receives a real sense of security, but at an early age he also begins to realize want and privation.

Holidays are a time of indescribable delight for small children. Eating meat, white bread, and cookies once or twice a year are events to be looked forward to. In their autobiographies, some of

[3] Sanders's remark is equally true for Orašac: "The Dragalevtsy child early learned the basic principle of action: if you want to stay out of trouble, keep out of the grown-ups' way. The child's greatest errors were those of commission rather than omission." Sanders, *Balkan Village*, p. 113.

the older men tell about the joy of receiving a new pair of sandals or even just a stick of striped candy on the rare occasions when they were permitted to go to town with their elders.

At an age as early as five, many children are entrusted with watching the pigs or sheep near the house, gathering kindling, and helping to pick fruits and vegetables. A real change in their lives occurs when they are seven and start school. Besides the new experiences, it is at school that they have their first real contacts beyond the neighborhood and meet children from other parts of the village. There are eight grades at the Orašac school, the first four being elementary school and the second four considered the lower half of high school. Going to school is an exciting and eagerly awaited experience. Once the initial difficulties of adjustment are over, most children take to it enthusiastically. They are taught at home to be polite and above all obedient to their teacher, and no child, so proud of his new status as a *djak*, or pupil, would think of behaving otherwise. Many men who wrote autobiographies recall their schooldays as the happiest in their lives and regard having been able to go at all as a great privilege. Some were keenly disappointed when they were forced to drop out because of work pressures at home. The essays of both older and younger children express the pleasures of learning. A third-grader summed up his thoughts on school in this composition:

I go to school every day. I like my teacher. My teacher is called Ljiljana. I am in the third grade in our elementary school. My name is Jovan Pejović. What do I like to learn from my books? I like history best and then geography and then the reading book and then natural science. And now I'm finished telling about school.

The same small boy had this to say about what he does after school:

At home I watch the pigs and sheep. I play while I watch the pigs and sheep. In the winter I ride on my sled and throw snowballs. What I like best of all is playing the flute. I can play the flute and the double flute. But how I would love to play the accordion! Of all the livestock I like horses best.

From the ages of seven to eleven or twelve, while they are pupils in the elementary school, all village children have definite chores at home. They are made very conscious of their responsibilities. A ten-year-old girl was informed that she could see a health film being shown that night at the school or else attend a neighbor's wedding the following day. She would have loved to attend both but could not because either she or her brother was obliged to watch the sheep during the day. Finally she chose the film, resignedly declaring, in the fashion of her elders, "*Čovek mora da radi*" (A person must work).

Not all children accept their duties so philosophically, and the adjustment involved in the assumption of new responsibilities is sometimes difficult. Bursts of temper are not infrequent, and occasionally older children tell their mothers or grandmothers to shut up. In return they get their ears boxed or nose soundly twisted, and eventually the storm passes. Extreme physical punishment is rarely employed.

Children in the upper grades of the village school view their life to date with mixed emotions. One of the chief reasons is that they were born in 1940, 1941, and 1942, when Orašac village was the scene of much fighting among the Partisans, Četniks, and the German troops who occupied the area. During 1942–44 many houses were burned and families were forced to flee to other villages. Several children did not know their fathers during their early years. Aside from disturbing experiences caused directly by war, several children had unstable family lives due to the death of one or both parents. On the other hand, some children describe losing their sheep or being caught in a storm as being the most serious events of their lives.

No matter what unhappiness has been experienced, everyday fun is combined with school and household chores. In the winter children frolic in the snow, on homemade skis or sleds, build snowmen, and have snowball fights. A favorite indoor game is *mica*, similar to draughts, played on a homemade board with vari-colored corn kernels. Fair weather outdoor games include a sort of blindman's bluff and another tag game called "cat and bird." A popular local sport is *klis*, in which players take turns flipping a notched stick on the ground by beating it with a staff. In the open yard near the church soccer, learned at school, attracts the older boys.

The following essays on "My Childhood" are selections from a group written by thirteen- and fourteen-year-old boys and girls.

A. I was born on December 26, 1940, in Orašac. I have a sister two years younger than I. When we were little we used to fight with each other. When I was three the Fascists began to burn our little neighborhood of Gajevi, and we were forced out of our house. I went with my mother and sister to Grandpa's in Gornji Kraj. They burned only part of Gajevi, but they didn't touch our house. When we returned we saw how they had broken into our house and opened my mother's clothes chests and stolen most of her things. They took my father with them. He escaped and came back. Later he went to fight in the war and disappeared. Finally all the fighting was over. I grew up a little and was able to drive the sheep to pasture. I followed the shepherds and ran and played in the meadows. Spring is the best time because the first flowers appear—violets, primroses, and other kinds. The second reason is that the baby lambs come at this time. When we are watching the sheep we sit near a brook and listen to the water and smell the flowers and are very happy. We gather bouquets and carry them until they die, and so we pass the day.

B. According to what my parents say I was born during the Occupation. My father was a prisoner of war in Germany. My life until 1945 was without any interesting events. Then one day my mother said to me, "We are going to Arandjelovac. Your father has returned." I sat in the cart with Mommy and my brothers and we went. I remember well that she led the cows. When we went over Preseka Hill she told us stories to pass the time. When we arrived in Arandjelovac we left the cows in the street in front of the kafana. They told us my father wasn't in there so we went to another restaurant, and there he was sitting at a table with my uncle. Although I had never seen him before I greeted him and kissed his hand. That was a joyful day for Mommy and even more for me. From Arandjelovac we returned home. I was given a chocolate bar on that day. Many of our neighbors came to talk to my father. After that my brother started school. He told me what he learned, but he didn't want to teach me. I was angry and complained to Daddy. I could hardly wait for the day when I could enter school and would not have to ask anyone to teach me. So my childhood passed until 1947 when I finally entered school.

Now I am in the sixth grade, and so far I have been a good pupil. That is how I spent my childhood.

C. As far back as I can remember I have had both good and bad experiences. My village is very pretty, with hills and pastures. I am very young but I know my village well enough to praise it. Where I live a little brook, Misača, runs through. I was bathed in it many times, more often crying than willingly. One day when I was watching the sheep with several other boys I went to drive some sheep back and accidentally slipped into the water. It was quite deep because the snow had just melted. I was lucky to have caught onto a branch or I would have been swept through the water. The other boys came to see what had happened to me, pulled me out, and I returned home. At home I have an old grandfather, over sixty, and when he gets angry all one can do is leave home. When he saw me all wet, he asked me why, and I started crying, convinced that he would beat me. He only made a serious face and told me to go change my clothes. He used to play the double flute very well. Whenever he had time he would play for us, and we children danced gaily. Then Grandpa was gay, too, but it happened very rarely. So I can say I had a fine time most of the time, but sometimes I deserved to be punished, especially when I played with the other children and my sheep wandered too far away. There are lots of other things from my childhood I could talk about, but they would be similar things.

D. I spent my childhood playing, working, and studying. Most of the time I spent and still spend watching the sheep. I have done it since my early childhood. When I was five I was allowed to drive the sheep to pasture. In the mornings my mother prepared a package of bread for me, and she drove the stock out for me. Then I took my bread and a switch and went to the fields. On my way I met my friends, and we went together and played for the whole day. In the evenings we all returned home. When I came home I drove the sheep to their pen and went inside to have some supper. It is this way most of the year. In the winter I help feed the stock. This means a yearly holiday for me because I don't have to watch the sheep. We play in the snow all day. When we come home we look as if we had been in water. When I began school I still had to watch the sheep, but less often than before. Today I have new friends, and I am always with them. We boys inherit games from the adults, for instance, *futbal*, which is our favorite game today. We had no such ball games formerly and played with balls made of rags. We used to play a lot, but now that I am in the seventh grade I have to study. When I was in elementary school I spent most of my time playing, studying, and helping around the house. Now there is less play and more studying. As a little boy I knew nothing about skis. In school I learned about them and made a pair for myself. Now it is winter and I'm going skiing today.

Until they are in their late teens, a boy is called a *dečko* or *momčić* and a girl a *devojčica*. In this period of adolescence their futures are determined. Of those who finish the eight-year village school, a fortunate few go on to complete the remaining four years of high school in Arandjelovac. A small number are apprenticed to craftsmen in town. This occurs especially in those households which have several sons and a very limited amount of land. An older peasant who had been away as a prisoner of war said, "We are not like the peasants of western Europe, where only one son remains on the farm. With us, all the brothers remain at home." Yet it is true that today the change away from this tradition is noticeable, and some parents conscientiously try to plan on sending a younger son to school or work. This transition has been encouraged by the free schooling available in the post-war period and the greater demand for urban workers of all types. One boy, one of the very few who disliked school, wrote:

when I entered elementary school I had to learn to study well for the whole year, because my parents forced me to. During holidays I played a little but also had to study. When I finally finished elementary school they made me continue on to high school because it would be impossible for me to remain a peasant. My parents can barely live on two hectares of land, and it would be hopeless for us three brothers, too. I didn't want to go to high school, but I had to. Now I am in the seventh grade, and I realize that it is impractical for me to remain a peasant.

The vast majority of post-school children stay on the land. They assume greater responsibilities, helping now with the plowing, hoeing, reaping, threshing, and other agricultural chores. Boys accompany the men to market and learn the skills of livestock trading. Girls are taught to cook and bake and to do all kinds of handiwork. It is at this period that the girl starts her *devojačka sprema,* or trousseau, increasing it year after year as she becomes more proficient in the various crafts.

The physical changes that accompany adolescence are regarded with secrecy and shame, in keeping with the severely repressive attitude toward sex. Information about menstruation is learned from other girls at school and not at home. After the onset, however, mothers, grandmothers, and aunts are full of advice and folk remedies which they readily pass on. One of the most popular is to smear a drop of blood on the forehead and leave it there for an entire day, after saying the words "night and day." This is supposed to curb the flow of blood for that month. In general, their periods last only three days and are not accompanied by any real discomfort. During this time all normal activities, including strenuous work in the fields, proceed as usual. A girl is taught to set aside her oldest skirt which she wears drawn through the legs, under the regular skirt.

Some boys go through a period of rebellion coincident with the lessening of parental authority. At present this attitude is of minor significance in Orašac, but the following recent examples indicate that it may become more of a problem in the future. In one case a village official was reprimanding a boy of sixteen who was accused of starting a fight during which several windows in the brand new Cooperative Home were smashed. He listened sullenly and, cursing, jeered that there was nothing anyone could do to him. It was only when he was told there was an excellent chance of his going to jail that he changed his attitude. Another time a fifteen-year-old was brought before the county court for beating an old woman in an argument over herding sheep in a certain pasture. Older men simply shake their heads, like their fellows all over the world, an mutter that things weren't like that when they were boys.

COURTSHIP

One of the high points in a person's life comes during his late teens. It is true that more and more adult work is expected, but the *momak,* or youth over seventeen, and the *devojka,* maiden over sixteen, are looked upon with envy by both the younger and older members of the community. Their new status as young adults means greater freedom and the climax of years of anticipation. This is not so much a looking forward to marriage, for that is considered inevitable and the only possible way of life, but rather to dressing up in the finest clothes their families can provide and attending the fairs and dances in the town. A major share of a household's annual clothing budget goes into outfitting a bachelor or maiden, who must have something new for Easter regardless of whether Grandpa needs a new šubara. When we made a present of a pair of socks to a villager in his late twenties, he promptly put them away in the chest. "Me, I don't need these fine socks," he said, "I'll save them for Rade to wear when he becomes a momak." Rade was eight years old at the time.

Nowadays youths seldom watch the sheep, for they are needed to help with more strenuous household activities. There are a number of folk songs romanticizing the rendezvous arranged while a girl and boy were herding their flocks, and they give an idea of sanctioned courtship patterns generally no longer practiced. These songs are sung by all age groups but apply only to young people in their late teens.

> Čuvam ovce dole u Jasenje,
> Gledaj, dragi, pa dodji kod mene.
> Samo pazi da ne vidi nana,
> Ti porani rano sa ovcama.
> Ako ne znaš gde ja čuvam ovce,
> Ti ćeš čuti na ovcama zvonce.
>
> Preko puta medenice zveče,
> Tu moj dragi svoje stado kreće.
> Stado kreće u sviralu svira,
> Srce moje ne daje mi mira.
>
> I'm watching the sheep down in the glen,
> Try, darling, to come to me there.
> Be careful lest my mother see you,
> So get up early with the sheep.
> If you don't know where I'm watching them,
> You will hear the sheep's bells ringing.

Across the road a brass bell is ringing,
And there my sweetheart is moving with his flock.
He's watching the sheep and playing his flute,
And my heart will not stand still.

Another popular one is presented below, followed by perhaps the best-liked of all, sung in responses to the accompaniment of a flute.

Čaj goro, lane moje,
Pričuvaj mi ovce.
Da ja sidjem, lane moje,
Dole do devojke,
Da ja vidim, lane moje,
Šta devojke rade.
One rade, lane moje,
Lepo cveće sade.

My dear wooded hill,
Guard my sheep for a while,
So that I can go down, dear hill,
Down to where the girls are,
To see, dear hill,
What the girls are doing.
They are working, dear hill,
Planting beautiful flowers.

Both: Jovo Ružu kroz sviralu zove:
Boys: "Ajde, Ružo, da čuvamo ovce."
Girls: "Ne smem, Jovo, karaće me majka."
Boys: "Ako kara, izbiti te neće,
            Ako kara beži mome dvoru."

Both: Jovo is calling to Ruža on his flute:
Boys: "Come on, Ruža, let's watch the sheep together."
Girls: "I dare not, Jovo, my mother will scold me."
Boys: "Even so, she won't beat you,
            And if she scolds you, run away to my house."

The Orašac maidens herd their sheep together, and if they cannot meet the boys they can at least sing about it. They also pass the time composing songs. The following two were made up one day while three seventeen-year-olds were out with their flocks. The sentiment expressed in the second one appears to be quite recent.

> Ala sam se karmenisala,
> Tri sam momka ja begenisala.
> Prvog Raju, drugog Radosava,
> A trećega Stanić, Milosava.

> How I rouged my lips,
> And made eyes at three boys.
> The first was Raja, the second Radosav,
> And the third, Milosav Stanić.

> Beli šeboj u čaši miriše.
> Imam Mila on pismo piše.
> Sve je dobro, samo jedno kvari,
> 'oće Mile da mi gospodari.
> Mile moje, nemam gospodara
> Dok ne vežem ruke kraj oltara.
> Dok sam dete i dok sam devojče,
> Neću dati da mi sudi momče.

> A white flower perfumes the vase.[4]
> I have my Mile who is writing me letters.
> Everything is fine, only one thing spoils it,
> Mile wants to boss me around.
> My dear Mile, I don't have a boss
> Until my hands are tied before the altar.
> While I'm still young and a maiden,
> No fellow is going to order me around.

A boy and girl have many occasions for contact, despite today's lack of the most idealized form of courtship, that of watching sheep

---

[4] A characteristic song pattern is for the first line to be unrelated or a nonsense line, used for rhyme alone.

together. Within the village there are dances and celebrations; in the town, markets and fairs provide opportunities for young people of neighboring villages to meet. A traditional courtship institution still very much in evidence is the *prelo*, or spinning bee. Each neighborhood customarily holds informal spinning bees attended by all the girls and many matrons of the komšiluk. During the summer they take place out of doors in the evening, at a place where several lanes meet or else in a grassy clearing in some central spot. In the winter the prelo is held in a peasant home.

The summer ones are much better attended, often with forty or fifty girls and women present. Each comes with a milking stool to sit on and a huge fluff of combed wool strapped to her distaff. There is a formal seating pattern, usually around a bonfire, which is lit when the night air cools: the married women sit next to each other and the maidens close the ring on the opposite side. It would be hard to say which work faster, fingers or mouths, as they spin and chatter on into the night. The girls are bright-eyed with anticipation. They know when the boys have arrived by the murmur of low voices behind them in the shadows. Under the watchful eyes of the matrons, boys and girls tease one another, joke, and sing songs. The boys' group starts the singing, and the girls, spinning all the while, return a song. The boys answer with another of their songs, and the girls again reply. Soon spindles are tucked under the low stools, and the boys move closer to the circle. Excitement mounts, and one girl exclaims, in the pattern of an old folk saying, "*Oj*, maidens, make up your eyebrows black,[5] for the devils have now become Don Juans!" There may be some small talk to mask an exchange of meaningful glances, and the young men take off down the dark lane, singing as they go. The maidens glow with pleasure and the matrons with nostalgia, as they pick up their spinning and stools and return home, all agreeing that it has been a successful prelo.

The songs sung by the maidens at the prelo provide an excellent vehicle for expressing attitudes on love and marriage. Many of them deal with a girl's relations with her future mother-in-law, reflecting her fears of being under the domination of her husband's

[5] Dark, well-shaped eyebrows are considered a mark of beauty.

mother and bringing out the culturally stereotyped role of the mother-in-law.

> Prete prelje, ne gledajte na me.
> Ja sam bila u selu na prelu,
> Oprela sam tri aršina platna.
> Biće mojoj svekrvi košulja,
> Sve se bojim dugačka će biti
> D' imam kade bi je podrezala.

> Spin, spinners, don't look at me.
> I was at the spinning bee in the village,
> And I spun three *aršina*[6] of cotton.
> It will be a shirt for my mother-in-law,
> But I'm afraid it will be too long.
> If only I knew how, I would shorten it.

> Mene moja svekrvica kara,
> Što joj nisam ja donela para.
> Svekrvice ti mnogo ne traži,
> Jer tvoj sinak za mene ne važi.

> My mother-in-law scolds me,
> Because I didn't bring a dowry.
> Mother-in-law, don't ask too much,
> Your son doesn't mean anything to me.

> Ja se mojoj svekrvi ne svidjam.
> Hvala Bogu često nju ne vidjam.

> My mother-in-law doesn't like me.
> Thank God I don't see her too often.

Other traditional prelo songs are teasing chants, sung to one girl by a group of her friends, linking her name with that of a village bachelor. When the boys hear it they whoop with glee and immediately retort with one of their own teasing songs. This is a song sung by the maidens:

---

[6] A Turkish measure of length.

Ajte, ajte, devojke na prelo,
I pones' te šareno vreteno.
Od' ovamo Ružo, od' ovamo lepa Ružo,
Da ti damo, Ružo, da ti damo lepa Ružo,
Lepog Raju, lepa Ružo,
Lepog Raju, lepa Ružo.

Come, come on to the prelo, maidens,
And bring along your colored spindles.
Come over here, Ruža, come on pretty Ruža,
So we can give you, Ruža, to give you, pretty Ruža,
Handsome Raja, pretty Ruža,
Handsome Raja, pretty Ruža.

Once or twice a year there are county fairs in Arandjelovac. These are especially important events for the young people, and the boys freely admit that they intend to look over the girls from other villages. The Orašac girls attend for the same reason, to be seen by bachelors from neighboring communities. Everyone wears his best clothes and goes in groups of three or four friends. A boy and girl would never go together to such an event unless they were officially betrothed, and even then they would most likely go in the company of friends. After the trading, games of chance, window shopping, and visiting, boys link arms and move through the street, nodding casually to girls they know. The girls reciprocate with cautious nods and then gather in a huddle to whisper and giggle as soon as the boys have passed. After the fair a dance is held on the churchyard hill above the market square. Accordionists have been hired to provide music, and two or three circles of young people form on the grass to dance the *kolo*.

When led by a particularly spirited young man, the dance circle opens and snakes back and forth, giving the bachelors a chance to show off their nimble, high-stepping footwork. The girls dance in a restrained manner, never with the buoyancy of the young men, and any maiden making herself conspicuous by dancing with too much enthusiasm would be regarded as behaving in bad taste. Sometimes several hundred young people from more than twenty nearby villages come to join in the fun, to see and to be seen. Any

courting done at these dances is very subdued. A boy interested in
a maiden he has never met may ask an acquaintance to act as a
go-between and introduce them. They exchange a few platitudes,
and if the feeling is reciprocated they will be sure to find each
other on the next market day. This is how many young men meet
their brides.[7]

When village girls get dressed up to go to town they carry their
good shoes and walk in everyday rubber sandals. Just outside
Arandjelovac they stop to change shoes, help each other smooth
their braids and eyebrows, and perhaps dab a bit of moistened red
crepe paper on their cheeks. "Who knows what [who] will be in
town?" is the reason.

The village itself provides ample possibilities for bachelors and
maidens to get together. On important holidays dances are held
near the village churchyard. Although they are not formally invited, boys and girls go to larger wedding parties after the feasting
is over and join in the dances, which last well into the night.
There are also dances and merry-making associated with the
komišanje and moba. In fact almost any event, even a political
meeting, is followed by dancing.

There are different rules of etiquette, depending on the conditions under which a dance is held. At those where the dance itself
is the main event, it is likely that only the young people will participate although men and women of all ages may be present. On
the other hand, everyone joins in at wedding parties and other
affairs that are less public. The dancing is always of the traditional
type. Some villagers are aware that Western-style dancing exists
and consider it "shameful to be in such intimate positions when the
whole world can see you."

Young men are permitted relative freedom in sexual matters.
When a certain mother was asked about her attitude on this question she replied indignantly that *her* son was a good boy. Later
the father was questioned in private, and he boasted about the
boy's exploits and laughingly called him a chip off the old block.

A girl who is not a virgin until she is married is severely censured
—one who violates the approved pattern is penalized socially in a

[7] For similar patterns in Bulgaria, see Sanders, *Balkan Village*, p. 80.

way that can change the whole course of her life. In Orašac a girl
of fifteen met her boyfriend after school one day and ran off with
him to another village. After a month or so her parents succeeded
in breaking up the affair, and the girl returned to her home in
the village and to her class in the eighth grade. Her readjustment
will be very difficult, for she does not fit anywhere into the well-
defined village age groups. In the eyes of the villagers, *"Ona nije
devojka, nije mlada—nije ništa"* (She is not a maiden and not a bride—
she isn't anything). A young momak would not think of marrying
such a girl, and her best hope would be a widower.

Among the lowest levels of Orašac society the penalties are not
as severe, particularly if the couple is eventually legally married.
The village was more amused than upset when a girl seven months
pregnant was married to a landless miner from a nearby village.
It was rumored that he was not the father of the child, but be that
as it may, the bride herself was apparently not too concerned.
She even insisted that we take her picture in the bulging, fitted
wedding dress that emphasized her coming motherhood. She was
the daughter of a widow, head of one of the poorest households
in the village, and her getting married at all was considered a
marked social step.

It must be stressed that these are two extreme examples. Il-
legitimacy and common-law marriages are very infrequent. Prosti-
tution is virtually unknown in the village, although there was one
young widow who granted favors in return for gifts of clothing
and jewelry. According to informants, this was a very recent development, and nobody condemned her too strongly because her
husband of several months had been killed in a tragic accident.

MARRIAGE

The status of momak or devojka lasts only a few years. Girls are
expected to marry in their late teens or early twenties, and boys
are supposed to cease being bachelors by the time they are twenty-
four or twenty-five. Within this approved pattern there is generally
little variation. In 1953 the youngest married male was only sixteen, and there were two girls married at seventeen. Of the entire
Orašac population over thirty years of age, less than 2 percent

were unmarried. They include German miners, sisters of the miners, and teachers; there is only one peasant woman over thirty who has never been married. She is another one of those rare members of the community with no clearly defined status in the social system and serves to reinforce the statement that marriage is considered the only natural way of life in the village.

The actual ages of brides and grooms at marriage were calculated for eight two-year periods, from 1881–82 to 1951–52. Of the 214 marriages considered, in just under 10 percent of the cases the bride and groom were the same age. The bride was older in about 30 percent of the cases while the groom was older in 60 percent. The older brides in this sample averaged two and half years older than their bridegrooms, and when the grooms were older they were on the average 4 years their brides' seniors. Over the years, then, the pattern has remained fairly similar, with the ideal age for marriage showing little change.

In addition to marriage being the only conceivable and completely acceptable pattern of life, another pressure on young people is that if there are several brothers or sisters in the household they usually marry in order of age. The only usual exceptions to this are boys who have continued with their education or who have learned a trade. Occasionally a younger sister is allowed to marry first, but this makes the position of her older sister difficult. In most cases today it is considered essential that the young man complete his compulsory military service before assuming the responsibilities of marriage.

Before the First World War arranged marriages were the rule, and all negotiations were carried on between the heads of the two zadrugas concerned. Marriages were sometimes prearranged by the parents while the prospective bride and groom were still children, although this was comparatively rare. The pattern has been altered in recent times so that it is very possible for a couple to meet at a dance and then seek their families' permission.[8] Parental consent is usually not too difficult to obtain. The only real objec-

[8] Meeting a girl at a fair or dance and marriage arranged by parents were not necessarily unrelated since parents often went with their children to the dances to help them select a suitable mate.

tions arise if there are significant economic and status differences between the families. A gazda is more likely to insist that his daughter marry the son of a family in a similar position.[9]

The geographic origin of brides has remained basically unchanged during the past eight decades, but there has been a slight shift toward a higher number of brides from within Orašac. In another sixteen-year sample, of 248 marriages approximately a third of the brides came from Orašac, a little more than a third from immediate neighboring villages, another third from other villages within a ten-mile radius, and less than five percent from a greater distance. In the entire sample no bride's village was more than twenty miles from Orašac.

There are several reasons for this pattern of distribution. For one thing, as we have seen earlier, there is considerable variation in the population size of the various villages. Even more important is the function of kin and friendship ties in the selection of brides. Outside the more common occurrence of marrying a girl from Orašac, parents are most likely to make arrangements with, or young men to meet, girls from families with whom they already have some sort of tie. Frequently an Orašac matron originally from a particular village will recommend a girl from her vamilija to someone in her husband's clan or to a neighbor.

In the event that there is severe parental opposition to their marriage a very determined young couple may elope, usually to the boy's house. Even in these cases an attempt is made to smooth the relationship between the two households. This is very significant because aside from obtaining a mate the bride is also marrying into a household. To have good relations with her in-laws is as important as it is with her husband.

At the other extreme are the cases of the occasional young man who for one reason or another cannot or does not wish to find a bride for himself. The parents then arrange a marriage for him. Even today the prospective bride and groom may sometimes not be aware of their impending marriage until a few weeks before it occurs.

[9] During the 1920s, when there was intense political activity in the villages, parents often sought spouses for their children from families of the same political party.

Despite the greater independence of young people, the characteristics desired in prospective husbands or wives still remain similar
to what they were fifty or even a hundred years ago. For a momak
it is most important that he "be from a good family." This means
that his vamilija in general and his household in particular be
respected in the village as well as at least moderately prosperous.
He should also be a capable worker and have some ambition. It is
equally important that the devojka come from respected people,
and her chances for a "good" marriage are increased if she has
the prospect of a significant dowry. A bride must be a good worker,
too, for no matter how prosperous her parents or how wealthy
the household into which she is marrying, the bride will be expected to assume her share of the agricultural and household work.
If there is any question as to her virginity her chances for marriage
are greatly harmed.

Most marriages are arranged in the fall, so that they can take
place in late October, November, or early December. This is the
time when the harvest is in, the households are well stocked with
food, and feasting is not restricted by the religious fasting which
takes place prior to Christmas. Another approved period for weddings is in the late winter and spring, before and after Lent.
Marriages also occur occasionally at a few other times during the
year, when not restricted by religious rules.

The few weeks before the wedding are a busy period for both
families. The bride has to fill in her trousseau and make sure she
has enough shirts, slips, towels, and knitted socks to present to
all her in-laws as gifts. The prearranged *ruvo*, which includes the
trousseau and all the furniture and personal effects she will bring
with her as part of her dowry, must be set in order. In a gaily
decorated wagon her future father-in-law comes to call for it a
few days before the wedding. All items are piled high on the cart
so that villagers and neighbors passed on the way can see the value
of the bride. When he returns home with the ruvo his wife and
other female relatives of the groom arrange it in the room the
newlyweds will occupy, all the while poking through the bride's
linens and passing expert comments on the quality of this or that.

The size of the dowry and trousseau depends to a great degree on the wealth of the bride's parents. The whole idea of a dowry is a comparatively recent development, springing from Western ideas and reflected in the Serbian civil code of the early twentieth century, in contrast to the traditional zadruga attitude which holds that there should be compensation to the girl's house for the loss of a working hand. In the period since the First World War there has been a very large increase in the amount and value of the ruvo.

About forty years ago an average bride brought little more than her painted hope chest filled with clothing and other items of her own handiwork. Today these articles still form an important part of the bride's trousseau even though every piece may not be handmade. Each bride now also brings some furniture. In the 1920s the daughter of a prosperous peasant brought a bed, some chairs, and possibly a small table, while now no bride, even a poor one, can bring less than an impressive šifonjer. It is not difficult to imagine the tremendous parental sacrifice this symbol of prestige represents. A rich bride today brings a complete set of bedroom furniture, in a few cases including a mattress made in town and a combination mirror and vanity table. Ten years ago these were unheard-of extravagances for a peasant dowry.

The *ženidba*, or activities at the groom's household, are even more extensive. Most of the pre-wedding tasks center about preparing the feast for the celebration. It can range from a modest meal for a few dozen guests to a huge banquet to which hundreds of people are invited. The father selects a number of male relatives and friends to help with the preparation of the food and serve the guests. They roast the pigs and lambs and prepare tremendous kettles of food, and the women assist with the baking. All these helpers are given gifts, such as socks or kerchiefs, which they wear sewn over their shoulders on the day of the wedding.

A professional *kuvar*, or male cook, is also hired. He is a peasant who makes this a part-time specialty and receives 1,200 dinars for his services. These include staying up all night before the wedding cooking special festive dishes such as *piktija*, or jellied pigs' hocks, a village holiday treat. For the wedding day at least one accordionist is hired and quite often there are several. Sometimes a Gypsy troupe, including a violinist, bass fiddler, accordionist, and girl tambourine player, is hired if the budget permits. Tables, benches, plates, glasses, spoons, and forks must be borrowed from relatives and neighbors, since one household never has enough to serve a large party. In view of all these expensive preparations, it is not hard to understand why poor parents sometimes encourage their children to elope.

Two or three days before the big event, the father of the groom fills a flask with his best brandy, decorates it with flowers, and, swinging a colorful woven sack over his back, sets out as a *buklijaš*, flask-bearer, to invite the wedding guests. He goes first to the home of the family's kum, the most important guest, since he will be the godfather of all the children resulting from the marriage. Next he calls on the *starojko*, the chief witness, another important partic-ipant in the ceremony and usually the groom's *ujak* (mother's brother). Then he goes to the *dever*, or best man, the groom's brother or best friend. After these calls the father visits the home of the bride and then the various households of his own vamilija. Finally friends and neighbors are invited. At each household the buklijaš ceremoniously offers a drink to his invited guest. Upon acceptance of the invitation, a toast is drunk to the health of the young people, and the guest refills the father's flask with some of his own brandy and pins a handkerchief, pair of socks, shirt, or towel on the sack. By the time the buklijaš has made all his calls he is filled with toasts and good cheer, and his *torba* is covered with gifts.

Early on the wedding morning the *svatovi*, wedding guests who go to fetch the *mlada*, or bride, assemble in the courtyard of the groom's father's household to prepare for the ride. A caravan of fiacres and buggies, many specially rented for the occasion, are festooned with garlands of pink, white, and gold chrysanthemums and green leaves, and the horses' bridles are trimmed with flowers, colored streamers, and long white scarves that fly in the breeze as the gay wedding party moves forward. In the first carriage ride the *mladoženja* (groom), his parents, and his godfather. Other members of the party, including an accordionist or two, follow according to their kinship to the groom. With merry whoops and cries the party is off, led by several bachelors on horseback. One of them carries a Serbian flag, an indispensable part of every wedding procession. It is an arresting sight to see twenty or more brightly decorated carriages filled with shouting, singing merrymakers racing across the autumn countryside.

As the svatovi approach the bride's house the *vojvoda*, or standard-bearer and leader of the procession, cautions the party to halt. He has to overcome an obstacle set up by the bride's family before the caravan can enter the courtyard. A swaying willow pole about ten feet high is lashed to a treetop. On top of the pole is a small gourd with a white handkerchief attached to it, the trophies he must retrieve before the party gains admission.

The vojvoda is "assisted" by the clowning antics of the *vojvodski momak*, a sort of wedding jester, who is encouraged to act silly, lead the merrymaking, and even sing lewd songs, all permitted in view of his specific function as a distraction for any evil spirits which might be present. Toward this end he is dressed in comic imitation of the bride, to confuse the spirits and keep the evil eye from falling on her. He wears a long braid of flax pinned to his cap and a necklace of red peppers, garlic, and corn kernels around his neck. A further embellishment is the decorated squawking hen he carries with him.

Amidst much good-natured fun and teasing the bride's male relatives finally come out to drink a toast with the svatovi and to admit them. Meanwhile, her female relatives line up inside the courtyard to survey them as they enter and to pass judgment on the groom with this song:

> Napred, napred, kićeni svatovi,
> Da vidimo, da vidimo, koj je djuveglija—ii ih!
> Da l' je lepši, da l' je lepši,
> Od naše devojke—ii ih!
> Što dadosmo, što dadosmo?
> Zlato za olovo—ii ii ih!!

> Come forward, come forward, beribboned wedding party,
> So we can see, so we can see, who is the bridegroom—ii ih!
> Is he better looking, is he better looking,
> Than our maiden—ii ih!

What have we given, what have we given?
Gold for lead—ii ii ih!!

The bride sits alone in a special room, waiting for her mother-in-law-to-be and her new female relatives, who come in and present her with a gift. Today it is a coat, some stout oxfords, or a pair of city stockings, but formerly the present was a necklace of gold coins. The bride is dressed by all the women. Her wedding finery, complete with the gifts she has just received, includes a long, high-necked, long-sleeved white wedding dress and gauze veil arranged in a huge puff around her head. Everyone leaves her then and joins the crowd eating and drinking at the long tables the bride's family has set up in the yard.

A shot is fired and the bride is ceremoniously led out by her brother and brought to the head of the table, where she respectfully greets all her in-laws by kissing their hands. She and the groom stand at the head of the table until the meal is finished, while her sisters, cousins, and girlhood friends pin corsages they have made onto the jackets of all the guests.

The dever, with a white sash draped across his chest, is the bride's official guardian until the wedding ceremony, and he rides with her in the lead carriage when the caravan returns to the groom's home or village. The svatovi depart, shouting and arms akimbo, waving brandy flasks in the air. The bride's relatives watch silently from their gateway. The procession gets livelier as it approaches the village church, and the poor bride sits pale and scared, all alone with her thoughts, a bewildered stranger among the noisy merrymakers.

The bridal party proceeds directly to the church for the *venčanje*, or marriage ceremony.[10] Before entering, the mother-in-law loosens the bride's shoes, "so that she will bear children easily." The ceremony itself is brief. The starojko stands behind the bride and the kum behind the groom, all four bearing decorated candles.

---

[10] Unlike before the war, when there were no civil ceremonies, today all marriages must be registered with the Village Council. Under the present law the registration and a brief accompanying ceremony, consisting of the Village Council President reading several paragraphs of the marriage law, is sufficient. Almost all villagers desire a religious ceremony as well. The only cases in which it is dispensed with are during periods of fasting, when no marriages are performed by the church.

The bride and groom must clasp their right hands during part of the ritual, and the joined hands are discreetly covered with a cloth, "for it would be shameful if everyone saw." The priest blesses two silver crowns and gives them to the groom and bride to kiss and then crowns them in marriage. The groom, bride, and principal witnesses each take three sips from a glass of wine and repeat a prayer, moving with the priest three times around the table at which the marriage vows are taken. It is a tense affair only for the nervous newlyweds, for the others often laugh and talk during the ceremony. Most of the party remains outside, joking, drinking, and dancing. As soon as the bride and groom emerge from the church everyone joins in a gay kolo.

As the carriage with the bride and groom enters the courtyard of the groom's house through an archway of entwined flowers, all the waiting relatives and guests cheer and shout, and the old women sing a song of welcome to the bride. Before she is allowed to alight she is given a baby boy to hold and kiss three times, "so that she will soon have children." Then she steps down onto a sack of grain and tosses corn in four directions and up on the roof. With a loaf of bread under each arm and a bottle of wine in her hand, the bride enters her new home.

Tables are lined up end to end in the courtyard, and the kum, starojko, and other honored guests are seated at the head. Others take their places according to their accepted social rank—old men, younger men, old women, and finally younger women and children down at the end. Those at the head of the table are served the wedding feast on china plates, with silverware, on a tablecloth. They also get the best cuts of meat and the most generous portions. Further down the table are enamel plates and metal spoons, and those at the foot of the table share a common earthenware bowl and eat with wooden spoons. There is no resentment of this procedure, and the pattern is accepted unquestioningly. During the entire wedding feast, which lasts for hours, the bride, groom, and best man stand at the head of the table and do not partake of the banquet.

Before the meal starts there is a presentation of gifts from the bride to her new in-laws. The jester acts as master of ceremonies, making everyone laugh as he describes each gift and throws it onto the shoulder of the recipient. He might say, "Now here is something really excellent, made by our lovely bride and presented to that good fellow, Uncle Tihomir. A fine shirt, and well made, too, but how will it fit over his fat belly?" After each presentation he throws back his head and calls in a loud sing-song voice, while the guests rock with mirth at his harmless teasing, "*Amin, amin!*" (Amen!).

A large, unleavened bread (*pogača*) is placed at the head of the table and passed down from guest to guest, each of whom resoundingly calls out his good wishes and places some money or a small gift for the newlyweds on the loaf.

The feast consists of several courses, beginning with a thick soup (*čorba*) followed by stuffed cabbage or cabbage minced and boiled with pork, and roast suckling pig and lamb. Wine and rakija are in abundance. For dessert there are cookies and cakes. In Orašac and surrounding villages the guests bring their own baskets of food and cakes to eat later on and to share with one another.[11] When the meal is over the cook wraps his hand in a rag and walks up and down past the tables, clutching his ladle and moaning, "*Jao*—I burned my hand cooking the wedding feast! Please help me out so I can go to the doctor!" People toss some coins in the ladle as well-deserved tips.

Later in the afternoon the *pohodjani*, the bride's relatives, arrive.[12] They are greeted with a flourish of music and are warmly welcomed by the groom's parents. Separate banquet tables are set up for them in the house. Meanwhile the outdoor dancing and singing which begin in the early afternoon is continued, and many young people and other uninvited guests come to join the merrymaking. With a leader waving his white handkerchief, the kolos become more spirited as the party progresses, and men proudly show off their fanciest steps.

At dusk the bride and groom are supposed to break away from the circle of dancers and slip into the vajat or, today, to their

[11] This custom is not practiced in some villages less than five miles away, where it is considered an affront to the host if his guests bring food with them.

[12] Formerly, when wedding parties lasted three days, the pohodjani did not come until the second day.

room. If the bride goes first it is said that the groom will be hen-
pecked. At this point some of the bride's sisters enter and present
her with a knitting basket containing started handiwork, to ensure
her a productive life. They must not speak to one another during
this little ritual or the spell will be broken.

The dancing and celebrating continues through the night. Later,
the vojvodski momak climbs up on the roof and sets fire to a bundle
of straw. As the others laugh and encourage him, he capers about
the roof silhouetted by the flaming straw, threatening that the
vajat (or cottage) will burn down unless the bride comes out and
tosses a gift up to him.

A week or so after the wedding the formal festivities are completed with the *povratak*, the bride's first visit as a married woman
to her parents' homestead. It is again an occasion for feasting and
dancing.

Kosmaj, Bukulja, Venčac . . . still rise clearly above Šumadija's undulating fields and meadows.

Attractive vistas open up as the road curves around Orašac.

The paths are used all year around, although wet weather churns them into practically impassable courses of famous sticky village mud.

*Plowing today
is done with
. . . a simple
double-handled
wooden plow.*

*Crude but efficient rollers
as well as simple harrows
are made by certain of the
village men.*

The two basic items of agricultural equipment remain the wagon and the plow.

Wheat is fed into the grumbling machine by hand, and at the other end women . . . fork aside the straw and dust that come spurting out.

Entirely of metal, the "apparatus" [for distilling brandy] is considered by the peasants to be a streamlined piece of equipment indeed; it is made in town by the kazandžije, *or coppersmiths.*

Costs can be cut down . . . by substituting mud bricks for fired ones . . . in building a zidana-*style house.*

The polubrvnara, *or half-log cabin, a few examples of which still exist in Orašac today.*

The bondručara *type of house is still used by the majority of Orašac households.*

Representing the greatest advance in Serbian peasant architecture, the zidana *house is a sturdy two-story dwelling of fired brick and concrete construction, with outdoor steps leading to the upper level.*

The vajat *formerly used for sleeping is now an additional storage house.*

Even the rudest homestead is entered through a gate of some sort.
. . . If a new kapija (covered gateway) is built, however, it is in
the modern style, with brick posts and a roof of tile.

Livestock stalls
. . . are con-
structed as they
have been in the
past—wattle
and daub huts,
straw or thatch
structures, or
woven twig
enclosures.

Almost without exception, all Orašac males, including the miners, wear the peasant britches.

As for underwear, they all wear long linen or cotton drawers (gaće), which also serve as lining for the scratchy woolen britches.

On Easter Sunday, everyone was dressed in his best clothes.

A number of the village youths sported high polished leather boots and freshly whitened sneakers.

*Colorful woven blankets . . .
knitwear . . . . characteristic
Šumadijan men's socks.*

*Today women of all ages wear modified
urban clothes.*

*They still wore . . . the leather sandals
with turned up "noses" in front, bound to
the legs with shiny leather straps.*

Over the blouse goes the prsluk *[women's
vest] . . . trimmed with intricate borders
and sprays of gold or silver embroidery.
. . . The* jelek *[men's vest] . . . trimmed
with silk cording and braid.*

When a celebration is held on the occasion of the child's first birthday the godfather is an honored guest.

It is at school that they have their first real contacts beyond the neighborhood and meet children from other parts of the village.

In the open yard near the church soccer, learned at school, attracts the older boys.

Girls are taught to cook and bake and to do all kinds of handiwork.

After the trading . . . boys link arms and move
through the street, nodding casually to girls they
know. The girls reciprocate with cautious nods
and then gather in a huddle to whisper and giggle
as soon as the boys have passed.

The father of the groom fills a flask with his best
brandy, decorates it with flowers, and, swinging
a colorful woven sack over his back, sets out as a
buklijaš, flask-bearer, to invite the wedding
guests.

One of them carries a Serbian flag, an indispensable part of every wedding . . . a sort of wedding jester . . . is dressed in comic imitation of the bride, to confuse the spirits and keep the evil eye from falling on her.

Fiacres and buggies . . . are festooned with . . . chrysanthemums and green leaves.

During the entire wedding feast . . . the bride, groom, and best man stand at the head of the table.

A large, unleavened bread (pogača) is . . . passed down from guest to guest, each of whom resoundingly calls out his good wishes and places some money or a small gift for the newlyweds on the loaf.

The cook wraps his hand in a rag . . . clutching his ladle and moaning, "Jao —I burned my hand cooking the wedding feast. . . ." People toss some coins in the ladle as well-deserved tips.

The larger weddings in the village are frequently classified according to the number of Gypsy musicians hired for the event.

The guslar, *closely akin to the wandering medieval bard of Western Europe . . . chanted heroic ballads. . . . Although the wandering* guslari *no longer exist, the* gusle *is considered the national instrument of Serbia, and many village men know how to play it.*

There are . . . dances and merrymaking associated with the komišanje *and* moba. *In fact almost any event, even a political meeting, is followed by dancing.*

As they advance in years women approach a status more respected than at any earlier period.

The priest says the final prayer and makes a cross with a mixture of olive oil and red wine.

A memorial feast is spread out. It usually consists of a roast pig or sheep, soup, gibanica, bread, brandy, wine, and cakes.

All the members of the funeral party line up . . . to take a spoonful of žito and a sip of wine, after crossing themselves and murmuring a prayer.

The women . . . spread cloths on top of each grave. . . . Meals . . . are arranged on them.

They think nothing of casually draping a torba over a tombstone.

Porcelainized photographs of the departed were mounted in the stones.

In the late nineteenth century small limestone tablets were used. These were made more ornate, with carved bas-reliefs of the deceased in folk costume.

The Gypsy beggars . . . ask for food and drink to honor the deceased.

To the individual household the most important holiday is the slava, in honor of its clan's patron saint. . . . The traditional main dish, roast suckling pig, is prepared by the men of the house.

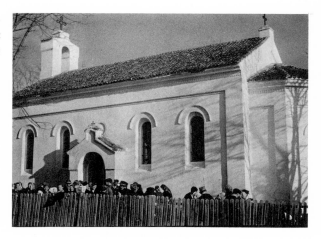

The Orašac church has white-washed outer walls and a small wrought-iron Orthodox cross on the roof.

The [Lenten] fast is broken by a picnic in the yard, and men press one another to sample their best rakija and wine.

The priest's views are respected and his advice often sought.

Children and adults alike enjoy the game of tapping Easter eggs.

At least one and often two members of most house-holds go to the market town every Friday.

. . . a turbulent mass of squealing pigs, placid cows, and animated villagers, clinching bargains, amidst shouting and hand-slapping.

The long, narrow row of shops lining the town's main street is occupied by various private craftsmen and several state-controlled stores.

Much of their town business is at the sandal-maker's, potter's, and tanner's.

Often some of the older men congregate in the sun in front of the tavern to smoke and discuss the weather, crops, and local gossip.

After the war the new government . . . built a mining colony . . . of barren, low buildings . . . not considered part of the village by the Orašac peasants.

The job of carrying out most government policies falls to the Village Council.

Today there is a monument to fallen Partisans near the Village Council building.

The peasants recruited from this area formed the Šumadijan Brigade. . . .
Their annual meetings are usually the occasion for important political rallies.

The basic policies and beliefs of the Yugoslav Communist Government
do not seem to have changed.

Everything indicates that all cultures are in a constant state of change—LINTON.
Above, agricultural homestead on main street of market town.
Below, new workers' housing development in Arandjelovac.

CHAPTER 9

LIFE CYCLE II

WE HAVE TRACED a villager's life through infancy, childhood, courtship, and the marriage ceremony. When a young man and woman marry, another period of life begins. For the bride especially, it means an entirely different phase of life. She must accustom herself to living and working with new people, in a new household.

EARLY MARRIED LIFE AND PARENTHOOD

Immediately after marriage the bride traditionally went through a period of trial and initiation in the home of her in-laws. She was expected to show the greatest respect for them, particularly for all the male elders. Acts of humility, such as the washing of the men's feet each night, were part of her duties, and other menial chores were performed. Cooking, a job for full-fledged women, was never entrusted to a bride. She did not eat with the family but served them all and took her own food later. In fact, during her first few months of marriage she was often treated little better than a servant—although the household was probably very proud of her. It was considered a disgrace if the bride retired at night before the others—a diligent new daughter-in-law was supposed to be busy constantly and to show her industry by outdoing herself carrying out small chores to win her in-laws' favor.

Since the period between the two World Wars and particularly since the end of the Second World War, few in-laws have been so demanding. A period of apprenticeship is certainly in evidence today, but the bride is made to feel more at home and part of the household group. This, too, is a reflection of smaller household units. Of course, the bride's desire to win the approval of her in-laws is just as strong as it has always been, for as was pointed out earlier she is not marrying only a husband but his whole household as well.

Patrilocal residence is the predominant pattern in Orašac. In the entire village there are less than a dozen cases of matrilocality, occurring most often when the bride has no brothers. It may also be resorted to when the girl's family is economically better off than the groom's or when the groom is the youngest of several brothers, but it is not considered a satisfactory arrangement. Indeed, in 1953–54 three such marriages ended in divorce or separation less than a year after they began.[1]

Besides strains resulting from incompatibility, sterility is the only other usual cause for divorce in the village. A sterile woman may consult a female *vračara* for special treatments, consisting of massage and incantations, although today she is more likely to go to the doctor in town for a series of "miracle *injekcije*." It is inconceivable that the fault may lie with the male. If a couple still remains childless they may adopt an orphan or the child of poorer relatives or friends who cannot adequately care for it. There are very few childless couples in the village.

A bride and groom do not receive the full status of *čovek* and *žena*, man and woman, until they have a baby. Most brides bear their first child within a year and a half of marriage. When it is known that a mlada is pregnant, all the members of the household are delighted. The proudest person in the family is her father-in-law. Outside the immediate family word of her condition is not advertised, in keeping with the general attitude of restraint in these matters. Although everyone loves and wants children, the physical events associated with bearing them are not discussed in public. Even if the mother-in-law, beaming, relates the news to a close female neighbor, the latter will reply matter-of-factly, "*Ako, ako*" (So be it), and pass on to another subject.

---

[1] Before the war ecclesiastical courts were the only authorities who could dissolve a marriage. Now divorce can be obtained more easily through civil courts.

A pregnant woman is considered ritually unclean. She is not supposed to eat the ceremonial cake at a slava. When the priest comes to the house to bless the water used in the preparation of these cakes, she must go outside. In addition, she must avoid having anything to do with death—being near a fatally ill person, helping to prepare food for the graveyard, or mourning—as it might be a bad omen for the unborn child. If a close relative dies, however, and she must attend the funeral, she wears a red string tied around her wrist, "for string and blood are one, and the baby will live."

She may get more to eat but is expected to fulfill her regular chores and work in the fields almost up to the time the baby is due. When labor pains begin a *babica* may be called in. There are several old women who act as midwives in the village although they have no formal training. If none is available, a female member of the family helps with the delivery, and there have been some cases where the husband has assisted. A favorite folk belief in aiding delivery is for the husband to stand with his legs apart and his wife to crawl through them. The actual delivery is achieved in a squatting position, and the mother is washed and put to bed. The infant is washed and warm lard is rubbed gently on his head; he is swaddled, bundled in clean flannel or bits of blanket, and tucked into bed beside his mother. She is permitted to rest a while, and usually within three days is up and attending to all but her more strenuous chores.

As was shown by Tables 10 and 11, there has been a marked decrease in the number of children borne by each mother. This condition stems from conscious birth control, in large part motivated by the decreasing ratio of available resources, which have remained relatively constant, to population, which has steadily increased. Also, there are much fewer infant deaths than formerly, and chances are better for a child born nowadays to survive. Undoubtedly the ideas and outlook of city people have had an effect, too. A few people in the village are aware of modern methods of contraception, learned or heard about while in the army. The most widespread type of birth control, however, is abortion. It is not at all uncommon for a healthy woman to have three or four

abortions.[2] Most of them are achieved with the assistance of a mid-
wife, by means of both internal and external manual treatment, or
by self-imposed paddling with a plank. In Orašac a drink of hot
wine and salt, taken several times a week, is thought to be of help.

The ideal number of children today varies between two and
four, especially if the first or second is a boy. Some people feel
that additional children simply are not necessary. One man was
overheard upbraiding his daughter-in-law: "What do you mean,
you're expecting another baby? I already have a grandson!"

THE PASSING YEARS

As the household size has become smaller, the relationship between
man and wife has become increasingly significant in the organization of the household. The man is still formally regarded as su-
perior, but women have been participating more and more in
discussions of budgets, plans for the future, and other things which
must be worked out to the advantage of the entire household.
On the other hand, emotional restraint is still the rule. Although
a great deal of affection is shown to children, and from children
to parents and grandparents, parents are never openly demonstrative toward one another. In fact it is still common for couples to
refer to each other as He and She or My Husband and My Wife.
Even when addressing one another directly, they rarely use proper
names. If a man calls to his wife, for example, he shouts, "*Ženo!
Odi 'vamo!*" (Wife! Come here!).

The husband and wife relationship is reflected in many folk
proverbs. One heard often in the village is, "*Žena muža nosi na
licu, a muž ženu na košulji*" (The face of the wife shows what her
husband is, and the husband's shirt shows what his wife is). There
are several sayings expressing the thought that there is no home
without a wife. At the same time proverbs such as these persist:
"*Žena će samo onu tajnu sačuvati koju ne zna*" (A woman will keep
only those secrets of which she knows nothing) and "*Žene su da*

---

[2] No statistical data on this subject are available for Orašac. In a survey of twenty
women taken before the war in a village near Belgrade it was found that the total
number of abortions were only a little less than the total number of living children
of the same women. See A. Petrović, *Rakovica*, pp. 25–26. On the basis of interviews
in Orašac, it would seem that the proportion of abortions is higher today.

zbore a ljudi da tvore" (Women do the talking and men do the working).

Men and women in their twenties and thirties are considered in the prime of their physical strength. They age faster than do their urban counterparts. Hands become work-worn and calloused, and faces are those of people who toil out of doors—ruddy complexion, furrowed brow, and crows' feet around deep-set eyes. Women soon lose their youthful figures and take to wearing somber clothing more in keeping with their station in life.

While people in their twenties and thirties do most of the heavy labor, prestige and authority still reside for the most part with their elders. This concept is relative, of course. By the time villagers have reached forty they are respected as elders by younger people; a man is called *čiča*, a general term for uncle, and may start carrying a cane when he goes to market, as a symbol of his advanced years. By the time they are about fifty, men and women are called Baba and Deda.

As they advance in years women approach a status more respected than at any earlier period and which more nearly resembles the status enjoyed by males. They are permitted a greater degree of freedom of conduct, hedged in by none of the restrictions imposed on them in their younger days. For example, old women may usually go where they please, whenever they wish. They can go alone to market, social gatherings, and weddings. In the company of their cronies they can dance, drink, tell jokes, and "whoop it up" at a gathering of relatives and neighbors without being condemned for their behavior. Of course, if they go visiting in another village, they are expected to conduct themselves with dignity.

Less than fifteen years ago there were several old women in the village who were practitioners of folk medicine, for curing diseases and predicting the future. Old women were thought to have supernatural powers and were somewhat feared. Today this attitude has practically died out, and with it the proverb: "Where the devil cannot cause mischief he sends an old woman to do it for him."

Most important in the consideration of old people is the position they hold in the household. In a society which normally does not have large surpluses, it is often a burden to support the aged. They must receive the same amounts of food and other material comforts while they can no longer do their full share of work. Most sons accept this responsibility unquestioningly. As was seen in Table 12, showing the Orašac population in relation to the heads of households, in many cases an older person retains the honorary position of head while in actuality a son, or sons, has taken over the reins. If the old person is not a parent, grandparent, aunt, or uncle, his lot is usually a hard one, for he is considered an obligation and an unnecessary burden. One man whose old mother-in-law, a widow, moved in with his household after all her daughters had married and left her, constantly went about grumbling, "My God, that old witch has more lives than a cat. When is she going to die?"

Perhaps hardest of all is the position of those occasional old people who live alone and who must constantly depend on younger relatives and neighbors to help them with tasks they cannot do themselves. The tradition of helping one's fellow man is certainly strong, and, as many villagers put it, "Someday I'll be old and helpless, too." Incidentally, it is only in this context that the villager will readily admit that he, too, is getting on in years—in other situations, such as when a man in his fifties tries to do physical labor his body can no longer take, he will very reluctantly, if at all, acknowledge the fact that he cannot do everything his sons can do.

LIFE IN RETROSPECT

How do Orašac peasants evaluate their own life experiences? What periods and which aspects do they consider most interesting or important? An attempt to find answers to these questions was made by obtaining several autobiographies. The seven selections included here were written by about as diverse a group of men as one could hope to find in the village, representing as they do various age levels, economic positions, personality traits, and political viewpoints.[3]

[3] Those asked to write autobiographies were the men who had been most articulate in interviews. Little attempt was made to determine their content except to ask the writers to discuss how times have changed and to describe the most important experiences in their lives. As might be expected, they vary greatly in emphasis and attitudes.

The first autobiography was written by a villager in his late eighties. Although literate, he is arthritic and partially blind, and his account, therefore, is transcribed as it was dictated to his thirty-five-year-old grandson. His focus is mainly on the changes which he has witnessed in his lifetime, and his reaction is mixed—he is conscious of a great rise in the material standard of living but at the same time feels that people are no longer true to the old ways.

AUTOBIOGRAPHY A

I was born in 1866. There were two of us brothers and four male cousins.[4]

We used to eat less than we do today. Our clothes were not good. We went without pants.[5] There was no doctor, no railway, and there were dense forests all around. We used to cultivate with wooden plows. It wasn't until the reign of King Peter I that we had iron plows and wagons, better houses, and all the rest.

I remember once when Milan Obrenović[6] came to our village in a horse-drawn carriage. He got out and walked through the village and talked to the people. At that time we paid one ducat for taxes on our property, which amounted to thirty hectares. There were only three stores in Arandjelovac then. We had no beds and used to sleep on the dirt floor around the hearth.

I took part in three wars—first, in 1885, against the Bulgarians; second, the Austro-Hungarian War, with my two sons, one of whom fell; and third, the terrible war in 1941, when the Serbs killed each other, one brother burning the home of the other. My youngest son became an invalid.

I used to go to the fairs in Milanovac on foot.[7] I remember six rulers,

---

The one characteristic all these men shared was the willingness to write an autobiography, although several were a little reluctant to begin. Once they were induced to start, however, they seemed to enjoy the work. They refused any compensation for their efforts, but with an eye toward practicality most of them asked for paper and pencils. Some of these essays have been shortened, especially those that go into great detail about military experiences and other material extraneous to life in the village. From the point of view of literary Serbian, most of the autobiographies contain mistakes in spelling and grammar, but in the broader sense of literacy the men succeeded in describing their views very clearly. It is regrettable that women's autobiographies could not be obtained satisfactorily. The women were mostly illiterate, and when attempts were made to transcribe their verbal comments, they seemed only to be able to answer specific questions but could not narrate nondirected accounts.

[4] Father's brother's sons (*braća od strica*), all living in the same zadruga.

[5] They wore long shirts over linen underdrawers. (See Figure 16.)

[6] He reigned from 1872 to 1889.

[7] About forty miles from Orašac.

the best among all being Peter I, who liberated Yugoslavia and enlarged it.

In the old days, when I was twenty, I used to plow with six oxen. At that time we had a wooden plow, while today we use a steel one with two cows. We did not have brick houses, nor did we know how to build them. A recruit used to go serve in the army on foot while today they all go by train. Until 1905 we all went everywhere on foot.

We used to eat corn bread, and nobody ever smoked or cursed. People were healthier than they are today. Holy things were respected and kept. Today all is different. A new life is coming, when one has to work more and harder to have less.

The next account was written by a man of sixty. In contrast to the first autobiography, there is little mention of social and cultural change here. Since he was from a very poor household with almost no land, he was forced to seek work outside the village for various periods. During the First World War he was a prisoner of war in Czechoslovakia—this must have been the most outstanding experience in his life as he describes the several years' confinement there in great detail. In fact about seventy percent of his autobiography is devoted to this period. The account is of further interest in illustrating how his mother, a widow with children, was forced to assume the role of domaćin.

AUTOBIOGRAPHY B

I was born in the village of Orašac, near the town of Arandjelovac, in the region of Šumadija. My father's name was Milorad and my mother was called Danica. They were rather poor, and if my father had only lived we would not have been too badly off. But he died in his forty-fifth year, leaving mother with three small children. I was only four, my sister Radmila eleven, and my sister Milica six. I was too small to help very much. All I did was play with other little children, and my mother had the hard task of fending for three small children without any assistance.[8] There was no social insurance, and it was her duty to feed and clothe us.

We also had many religious customs which included that every Serb have his slava and keep many other holidays. My mother could not send

_____

[8] Usually in such cases, if they were members of a large zadruga, their father's brother or grandfather would take over the responsibility of caring for them, but this appears not to have been the case here. It is likely, however, that they received some assistance from fellow clan members.

my two big sisters to school because we were so poor and as at that time very few girls went to school. They had to go out to work in the village to earn themselves food and clothing and to bring something home for me to eat. They sometimes had to go seven or eight kilometers away to rich peasants to work. Their work was physically difficult, so that they actually worked sixteen hours a day for very small wages. We had barely enough to live on.

As the smallest, I was left at home to watch the chickens and hen, and sometimes we had a piglet tied with a piece of string. Without my mother and my two sisters, who went to the orchards to work, I was left alone. In the evenings when they came home they used to find me asleep in the yard and would carry me to bed. We slept on straw pallets and had very little to cover ourselves with.

My mother was able to earn only a little money, but even we, as poor people, always celebrated our slava, the happiest day for us. It was St. Nicholas' Day. Although I was so little I still had the honor of breaking the slava bread with our guests, but as I was smaller than the table I had to get up on a chair to do it. Then I prayed to God and burned incense with our guests, for those are our religious customs. This is how I spent my life from my fourth to my eighth year.

In my eighth year I started school, with a striped carrying sack over my shoulder. I didn't like school very much and I used to run away, but in spite of this I was a good pupil and finished the four-year elementary school.

During these years my sister Radmila got married, and with my mother I went visiting there. I shot off a pistol with great happiness. At this time I was fourteen.

Now it became high time for me to go to work. I went to work in a dry goods store. My master was called Vojin Simić. He had two stores, and I was the sixth apprentice and the youngest. I had to work for three years without pay, and to clean the kitchen and look after my master's children. If they cried then I was beaten. It was my lot to be beaten by all of them. I didn't like this and left my job. My mother was very cross, but I continued working as a peasant with my sister Milica, who was not yet married.

We used to work fifteen days for a lamb or a little pig, and the daily wage was usually one dinar for twelve hours of work. Then my second sister got married. I was at that time sixteen years of age, and alone with my mother. When I was seventeen I worked wherever I could get a job. When I was eighteen I went to work as a miner in the coal mine in Orašac. I worked there for two years. I was then twenty years of age, and in November, 1914, I enlisted in the army.

We didn't have much time for drilling, only two months, as there was a great shortage of men. We had to wear our own clothes. We slept on straw in Turkish-style houses, and we had just one blanket to cover four of us. In the month of January . . . we were assigned to reserve regiments . . . we were attacked by the Germans and Bulgarians . . . we were wiped out . . . I was wounded and taken . . . to an English mission hospital, and when the Germans arrived we became slaves. I spent fifteen days in the hospital, and then they loaded us in a truck under guard. We traveled with horses and other animals. In this manner we were transported to Kragujevac, and there I was left as a wounded man in a hospital.

He then describes how, in being sent from Kragujevac to Belgrade, he escaped and returned to his village, where after several days he was captured and sent to Czechoslovakia. There he worked for a brief period in the mines and later as a servant in a prosperous Czech farm home. In his autobiography he dwells at some length on the Czech girls and his romances. He returned home to Orašac late in the fall of 1918.

At home I found my mother. I knew that she was alive and well because we had been writing to each other. The situation at home was what might be called bad. We didn't have anything—just one bed and one table, two meters long. I slept on the table. I had one blanket to cover myself. The house was old and in poor condition, and the roof leaked. It wasn't easy. My mother wanted me to get married and I did. I took a girl, and there was a small celebration, but I didn't have any luck. The girl was ill, constantly going to doctors, who said she couldn't have children.

I joined the army again for twelve months, returned home, and was divorced from my first wife. I remained alone with my mother and went to work in the mine. This was in 1920. I married my second wife, Zorka, who was a widow. She brought with her a child—a little girl of seven. The second year, I got my son, Dragoljub; after three more years my son, Dragan, was born; and after five years, a daughter, Stamenka. And so I worked in the mine until 1934. The situation in my home improved.

My wife was good. In 1935 I opened a store with a friend in the nearby village of Misača. I worked until 1940 and earned my best living there. And now the war came again, and the Germans once more overran

Yugoslavia. I took part in this war only for a month. Then the occupation troops came and I returned home. In 1942 I married off my daughter in Belgrade. With her first husband she didn't have much luck, for after several months he was killed. She married again and now is happier, with a son and a daughter. My mother died in 1943, and my wife also.

When the German occupation troops came the war turned to guerrilla fighting. There were about five different groups in Yugoslavia, all armed, all fighting, all killing. My son Dragoljub joined the army when he was eighteen years old. He was a Partisan[9] in the Šumadijan Brigade. He fought as a good, courageous, and brave soldier. He was wounded but stuck it out to the end.

He came home and married a girl, Ruža, and he has two sons, Milan and Radivoje. Dragoljub is a miner and now earns about 10,000 dinars a month. My son Dragan was sent by the mine to attend a course to become a mechanic. He finished the course and got a diploma as a skilled worker. He was then called to serve his term in the army. He proved himself a good soldier, and today he has left all this and has become a good peasant, helping me work the land.

And I, as an old man, work a little. I am sixty years old and have written this account of my life myself. I drink a little brandy and slowly wait for death.

The following autobiography is interesting as an account of a villager who, outside of serving in the army, has never done anything but till the land. It also gives a glimpse of zadruga life, from modest circumstances to a gazda. In addition, it is one of two accounts submitted commenting on political issues and post-war government policies. The man who wrote it is considered somewhat of a reactionary by the present local officials, and much of his land was confiscated for his failure to meet delivery quotas. He was also imprisoned for a brief period. At present, however, he manages to live fairly well by concentrating on livestock breeding. His son has written a letter to Tito protesting what they regard as the unjust confiscation of their land.

AUTOBIOGRAPHY C

I was born in 1880 in the village of Orašac. I spent my childhood in my birthplace. At that time my parents were poor, so they rented some fields

[9] Many of the peasants were recruited by the Partisans during the last year or so of the war. By this time the Partisans had become the Yugoslav National Army.

and we cultivated them. When I was four they bought a small bit of land in Orašac, near Stojnik, and took me there to watch the sheep. That was during the reign of King Milan Obrenović.

I lived on our land with my uncles who were together with us in the same household. I was the oldest child so I began to help them very early. We used to spend most of the year in a hut which had only one room. Inside the hut there was a fireplace and a chain hanging from the ceiling suspended over it. It had a hook where we hung the copper kettle in which we boiled milk. Our bed was made of straw and flat boards. The hut had walls of logs and a roof of wooden shingles.

My clothing was handmade, woven of flax by my mother. We used to eat well. The only trouble was that we ate corn bread in order to save wheat to be sold, for my parents wanted to buy some more land. Thus I can say that my childhood was a hard one. I used to come home on Christmases, Easters, and a few of the other big holidays. I liked the holidays very much because on those days bread was baked of white wheat flour.

I spent all the time before entering school as a shepherd. In 1889 my father registered me at the school. I had attended it for only fifteen days when the school teacher was transferred, and I returned again to my sheep. Two years later our village got another teacher, and my younger brother went to school. From him I learned to write and read, and soon I was better than any of the pupils who went to school.

When I was ten I was allowed to feed the bulls, cows, and calves we bred for sale. In the summer I helped my parents with hoeing, and when I grew up I worked in the fields with my oxen.

I married when I was eighteen, to a girl from my own village, and in a few years after that I had a son and a daughter. I joined the army in 1905 and was put in the infantry. This was during the reign of King Peter I. My term of service was shortened, so I stayed in the army for only six months. When I returned home I felt myself to be a mature man. Up to 1912 I worked as a farmer with my brothers and uncles. When the Turkish war broke out I was mobilized in the reserves in the Šumadijan division.

We met the Turks at Prepolac, drove them back, and reached Scutari in Albania. . . . In 1913 I fought against the Bulgarians, and this war lasted about a year. After that I was released, but not for very long, for only a month later the Albanians started a revolt and I was immediately called to duty at Debar. We met them at Tirana. After sixty-nine days in Tirana . . . I returned to Debar, when a new frontier was set up between us and Albania. In 1914 I was released, so once again I continued my work at home.

But in 1914, when Austria attacked Serbia, I was mobilized again. . . . I fought near Šabac and Smederevo, and later we were driven out of our country. I retreated through Montenegro and Albania to Skadar, Drač, and Valona. . . . In Valona I boarded a ship and went ashore on Corfu. From there I went to Salonika, where we were engaged in a battle with the Bulgarians in 1916. In 1917 I was in Africa on a rest leave, namely in Bizerte, Sebi Abdole, Algiers, and then to Constantine, where I spent six months and was sent back to the war. I was always in the first ranks but I was never wounded. After a few big battles we broke through Bulgarian lines, as well as the Austrian lines, and headed toward home.

I returned home in 1920, and with my brothers I continued my work in the fields. We divided the zadruga in 1921, when I was elected a member of the County Council of Jasenica, which consisted of thirty-one villages. During all that time I belonged to the Democratic Party of Ljuba Davidović. I held my position as a member of the Council until 1929, when Petar Živković took the power in his own hands and I resigned.[10] I worked on my land, which consisted of twenty-five hectares.

After the Second World War, I was given a bigger quota than I could fill and was asked to pay more taxes than I could pay. So I was sentenced to four years in prison but stayed only four months. I then returned home, but our land had been sold to pay expenses.

The other biography that mentions politics follows. In contrast to Autobiography *C*, this one is written with emphasis entirely on the mine and political matters. Its author is a retired miner, a member of the Communist Party and influential in village politics. A man in his fifties, he makes little mention of his life as a child and of the village institutions as they affected him. Instead, almost the entire brief account deals with social issues. Although he suffered poverty in common with most others, his reaction to it was quite different.

AUTOBIOGRAPHY D

I was born in Orašac in 1900. My father was Svetozar and my mother, Radojka Filipović from Misača. My parents were poor peasants with

[10] The Premier when King Alexander I dissolved the Parliament and proclaimed a Royal Dictatorship.

about two hectares of land. They had four of us children and barely supported us, by renting some land from a rich peasant. Three members of my family died of various diseases, so I remained alone. While I was in elementary school my father died and my condition became still harder. As soon as I finished the fourth grade I had to serve rich peasants, that is, to watch their stock and do heavy physical labor.

In 1920 I began working as a miner in the coal mine in Orašac. I continued at that job until September, 1952, when I retired. In the beginning the working hours in the mine were twelve hours daily, and the work was done in the most primitive way. The salaries were miserable, that is, just minimal, so a worker could hardly earn his bread. That lasted until 1941, when our country was occupied by the Germans. Work in the mine continued with as many workers as remained in the village. Work was compulsory, and whoever didn't want to work or refused was shot or interned.

Our village was liberated in October, 1944, by the National Liberation Army, and they immediately began to modernize and rebuild the mine. The operation of the mine was at first very primitive, but later it was mechanized so that today it even has machines and electric lighting. From the beginning [of the modernization], the mine was governed by leaders of the union in accordance with the directors of the mine. Toward the end of 1950 the first Worker's Council was elected. They change every year, and they govern the mine. After the liberation a great deal of effort has been made in behalf of workers in the building of homes for them and on cultural matters. Today the miners are their own masters, the surplus belongs only to them, and they share it at the end of the year.

By way of contrast, the next autobiography was written by a man of the same age as that of the author of Autobiography *D*, yet the emphasis here is exclusively on personal recollections and vignettes of his early life. Only the first part of his autobiography is quoted here, because the remainder deals largely with army experiences similar to those already presented.

AUTOBIOGRAPHY E

I was born in Šumadija in the village of Orašac in the District of Kragujevac in 1900. And today, on Easter Sunday, with a glass of wine in my hand, I'll try to tell you my life story from the time of my birth. When I talk to people about how I look now, completing my fifty-fifth year,[11] they say I don't look over thirty, so I begin to tell them something about myself.

I was the eldest of five brothers and worked at home in a big zadruga. There were five of us brothers, as well as my father, grandfather, and great-grandfather, who was a trader. We had a lot of land. I remember many things, and here is the first thing about me: I was never ill. For fifteen years I ate corn bread, and white bread only on Sundays. This was before the Turkish War, and the rest of the peasants used to do the same. On Wednesdays and Fridays everybody fasted, as well as before Christmas, St. Peter's Day, and other important holidays. Our storehouses were full of wheat, and yet there was bread only on Sundays.

When a pig was slaughtered, one didn't dare touch his lips with his finger while we cut and prepared the meat. After the work we washed the knives in ashes and dried our hands with the stubble of hemp plants. The pigsty was full of pigs, and the house was full of pork carcasses hanging in a row under the eaves, but if it was a Wednesday or Friday the only thing one could do was to look at them.

I used to go with my youngest uncle to the market, where fat oxen and other livestock were sold. Before I was fifteen I didn't know what a market place was although it was nearby, some three or four kilometers away. One day my grandfather took two wagonloads of rakija to market, and I went with him for the sake of the white bread.[12] It turned out that Grandpa didn't take any bread, but I was given money to buy a quarter of a loaf. I begged him to give me twenty para so that I could buy half a loaf, but he refused. Then I begged him to buy me a pair of opanke, so he bought them, a pair of red ones for half a dinar. I asked him to add another twenty para to buy me better ones, but without success. . . .

Written by the youngest contributor, a man in his late thirties, the next autobiography is the longest and most detailed one submitted. Despite their troubles, the other men seem to have felt basically secure and self-confident, especially the author of the preceding selection. But the following account appears to be largely an attempt by its author to bolster his self-esteem. This is closely related, no doubt, to his unhappy childhood experiences in the households of both maternal and paternal grandparents, each torn

[11] Age is reckoned in terms of the number of years one is about to complete.
[12] Peasants from more prosperous households always carried white bread with them when they went somewhere, so that others would not think they were poor.

by conflict and dominated by an unreasonable grandfather. In his own household today this man is very much dominated by his wife and mother.[13] His insecurity, however, appears to have made him more introspective, for besides portraying his own personal development his biography presents valuable detailed descriptions of various aspects of village life.

AUTOBIOGRAPHY F

If I remember everything correctly I shall write in this copybook all my work and everything I have experienced.

I was born in 1916, in my paternal grandfather's house. My grandfather Života had a wife and five sons: my father Radosav, and my four uncles, Čedomir, Branislav, Miodrag, and Slobodan, and two daughters, Desanka and Darinka. My uncle Miodrag and aunt Darinka died before my mother married my father. When my mother married my father there were eight in my grandfather's house, including my great-grandfather, Marinko, and his wife, Zagorka.[14]

Grandfather Života was the only son of his father. He never went to school and was illiterate. But he was the starešina, and no one dared do anything against his will. He had bad friends. He visited other women. He was always willing to vouch for the debts of others and never discussed anything with his sons. His parents used to chide him, "*Oj*, black Života, why don't you discuss your affairs with someone? If you don't want to do so with your father and mother then do it with your sons. If you don't want to do so with them, discuss your affairs with the mouse in the wall. May God kill you. Stop wandering. Don't you see that the house is going bankrupt because of you? The children are working and you are wasting."

But grandfather continued to go his way without listening to the advice of his parents, doing stupid things in his own village and surroundings. Before he started losing his land he was famous as a good gazda, a healthy, strong young man. In addition to his own wife he had many others. Men who noticed that he paid attention to their wives didn't dare tell him anything because their wives worked for him and they were poor . . . they planned their revenge on the sly . . . by stealing his stock, setting

---

[13] It was extremely difficult to interview him, in fact, because his wife and mother constantly interrupted and because he frequently paused during conversations to confirm a point with them—a rare situation in a male-dominated society.

[14] The position of household head was turned over to his grandfather because of his great-grandfather's senility.

his hay on fire, and cutting down his trees. All this happened because he was illiterate and an only son. He was both spoiled and neglected.

My father, Radosav, and the rest of his children went to school and understood things much better. They tried to explain things to him but he rarely listened. When he got angry he used to tell them, "Whoever doesn't want to do as I order shall leave home."

Because his sons were married, grandfather never bought clothes or opanci for the women or children. The women had to steal wheat, eggs, chickens, cheese, kajmak, and other things to sell to be able to buy what they needed.

Very soon quarrels started between the brothers and their wives, all because of the thefts. My father tried to prevent further stealing, but that was impossible because my uncle had so many children. During that time I lived with my mother's parents. When my father realized that nothing good could come of the situation he decided to go and take care of the stock at the shepherd's hut, three kilometers away from the house. My mother went with him.

He was very fond of hunting rabbits, wild pigeons, and other small animals. He liked good company and people liked him, too. His care of the stock was negligible, so my mother had to do all the work. He was a merchant, too. He bought plums, dried them, and sold them as prunes. At one time he worked as a buyer for other merchants, buying plums, grapes, and other articles. He was also a contractor for road building, because after the War[15] a great deal of attention was paid to the restoring of roads and the building of new ones. He gave the money he earned working at all these jobs to his father, Života, since he was the head of the household. He used to tell me a great deal about his work, teaching me not to steal, not to think badly of others, not to speak nonsense and profanities, to obey others, and so on.

During this time I lived at my maternal grandparents', and it was nice. I still remember well how there were four of us in the house, Grandpa, Grandma, my Aunt, and me. It was the same house in which we are living today, but the arrangement was quite different then. . . .

. . . . As a little boy I watched the sheep before I started school. In the summertime I wore a shirt and drawers with a woven belt and without pants. I often lost my things, such as the straps of my opanke, belt, and so forth because I was a very restless child. My grandparents loved me and even spoiled me a little. Grandma was nicer than Grandpa, who was

[15] The First World War.

a very, very stern man. In the first year of my schooling I didn't take it seriously. I went around with bad children, I fought, and I liked to steal a nice pencil, an eraser, a ball, and so forth. I never stole all by myself but always with the others. I was punished severely by the school teacher and my grandparents. Now and then my father came to visit me, and if I did some stupid thing he took off his leather belt and lifted my shirt and spanked my bottom. I cried and cried in pain, promising never to steal anything again.

My people instructed me and I improved. They showed me the example of the good children in the neighborhood and I began to play with them. When I was in the third grade I was among the best pupils, eager to be a still better student. In the beginning they had to force me to be good, but as I grew older I realized the necessity of knowledge. I finished the third grade with very good grades, and the fourth grade with excellent, both in studies and conduct. My elders used to tell me stories in the evening.

My grandparents were not rich—they owned five hectares, under forest, vineyard, orchard, and cultivated land. We were always short of forage for the stock. We used to have one or two cows and five or six sheep. Every morning I would have to get up early to take the sheep to graze before seven o'clock, because at eight I had to be in school, and it took me an hour to walk there. Sometimes I was late, and the teacher cursed me. In the afternoon as soon as I returned home from school, I had to help my grandparents with the work, especially in the plum-picking season. I was always afraid of my grandfather, who was very severe, so I kept picking plums without straightening up. My legs ached terribly, and I could hardly wait for the day to end.

When I finished the fourth grade I wanted to continue my education, but children were rarely sent to high school at that time. As my grandparents were the only workers at home, I forsook going on and resumed work. My life was pretty hard. My grandfather forced me to do much work, and being small I could hardly bear working with him. He had a bad temper and frequently beat me. I cried a million times but that did no good.

My parents didn't even want to hear or protect me from these tortures. I dreamt about the time when I'd be grown up enough not to be afraid of anyone. So year after year I grew older and bigger. At one time my grandfather and grandmother fought about a woman in our neighborhood whom he visited on the sly and slept with. Grandma scolded him, as every woman does, and he, being very temperamental and wild, beat her. That happened thousands of times.

During the day all three of us worked in the fields, and toward evening Grandma used to leave us to prepare supper and do some work around the house. We two continued our work until dark, and when it was impossible to work any more my grandfather told me, "*Ajde, kući*" [Go along home]. I collected our things in a hurry and ran home as fast as I could, being terribly afraid of the dark and wild animals. You see, I worked the whole day, and in the evening I trembled with fear, and when I reached home my heart was beating like a sparrow's.

At home my grandmother had milked the cows, done her chores, and put the milk in the kettle to cook. I used to sit near the hearth and tend the fire so that the milk would heat up quickly. When it was ready Grandma brought a wooden bowl, took the skim off the milk, and poured me a bowlful of hot milk. I sat on a little stool, Grandma turned over a large pan and placed the little bowl on it, and I had supper, fearful lest Grandpa would come and start cursing Grandma.

In the meantime I helped her prepare for the next day because she had to bake bread in the evening, being busy in the fields all day long. I never had the courage to go to bed before Grandma because I was afraid that Grandpa would kill her. I loved her more than my own mother because I never lived with my mother. When Grandpa came he started shouting and beating Grandma, and I always defended her. Many times he kicked us out of the house, so we had to spend the night out of doors. That's how things were.

In the further development of my life there were many hard days and difficulties. My friends were children of good parents, and I was told about their good parents by my grandmother. I used to be worried and full of thoughts. I worried about my grandmother and myself always being scared of my grandfather. It got so bad that I forgot even my own parents. But I was a strong boy so I overcame all the difficulties. I encouraged myself, and when I was blamed or beaten by my grandfather I drove the sheep to the pasture and began singing louder and louder.

I sang together with the girls, and both the girls and boys liked me. . . . The fear that vibrated in my nerves then disappeared and was forgotten during my playing and singing with the children. My thoughts at that time, if I still remember well, were the following: I thought about my future, I wanted to be good and be loved by everyone. I wished not to be scared of older people and not to be cursed and beaten. I wished to be better than these children. I wished to be better even than those children who my parents had told me were good children.

Everything happened in the best possible way, although with a lot of hardship . . . I used to pray to God to help me, and, if I remember well, there was hardly an evening in which Grandma and I did not light incense and a candle in our little room and pray to God. We prayed first for our health, and that everything in our home be peaceful and blessed. We prayed for the health of the stock, we prayed to God and all the Saints that our plum trees would bear a rich harvest and that there would be peace among our people. While my grandmother said all that she used to take the incense holder with some hot coals and incense and waft it toward me while I stood piously with bowed head, crossing myself and repeating the words she taught me.

. . . . I grew older as years passed by, and I came to have a normal way of living. My grandfather lived again happily with my grandmother. He stopped cursing her and liked me more. I was older and was able to help him in all work. The previous hardships I almost forgot. My grandfather always allowed me to go to the market in Arandjelovac, and on Easter, Whitsuntide, and Holy Trinity Day there was a fair near our church and school.

They bought me a fine Šumadijan costume of woolen stuff, with a vest and a jacket trimmed with black and cherry-red silk braid. The vest, jacket, and britches were light brown. They bought me a pair of fine Šumadijan opanci with black leather straps. I remember well that when I put all these new things on I went to church with my grandmother, because it was Easter Sunday. She wouldn't allow me to wear my new clothes before going to church in them because that was the custom. I was thirteen. My mother and father were there in the church, too.

My father gave me a dinar to buy some candy, and before I went to church I was given a dinar by my grandfather to buy some candy and one dinar to give to the church. So I had one and a half dinars in my pocket to spend because I bought candy for one-half a dinar and the rest I saved for another time.

After Mass was finished we had our breakfast in the churchyard. Although I shouldn't have been listening, I heard my elders talking about me. My grandfather turned to me and patted me, saying, "I am very pleased that people praise my grandson. Try always to be good." I answered that I would and kissed his hand because my grandmother taught me to do so, and to take off my hat whenever grandfather was teaching and advising me.

Sometimes I wished I could tell him not to beat and curse me but I never dared. As I tried to be better day after day the cursing and beating became rarer. By my fifteenth year I wasn't beaten anymore, only yelled at for some careless acts. That same year grandfather became ill and died. Soon my mother and father joined us. We now had only three hectares of not very good land.

My father was a merchant in prunes, and the three of us—my mother, my sister one year younger, and I—cultivated these three hectares.

According to Serbian custom, especially in Šumadija, bachelors and maidens wear nice clothes after they are sixteen, and do so till they are twenty or at most twenty-five. They usually marry at the age of eighteen to twenty-three.

I was in my seventeenth year and my sister was sixteen. We had reached the age of dressing nicely. Although our parents were short of money they bought us nice clothes. They bought a dress of dark blue fabric for my sister and gave her the twenty ducats which she wore as a maiden, for it was our custom that a girl shall wear ducats if her elders can afford it. They bought me a fine outfit and a new hat. I still have all these clothes. So my sister and I renewed our wardrobe for the holiday, and on Easter Sunday, following the custom, we went to church and later to the dance. We also went to the dances at the fairs.

Being good children from our childhood on, my sister and I were among the best, although we were poor. We always had the company of the daughters and sons of gazde. Some of them were bad—they gambled, drank, and did foolish things, and some of the girls were spoiled and disobedient and too proud. There were some of the same kind in the lower class, that is, among the poorer ones. My sister and I were poor, too, because our parents didn't own more than three hectares of land. But we were accustomed to work, obedience, and diligence, and we weren't shy. Whenever we went to a fair we were liked and respected. I behaved well, avoiding making others angry, and so did my sister.

My sister was married at the age of eighteen, and I prolonged my bachelorhood. When I was twenty I joined the army and served in the First Cavalry Regiment of the King's Guard. The life of a soldier was good although a little hard. I was careful and diligent. I obeyed my superiors and was among the best in learning. . . .

. . . . When I came home[16] my people wanted me to get married. They kept trying to talk me into it, and I obeyed. I wanted to find a good girl, of good parents, who would make a good housewife and help me in

[16] He became ill and was temporarily discharged.

my work because I wasn't physically strong. Our girls like to marry only sons, because in that case there was no dividing the property and, aside from that, where several brothers lived together there was always some quarreling. I had many chances to get married, but I hesitated in order to find a good girl. Thank God my wishes came true.

I found a girl about ten kilometers from our village, and we arranged the wedding and did everything according to Serbian customs. The girl was a good one, and she is still my wife. She is able to do all work and she is a fine housekeeper. I was married at the age of twenty-one, and she was about the same age. Being a child of good parents, she is a hard worker, and we devoted ourselves to work successfully. In January, 1938, a daughter was born to us. In May I went to finish my term in the army. I was ordered to report to the second squadron of the cavalry at Niš. My duty was not new to me, and I had fifteen more months of training before me. My life as a soldier was as good as it could be. In November I got a letter from home that my son was born, and all the officers and fellow soldiers congratulated me. Toward the end of 1938 the army was alerted and some new reservists were called up. In 1939 I was released. . . .

The final selection is the most sophisticated in content. The author, a villager in his seventies, is the same one who wrote the account of life at the time of the First Revolt, quoted in Chapter 2 and is considered by the other peasants as the authority on local history. His autobiography is less emotional than the others and is the only one that attempts to describe the culture from an objective point of view. Below are comments on his own life; his thoughts and analyses of social change are included in Chapter 13.

AUTOBIOGRAPHY G

My father, who was born in 1843, told me about the situation after 1850. At that time life and social structure underwent great changes, the zadrugas divided and dissolved, the population increased, there were less woods and forest. Faith remained strong but the customs changed, as well as the costumes and behavior of the people. Laws became effective and courts were established because there was already some crime. New ideas were in conflict with the old ones, but an honest word and the oath were still holy. This state of affairs lasted until 1880.

People loved freedom above all but they also loved their weapons, their hunting, good horses, good clothes, and songs. Better houses were built, with two to five rooms, better wagons and plows were used. The land was very fertile immediately after clearing the forest. The relations between members of the zadruga were equal. New roads were built and the old ones improved. A few schools were opened, and in some villages there were a few literate people. That was the situation before I was born.

And now something that I myself remember: I was born in 1881 in Orašac. My father was Milenko and my mother Leposava. My father was born into an old and rich zadruga. His father, Milivoje, who had no brothers or sisters, left the zadruga with his wife Ilinka, who gave birth to ten children: eight boys and two girls. She died when she gave birth to her tenth child. So my grandfather married Jelena, a widow from Bukovik. They had two more sons and two more daughters so that the total number of his children was fourteen: ten boys and four girls. Six sons and two daughters grew up and married while the rest died as children. After my grandfather's death, my father, being the oldest, remained the head of the zadruga while two of his brothers became good merchants in Belgrade.

My father married twice. With his first wife, Ljubica, he had two sons, both of whom died in the same year, aged nineteen and twenty, and two daughters who died as children. The second time he married Radojka, a widow who brought him three children. With my father she bore four sons and a daughter, among whom I am the only one alive.

I married and I had three children. One son died in his sixth year, and the other is an engineer. He is married and has a son and a daughter. My daughter is married and has two sons. So much for my family, and now in brief a few words about my education, occupation, life, and other circumstances.

When I was born my father had two sons by his first wife and the zadruga was divided. My father got about three hectares, a house, and two outbuildings. I was eight when both my elder half brothers died, and as my mother and my father were already pretty old it was a great shock for them. We were not rich, but after this what little we had began to go. My father's earnings weren't equal to our basic needs so he began going into debt at a high rate of interest. Day by day things got worse and worse.

I was old enough for school, but because of the lack of room in the school I had to wait and wasn't accepted until I was ten. I was accepted then only because of the tears of my parents. The teacher agreed, but he told me to bring a stool if there were not enough benches. There was only one teacher for all four grades.

As for myself, I didn't continue my studies although I liked them very much, being a good pupil. Nor did I enter a trade or become an apprentice to a merchant. I remained at home, following my father's advice. He used to teach me to be a good and honest man, not to steal, not to lie, and not to make friends with bad people, to respect old people and to be kind to everyone.

So time passed, I grew up, and I worked on our land and for others, too. When working, my daily salary was one dinar except for reaping, which paid two dinars a day. In the meantime another brother died so our economic position became still worse. We lost all our stock, which is the worst thing that can happen to a peasant's economy. When I was twenty my mother died, and when I was twenty-two I joined the army. That was in 1903. After having been discharged from the army I continued working at home until 1905, when I became a clerk in the *opština*.[17] I remained at that position for three years and then returned again to working on the land as a peasant.

In 1912 when the war against the Turks broke out I was mobilized. After this war and a short interval of peace, the war against Bulgaria started, and after that there was constant drilling. In the month of May, while I was returning home from military service from Prilep, I stopped in the county of Veles.[18] There I was a clerk, and because I had no rank in the army I wasn't mobilized during the Serbo-Austrian War.[19] I remained at my work there until October, 1915, when I fled to Greece before the enemy. In Salonika I joined the army again and continued fighting on the Salonika Front until the liberation in 1918.

When I was demobilized and ordered to my previous duty I returned home because in the meantime all the members of my family had died except an unmarried sister.

At home everything was ruined, so my marriage, which took place the same year, was held without any of the customary wedding ceremonies. In 1920 I was again a clerk, but this time in Arandjelovac. My job lasted until 1940. Then I became very ill and was forced to lie in bed, where I spent the Second World War and the accompanying occupation. During my life I recovered from pneumonia, dysentery, cholera, yellow jaundice, malaria, and a nervous breakdown that lasted for three years. I still feel very ill. . . .

[17] Pre-war name for Village Council, now called *odbor*.
[18] In Macedonia.
[19] The First World War.

In addition to life patterns, attitudes, and incidental descriptions, these autobiographies also serve to illustrate two aspects of the husband-wife relationship not yet discussed: adultery and widowhood. Extramarital relations are not common in the village, although some informants felt that since the war morals have changed considerably. This means that both grandfathers of the writer of Autobiography F were atypical. In a discussion of the subject with three male villagers, one interrupted another: "What are you saying, *bre*? Sure such things went on in the old days, only people didn't go around talking about it." After a moment's reflection he added, "They don't talk about it today, either."

The third concluded, "Eh, we don't have a movie-house, we don't have a theater—we have to have *something* to amuse ourselves."

Even in those cases where adultery does occur and is recognized, it generally does not interfere with the stability of the marriage. One man explained that if he ever got the notion to go to another woman he would wait until his daughters were grown up and married, for it would be a disgraceful reflection on them. By the same token, if a married man had relations it would never be with an unmarried girl or a young matron, but generally with a widow.

On the subject of widowhood, the autobiographies point up the fact that after the death of one's spouse the usual procedure is to remarry. The mother of the man who wrote Autobiography B is an exception to this rule. His account illustrates sterility as a cause for divorce, as in the case of his first wife and his remarriage to a widow, although he himself was not a widower. Other cases, where a widow is married by a widower and brings the children of her first marriage to the new husband's household, are brought out in Autobiography G. The basic reason for the high incidence of remarriage is simply that it takes a man and wife working together to achieve a satisfactory way of life in Orašac.

DEATH

To the people of Orašac death is an acceptable, inevitable event. Although it may not be in accord with official theology, they feel that the deceased simply continue their life in another world. There is a great deal of highly ritualized mourning but seldom deep grief outside the most immediate family, except for the death of a child or young person.

The declining death rate has brought about a marked change in the age structure of the population, with a much lower incidence of infant mortality and with a higher life expectancy now. As to the causes of death, local records are inconsistent and unreliable. All those of children are simply registered as *fras*, a German term pertaining to childhood, without listing the actual cause. Old age is the reason registered for most deaths of people over sixty. It can be said, however, that communicable diseases, especially tuberculosis, are one of the most common causes. In addition, from time to time there have been epidemics which took high tolls, such as that of influenza immediately after the First World War.

The villagers attribute the lower death rate to their more *higijenski* life today (although the author of Autobiography A felt that life was healthier when he was a youth). "Hygienic" means having more windows in the house and sleeping in beds raised off the ground. Lined wells, toilets, washing one's hands after handling livestock before meals, and not sharing a common food bowl are not included in this definition.

The older people feel that doctors are useful only when surgery is necessary; otherwise "a little hot wine or rakija and a heated brick held over the part that hurts" is considered the best treatment for all ills. For infants' and small children's disorders mothers still visit a vračara. In one instance a baby with digestive difficulties was brought to the home of a relatively young vračara, who claimed she learned her skills from her mother. She supported the infant's chin in one hand and pressed the unwashed index finger of her other hand hard against the roof of his mouth. He cried lustily, and she told the mother to nurse him immediately. The baby refused, and the mother was told to return with the child the next day. The pressure was repeated, the baby did not cry, accepted his mother's breast, and was apparently well again. Whatever the factors involved, the mother was satisfied with the results and confided that "such treatment is better than what you can buy in bottles."

When it is obvious that a person is sinking, especially an old person, his family passes the word that he is *gotov* (far-gone, or ready for death) and makes sure his best clothes are set aside for the burial. If the cause of death is a "dirty disease," such as tuberculosis, the old clothing is burned.

There are many beliefs surrounding death. Someone must constantly sit guarding the corpse, and candles must be burning. The windows are closed, mirrors are removed, and no cats are allowed to enter the room. These are precautions to prevent the spirit of the deceased from leaving. A piece of bread, some salt, and a glass of red wine are left on the table, so that the spirit can have something to eat while it remains in the house.

The funeral always occurs the next day. Usually the same people are invited to a burial who would be guests at a wedding in that household. They gather at the home of the deceased and are served slatko or a lump of sugar, to dip in water, followed by Turkish coffee and a glass of rakija. Even in times of sorrow traditional customs of hospitality are observed. Large numbers of people crowd the room where the corpse now lies in an open coffin. From outside the house piercing wails of the mourning women (*kukati*) can be heard. The men of the household, although they may be deeply moved, do little more than bite their lips, for it is considered unmanly to display grief openly. When the head of the household decides that all is ready for the burial the priest says a few brief prayers and the coffin is closed. A male relative leads a procession to the graveyard, bearing the wooden cross which will be placed temporarily over the grave. He is followed by another male relative carrying bowls of *žito*[20] which are decorated with crosses made of colored candies. Then come the close relatives of the deceased and after them a sled bearing the coffin. The other mourners follow behind.

As the procession approaches the church the bell begins to peal. This is considered an important part of the ceremony, and although there is usually a fee it is done free for those unable to pay. Inside

[20] A ceremonial dish made of boiled wheat, sugar, and nuts.

the church the priest performs a service with the members of the funeral party standing in a circle around the coffin holding lighted candles. Before the coffin is closed close relatives kiss the cross which has been placed on the corpse and then kiss the forehead of the deceased. After the conclusion of the service the procession makes its way to the cemetery, again to the accompaniment of the tolling church bell. Midway to the graveyard they halt for a prayer, intended to give the soul of the deceased a last glimpse of his village.

At the cemetery the coffin is opened for the last time. The priest says the final prayer and makes a cross on the body with a mixture of olive oil and red wine. A close relative usually places some money in the hand of the deceased, "for the journey." The bottle of wine and oil is broken on the closed coffin, and each of the relatives and friends throws a handful of soil on the grave.

All during this time the women mourn in loud, singsong chants. Much of the mourning is mechanical, according to familiar traditional patterns, with some improvisation to suit the person mourned. They express woe and loneliness, eulogize the deceased and send messages to other departed relatives whom he will soon be seeing. When the deceased is a young person and the grief very deeply felt, then the chants are personal and most poignant. This plaintive lament was chanted by a mother over the grave of her seven-year-old daughter:

> Jao, Dano, slatka ćeri,
> Sačekaj tvoju baku, sine, tamo,
> Pa u ruke poljubi,
> Pa baku, sine, slušaj tamo,
> Baka ti je bolna i prebolna.
> Ti ćeš kćeri baku poslučati,
> Pa ćeš baki vrata otvoriti.
> Baka će tebe, ćeri, u školu spremati,
> Pa će tebi baka kosu češljati,
> Dano, slatka ćeri,
> Tebi će baka češalj doneti,
> Tebi je mama češalj pratila,
> Da te baka očešlja, sine.

Slatka majko, ponesi poklon mojoj ćeri Dani,
Evo tebi, majko, poklon za materice,
Mojoj Dani, mojoj miloj ćeri,
Majkinoj vodonoši,
I majkinoj posluzi,
Majkinoj čobanići,
I majkinoj gostilji,
A ja tebe, ćeri, više, neman.
Jao, brate, milo moje.

Oh woe is me, Dana, sweet daughter,
Greet Grandma there, my child,
And kiss her hand,
And obey Grandma, my child,
For she is sick and very ill.
My daughter, you will obey Grandma,
And open the door for her,
And Grandma will prepare you for school,
And she will comb your hair,
Dana, sweet daughter,
Grandma will bring a comb,
The comb Mommy has given you,
So that Grandma can comb your hair, child.

Dear Mother,[21] give a present to my daughter Dana,
Here, Mother, is a present for Materice,[22]
To give to Dana, to my dear daughter,
To my little water-carrier,
To Mommy's little helper,
To Mommy's little shepherd girl,
And Mommy's little hostess,
And I no longer have you.
Oh woe is me, my darling.

Over the grave of a man the women chant about his good work and heroic deeds and tell him what his death means to his loved ones. Laments about women tell of their pure characters and good hearts. While a middle-aged man stood with bowed head beside

[21] Mourning mother is now addressing her own mother.
[22] A holiday preceding Christmas when mothers give their children small gifts.

the grave of his wife, two women who were her neighbors and good friends called to her:

> Kuku mene što ostavi tvoju decu.
> Ko će nji gledati kad njima majke nema?
> Godina po će godina proći,
> Druga će se oženiti i njemu ljubu dovesti,
> Ali njima majke nikad ni dovek.
> Od tudje majke tuga bije.

> Woe is me, that you have left your children.
> Who will look after them if they have no mother?
> One year after another will pass,
> Your husband will remarry and bring another his love,
> But your children will never have their own mother.
> From a strange mother only sorrow comes.

When the burial is complete the wooden cross is placed at the head of the grave. The male elders signal to the women to cease wailing, and they decorate the surface with fruit, sprigs of sweet basil, and fresh flowers. In the winter dried basil and crepe-paper flowers are used. All the members of the funeral party line up, old men first, to take a spoonful of žito and a sip of wine, after crossing themselves and murmuring a prayer.

Everyone sits on the ground in a long double row between the tombstones, and a memorial feast is spread out. It usually consists of a roast pig or sheep, soup, gibanica, bread, brandy, wine, and cakes. If the funeral occurs during a period of fast then only bread and a special bean gruel are served. Before partaking of the food, each person again crosses himself and says, "*Za* —— *dušu, večna pamet, Bog da ga prosti*" (For the eternal memory of ——'s soul, may God forgive him his sins).

The funeral is only the beginning of the observances for the deceased. A large feast is held at the grave a week (or the first Sunday after the burial), forty days, half a year, and a year after the death. The immediate family goes to the graveyard every week during this period. The women wear black kerchiefs and the men black arm bands. The same people attend each of the four other times, and the grave is decorated, candles lit, food prepared. Each time, too, the women take up their sorrowful wailing.

These are not the only ceremonies held at the graveyard. Three times a year, during Lent, during Christmas, and in the summer, *zadušnice*, memorial feasts for the dead, take place. On these days all the households in the village go to the graveyard to honor their departed relatives. If there is snow on the ground the individual graves are carefully cleared and the meal laid upon them anyway. Each household goes first to its ancestors' graves, kisses the stone, and lights small yellow candles at the base. The women mourn, red-eyed and convulsed with grief, and then suddenly straighten up and methodically spread cloths on top of each grave or on small makeshift tables. Meals of roast chicken, dried meat, cheese, bread, dried fruit, cakes, and cookies are arranged on them. Special small loaves of bread, stamped with the *slovo*, or holy symbols, are prepared in advance.[23]

After each family has formally mourned its own dead, the villagers call one another to partake of food in memory of the relatives of the others. This is considered an honor. When one household calls a member of another the domaćica gives him or her a memorial loaf and some food and sweets, saying, "*Ovo mojem —— zadušu da pojede*" (Eat this for the soul of my ——). The invited person, in accepting, kisses the offering and replies, "*Bog da mu dušu prosti laka mu zemlja gde leži*" (God grant his soul an easy resting-place). Food acquired in this way is set aside in the basket in which a household's own food was brought, and many people return home carrying baskets heavier than they were when they came.

One feature of zadušnice in Orašac is the Gypsy beggars. There is a colony of Gypsies in nearby Ranilović village, and many of them come, carrying sacks over their shoulders, to ask for food and drink to honor the deceased. They are scorned, reprimanded, and sometimes ignored at first, but almost everyone eventually gives them something.

Despite all the elaborate and patterned ritual, behavior at the

---

[23] They are supposed to be baked only by ritually clean women although this taboo is not strictly observed today.

graveyard is rather informal. The villagers' attitude toward their ancestors and departed relatives is the same as the warm, intimate one that they maintain toward each other, devoid of awe or fear. They think nothing of casually draping a torba over a tombstone, parking a šubara on a cross, sitting on the grave itself, and even telling stories and jokes after the religious rituals are completed. Much of the ritual is perfunctory, performed in an easygoing manner, and the opportunity for gossiping and visiting is an important part of the ceremony.

Perhaps formerly these matters were taken more seriously. Today the people continue to observe the customs because of the weight of tradition and in spite of themselves rather than because of any belief in their religious or spiritual efficacy. In fact, in discussions of the graveyard feasts with various villagers, the adjectives commonly used to describe the custom were "stupid" and "wasteful." "We could build a factory with the money and effort we spend on these customs," one man declared. Some of the more sophisticated peasants stated outright that it was pretty humorous to first mourn woefully and then sit down to a fine meal with all the trimmings.

When asked why they continue these ceremonies they answered, "Because everybody does" or, in the case of an individual death, "My ―― [a relative] was no servant. Why shouldn't we give him a decent burial?"

These graveyard feasts are in a sense akin to the potlatch ceremonies of the Indians of the Pacific Northwest Coast. They are certainly a very substantial economic drain on the community at large and on the individual households and at the same time cannot be considered festivities or joyous occasions. They are definitely competitive. Each domaćica is very conscious of the fact that what she prepares and brings to the graveyard will be closely scrutinized by the other village housewives, and no one wants to be outdone.

Nor are the memorial feasts the only expenses connected with death. The family must erect a fitting tombstone. The Orašac graveyard and the one in Vrbica, along the trail over Preseka Hill, show an excellent sequence of tombstone types. The earliest are wooden crosses. In the late nineteenth century small limestone tablets were used. These were made more ornate, with carved bas-reliefs of the deceased in full folk costume. Many from this period show men wearing the fez and baggy pants and women in ankle-length pleated skirts. The stones were later simplified, with carved crosses and the name and date. About 1920 porcelainized photographs of the departed were mounted in the stones, and today the most envied tombstones are of polished dark marble, from the quarry at Venčac, with gilt trim on the engraved lettering. They are very expensive, but as one woman put it, "The graveyard is in the center of the village, and everyone can see it."

CHAPTER 10

RELIGION, HOLIDAYS, AND FOLK BELIEFS

THE ROLE OF RELIGION, THE CHURCH, AND THE PRIEST

IT CAN BE SEEN from the preceding discussion that the village graveyard is a very important ceremonial center. The only place that
exceeds it in significance is the individual home, with the church
itself of distinctly tertiary importance. Religion, like so many of
the other village institutions, is a casual thing, taken for granted,
and intimately bound up with the whole way of life. The villagers
are well acquainted with God—they feel respect and reverence but
not fear and wonder. They are on speaking terms with God—
they feel that He understands their needs and problems. All of the
saints, too, are part of the peasants' life, not only individually as
special patron saints of the various clans, but also for the numerous
saints' days celebrated throughout the year. The Orašani never
refer to events by the formal calendar but use the one most practical for their means: the dates when the first snow falls, when the
grapes ripen, when Branko returned from the war, and when
Slobodanka's baby is due are all reckoned in terms of their relation
to a particular saint's day.

By the same token, the village church is an informal place.
Villagers go in and out at will, just to cross themselves and to kiss
the icon on the table before the altar. This is true on ordinary
days as well as on holidays, and low talking and moving around
are not infrequent even during services. The Serbs, and Šumadijans
in particular, are not regular churchgoers. They attend when they
wish to, and, for all the people the Orašac church serves, there are

never more than fifteen or twenty there for a Sunday service, and usually less. The only time when there is a sizeable attendance is Easter. This tradition is said to be an outgrowth of conditions at the time of the Turks. During that period churches in the woods were few and far between, and people got in the habit of going only on the most important holidays. This also helps to explain the development of the home as the main ceremonial center.

The real significance of the Serbian Orthodox faith and the local church is found in part in the ceremonial observances at home and also in the complete identity of faith and nationality. The Church played a most important role in maintaining a national consciousness during the hundreds of years of Turkish rule, as was brought out in Chapter 2. Serbia has been relatively homogeneous, and to say that a person is a Serb also implies that he is a member of the Orthodox faith. During the existence of Serbia as an independent state and later, after the formation of the Kingdom of Yugoslavia, the Orthodox religion remained in effect the official Church of Serbia. The peasants have always identified themselves as closely with the Church as with the State.

Until 1863 there was no church in Orašac, and the villagers attended the one in Bukovik. Under the leadership of their first priest, who was himself born in Orašac, an attempt was made to enlist the support of people from Kopljare and Orašac villages to help build a local church. There was great difficulty deciding on a site, because the people of Orašac wanted it built in the center of the village while those from Kopljare wanted it in their village. A compromise of sorts was reached when it was decided that the church would be built in Orašac and the priest would move his residence to Kopljare (it was later moved back to Orašac). Construction was started in 1868 and was completed in 1870, the peasants themselves supplying most of the funds and labor. Until 1950 all the priests in the Orašac-Kopljare parish were born in villages in the Jasenica region, providing a further bond between the villagers and their church.

The present Orašac *pop*, or priest, more formally called *sveštenik*, happens to be from Montenegro and is the only one to have come from outside the immediate area. His views are respected and his advice often sought. Before the war, however, the village priest had more influence. Together with the teachers and President of the Village Council he helped determine village policies.

Economically the priest fares only a little better than the average peasant. His income is derived from fees at christenings, betrothals, and weddings as well as from his yearly calls to each household to bless the water used in making the slava bread. Payment is not compulsory, and almost one-third of the families claim that they are too poor to give him some money for his services. The priest and his family are provided with a rectory next to the church. It is by no means the best home in the village but is considerably better than most peasant cottages. On his one hectare of rent-free land he can keep some chickens and a pig or two and raise an adequate amount of vegetables and fruits for his own family's need. He is also supplied with wood for cooking and heating.[1]

The church itself gets its income from contributions, the sale of candles and fees for holding special services. It is never particularly well endowed, as was seen by the sample budgets. Church affairs are managed by an elected council composed of peasants from Orašac and Kopljare. The priest is assisted by a villager, who acts as a part-time singer and sexton, a position of substantial prestige which brings a token payment each year.

The Orašac church has whitewashed outer walls and a small wrought-iron Orthodox cross on the roof. Inside, the floors are paved with flat stones and the walls are covered with pastel-tinted and gilt frescoes. In a rounded apse the altar faces East and is separated from the congregation by a characteristic decorated screen which has three doors, from which the priest passes back and forth from altar to worshipers. As in all Orthodox churches, there are no seats or benches, and the people stand during services. Formalized segregation is not practiced, but women tend to cluster on one side and men on the other.

Religious observances no longer followed include the keeping of frequent and lengthy fasts. In addition to fasting on certain holi-

---

[1] The present priest and his wife have five children, three of them attending high school in Arandjelovac, and they find it difficult to make ends meet.

days all Orthodox Serbs were expected to honor every Wednesday and Friday of the year as fast days. When asked if he still abided by these rules one villager replied, "Fifty years ago almost everyone observed the fast, but today only the priest does, and he has to." Today most people fast for a few days only, before the important holidays. If a graveyard feast is held during a period of fast, the bereaved family always serves special food in place of the usual spread. It shows the other villagers that the family is religious, and it is, of course, also much more economical for them. Food prohibited during fasts include all meat and meat products, milk, cheese, and eggs. Only in the case of lard, and to a lesser extent cheese, is the fasting a sacrifice, because the other foods are not staples in the normal diet. *Posni pasulj* is made with beans boiled in salty water and perhaps flavored with paprika. It is flat and unpalatable, and only the occasional remaining devout households prepare it for every fast. The prevailing attitude is, "May God forgive me if I fast in spirit only, for I can't stand my pasulj without lard!"

The yearly cycle of holidays connected with religious observances points up the role of religion in the everyday life of the villagers. The most important ones are listed in the accompanying chart, "Yearly Cycle of Traditional Holidays and Observances in Orašac."

Yearly Cycle of Traditional Holidays and Observances in Orašac

Nova Godina, New Year's Day   January 14
    Pre-war celebration at school, celebrations still held at home, with
    special fried cakes and shooting of pistols on New Year's Eve

Krstovdan, Saint John the Baptist's Day   January 18
    Fast day

Bogojavljenje, Epiphany   January 19
    Water brought to church to be blessed

Sveti Sava, Saint Sava's Day   January 27
    Day of the patron saint of Serbian education, an important pre-
    war holiday; also, traditionally coldest day of the year

Sretenje, Visitation of the Virgin   February 15
    Slava of the Orašac school, commemorating day of its dedication
    on anniversary of First Revolt

Zadušnice, Memorial Feast at Graveyard   February 27

Yearly Cycle of Traditional Holidays and Observances in Orašac (Cont.)

Bele Poklade, White Shrovetide　　　　　　　　　　　　　　March 7
Last Sunday before Lent, confessions, enemies forgiven; also, no
marriages performed by church until St. George's Day; children
masquerade from house to house

Čista Nedelja, Clean Week　　　　　　　　　　　　　　　March 8–14
First week of Lenten fast

Pačista Nedelja, Second Clean Week　　　　　　　　　　　March 15–21
Second week of Lent

Mladenci, Day of Young People　　　　　　　　　　　　　March 22
Young couples married during year attend special service at
church

Krstopoklona, Week of Homage to the Cross　　　　　　　March 22–28
Third week of Lent

Sredoposna Nedelja, Mid-Lent Week　　　　　　　　　　　March 29–
Fourth week of Lent　　　　　　　　　　　　　　　　　　April 4

Svetla Nedelja, Week of Light　　　　　　　　　　　　　April 5–11
Fifth week of Lent

Cvetna Nedelja, Week of Flowers　　　　　　　　　　　　April 12–18
Sixth week of Lent

Lazarova Subota (*Vrbica*), Lazar's Saturday (Willow Day)　April 17
Formerly a school holiday, with village procession

Cveti, Flower (Palm) Sunday　　　　　　　　　　　　　　April 18
Service at church, where children receive blessing

Velika Nedelja, Great Week　　　　　　　　　　　　　　April 19–25
Final week of Lent

Veliki Četvrtak, Great Thursday　　　　　　　　　　　　April 22
Evening church services, Sufferings of Christ read

Veliki Petak, Good Friday　　　　　　　　　　　　　　　April 23
Church service, market, and promenade in Arandjelovac

Uskrs, Easter Sunday　　　　　　　　　　　　　　　　　April 25
Sunrise church service, picnic breakfast; village dance in afternoon

Uskrsnji Ponedeljak, Easter Monday　　　　　　　　　　April 26
Memorial feast at graveyard

Djurdjevdan, Saint George's Day　　　　　　　　　　　　May 6
Slava of Nedić (45 households), and Petrović (9) clans; also,
spring festival, with dancing, gathering of boughs and flowers to
decorate houses

Sveti Jeremija, Saint Jerome's Day　　　　　　　　　　　May 14
Fair in Mladenovac

Yearly Cycle of Traditional Holidays and Observances in Orašac (Cont.)

Spasovdan, Ascension Day
   Slava of the village church, in memory of the day it was conse-
   crated
	June 3

Trojice, Holy Trinity Day
   Pre-war procession of officials and children through village, fol-
   lowed by dance
	June 13

Sveti Arandjel (letnji), Saint Archangel (Summer) Fair in Arandjelovac	June 26

Vidovdan, Saint Vitus' Day
   Anniversary of Battle of Kosovo, as well as day Archduke Ferdi-
   nand was assassinated and day of signing of Versailles Treaty,
   creating Yugoslavia; before the war, biggest state holiday, special
   church service to read names of all villagers who died in past wars
	June 28

Petrovdan, Saint Peter's Day
   End of fast beginning on first Sunday after Trojica, church service
   to bless children; fair in Topola
	July 12

Sveti Arandjel Gavrilo, Archangel Gabriel's Day Orašac village slava, church service followed by dance	July 26

Sveti Ilija,[a] Saint Elijah's Day
   Slava of churches in Bukovik and Banja; Elijah believed to be
   responsible for thunder
	August 2

Preobraženje, Transfiguration Grapes brought to church to be blessed; dance in Arandjelovac	August 19

Velika Gospojina, Feast of the Assumption
   Church service, breaking of fast begun two weeks earlier, picnic
   in churchyard; dance in Arandjelovac
	August 28

Mala Gospojina, Nativity of the Virgin Mary Fair in Topola	September 21

Sveti Joakim, Saint Joachim's Day
   Slava of Jakovljević (19 households), Janić (2), and Sekulić (1)
   clans
	September 22

Krstovdan, Holy Cross Day Fast day; fair in Palanka	September 27
Novi Vašar, New Fair Large livestock fair in Arandjelovac	October 9
Petkovdan, Saint Petka's Day Slava of Starčević clan (19 households)	October 27

Sveti Luka, Saint Luke's Day
   Slava of Joksimović (30 households), Maričević (25), Gajić (1),[b]
   Pejović (14), Minić (8), Obradović (7), Jovanović (5), Vasilić (1),
   Dimitrijević (4), Todorević (2), and Radojević (2) clans
	October 31

   [a] Many saints' days can be referred to by naming the saint or by naming the day as his day; these days are listed here as they are known in Orašac, but Sveti Ilija can also be called *Ilindan*, Sveti Nikola, *Nikoljdan*, etc.

Yearly Cycle of Traditional Holidays and Observances in Orašac (Cont.)

Mitrovdan, Saint Dimitri's Day Fair in Velika Ivanča	November 8
Sveti Arandjel Mihailo, Archangel Michael's Day Slava of Stojanović (19 households), Vasiljević (18), Matijašević (17), Lazarević (13), Gajić (9),[b] Anić (16), Pajević (7), Pavlović (10), Stanić (13), Vasilić (7), Lukić (6), Lucić (8), Jokić (6), Milovanović (4), Stevanović (6), Simić (4), Andrić (4), Ilić (3), Vasović (2), Perišić (2), Filipović (1), Petrović (1), Petrović (1), and Todorević (1) clans	November 21
Božični Post, Beginning of Christmas Fast	November 28
Vavedenje, Purification of Mary Dance held near the church	December 4
Sveti Nikola, Saint Nicholas' Day Slava of Milojević (9 households), Miloradović (4), Todorević (1), and Bogdanović (1); also, traditional time of first snow	December 19
Materice, Mothers' Day Mothers give children small gifts	December 26
Očevi, Fathers' Day Fathers give children small gifts	January 2
Tučindan, Day of the Killing Christmas sheep or pig slaughtered	January 5
Badnjidan, Christmas Eve Yule log cut	January 6
Božić, Christmas Day Church service, ceremonies at home	January 7

[b] In a few cases the entire clan does not slava on the same day; for example, the Gajić slava is on November 21, but one Gajić household slavas on October 31, out of respect to the father of one Gajić wife now residing with them.

THE FEAST DAY OF THE PATRON SAINT

To the individual household the most important holiday is the slava, in honor of its clan's patron saint. It is thought by some observers that all clans who "slava" (*slaviti*) on the same saint's day were originally from a common ancestor, and until the last century it was considered improper for people who shared a slava to intermarry even though they were not otherwise related. In Orašac almost half the peasant households slava on Archangel Michael's Day in November, so that most of the village is acting either as hosts or guests on that day.

Preparations for the slava start days in advance, with the coming

of the priest to bless the water. The women spend long hours
marinating and stuffing cabbages, slivering raw cabbage for salad,
cooking piktija, making homemade noodles for a rich chicken soup,
baking half a dozen kinds of cookies covered with coarse grains of
sugar, boiling and kneading wheat for žito,[2] and baking the special
slava loaf, the *kolač*. The traditional main dish, roast suckling pig,
is prepared by the men of the house.

Formerly the slava lasted for three days, but today it is celebrated on one day and part of the next. Guests are best friends,
neighbors, and usually some in-laws. It is common for men to
attend without their wives and women without their husbands,
for often they are invited to more than one slava and must decide
who should go to each. The current pattern of smaller-sized households also means that sometimes one spouse has to remain at home
while the other goes out as a guest.

On the morning of the slava the žito and kolač are taken to
the church to be blessed. Guests start arriving at about noon,
although no prescribed time is set, and are brought to the good
room. The entire cottage has had an annual cleaning, and the
walls are bright with fresh whitewash. The best linens and blankets
are brought out of the chests, to be displayed along with family
photographs and other treasured possessions. Eight to a dozen is
the usual number of guests nowadays. They are seated, in order
of social rank, at a large table that all but fills the room. It is covered with a cloth or, more commonly, sheets of grease-absorbent
paper, on which a vase of flowers, a holiday candle with small
flowers stuck in the base of the holder, the ever-present brandy
flask, and a pitcher of sweet wine are arranged.

In his capacity as host, the domaćin stands at the head of the
table during the entire feast. The celebration begins when he lights
a tall wax taper and crosses himself three times. He fills his earthenware incense holder with burning embers and a few pellets of
incense, letting the fragrance rise to the saint's picture on the wall.
The ritual continues as he wafts incense toward himself and each

[2] Žito is only served at the slavas of saints who are believed to be dead, for it is a
ceremonial offering associated with death. None is made by households who slava on
Archangel Michael's Day, for example, "because he is still alive."

guest, and blesses them and his family. The invited people reply with toasts to the health and prosperity of the host's household, punctuating every wish with murmurs of "God grant it!" A young girl or a ritually clean woman carries in the slava kolač, which is adorned with the holy seal, a small serpentine candle, a red apple, and a sprig of sweet basil, and she places it before the domaćin. With the assistance of the guest of honor, he performs the bread-breaking ceremony, considered the most important part of the slava. The loaf is cut along the lines of a cross, turned by both pairs of hands and broken into quarters. A few drops of red wine are poured on the cut surface and the men declare in unison, "Christ is in our midst, now and forever, Amen." The ritual is performed three times, and each time the men kiss each other on the lips and on both cheeks.

Portions of the holy bread are distributed to everyone, and then the bowls of holiday food are brought in. Cubes of roast pig, with creamy layers of fat and crackling brown skin, are eaten with the fingers, with the aid of a pocket knife. The host never lets his guests' glasses become empty. Even when the feast is officially over platters of meat and cookies are put on the table for people to nibble at as they sit drinking, singing, and telling stories. The party lasts well into the night, especially if someone present plays the gusle.

EASTER, THE PRINCIPAL CHURCH HOLIDAY

Easter is the Orthodox Church's greatest festival, *Velki post*, the Great Fast, or Lent, lasts for seven weeks before Easter. Each week is known by a special name and is accompanied by rituals of cleansing, rejoicing, or solemn reflection. On *Lazarova subota*, Lazar's Saturday (or *Vrbica*, Willow Day, as it is also known), before the war the priest and the school teachers used to lead the children out to the meadows to gather flowers to adorn the church. The children were dressed in their best outfits and it was a gala day. On the next day, Palm Sunday, children were taken to church to receive the priest's blessing, but this, too, is no longer practiced by most people.

The village church is crowded on Great Thursday, when the

story of the Crucifixion is read. Everyone holds a lighted yellow candle in the shadowy church, and alternately extinguishes and relights it at prescribed times during the reading of *stradanje hristovo*, the Sufferings of Christ. The glow of hundreds of candles shimmers on the walls, and the thick, sweet smell of incense fills the air.

Another important event of the Easter season is now *veliki petak*, Good Friday, which is also a regular market day in Arandjelovac. Everyone, but especially the young people, dress in their holiday clothes and promenade up and down the town's single cobble-stoned street.

As early as two or three o'clock in the morning, villagers arise on Easter Sunday, pack a breakfast in their carrying sacks or wicker baskets, and set out over the dark lanes for the church. Upon entering church, each person kisses the icon and places an offering of hyacinths and other spring flowers on the side. Soon the little church is filled to overflowing with a capacity congregation that will not occur again until the following year. Individual candles are lighted from a great taper on the altar, and the villagers, bearing their flickering lights, form a procession following the priest outside the church and moving three times around it. Communion is given when they return inside, and at sunrise the service is over. People step out into the early morning sunshine joyously calling, *"Hristos vaskrese!"* (Christ is risen!) and receiving the reply, *"Vaistinu vaskrese!"* (Indeed He is risen!). The fast is broken by a picnic in the yard, and men press one another to sample their best *rakija* and wine. Children and adults alike enjoy the game of tapping Easter eggs, colored with homemade onionskin and berry dyes, and collecting those they have won by cracking them in the contest.

SOME BELIEFS AND CUSTOMS

Some traditional observances are often closely bound up with folk beliefs and customs not directly connected with the church. One of the most interesting which still persists occurs early in May, on the eve of *Djurdjevdan*, Saint George's Day. During the night youths and maidens and even some older people, sometimes accompanied by an accordionist, meet out in the moonlight in a meadow or grassy dell, where they sing and dance and pick boughs of willow, dogwood, beech, and hawthorne. The girls bend willow branches to wear as wreaths around their waists and later carry armloads of boughs home to decorate the cottages. Each type of branch is thought to have a symbolic significance—growth, fertility, health, and so on. This event is known as *uranak* and locally as *hajdučki sastanak*—named after the times when the highwaymen met after leaving their winter quarters. The girls wash their faces in the dew on the grass and flowers, "to give us beautiful complexions." They weave wreaths of field flowers to toss over the gateposts, on the roof, and in the well of each home, for good health and good luck. The whole custom has nothing to do with St. George's Day itself except in the sense that his day represents a sort of May Day heralding Spring.

Both this festival of Spring and the *dodola* rain-making rites described below are folk customs which probably date from pre-Christian times. In Šumadija rainfall is fairly equable throughout the year, but sometimes there are severe droughts which can ruin the crops and the peasants' economy for the year. When such a disaster seems to be at hand, villagers invite a young Gypsy girl. They dress her in a skirt and cape of thick leaves, and she is led from household to household where she dances and sways, chanting for rain. This is a well-known rite in many parts of eastern Yugoslavia, and the version of the chant sung in Orašac is:

> Oj, Dodo, Dodole! Da porosi rosna kiša!
> Oj, Dodo, Dodole! Da nam rodi pšenica belica!
> Oj, Dodo, Dodole! I u polju vinova lozica!
> Oj, Dodo, Dodole! I livade i travica!
>
> Oh, Dodo, Dodola! Let the gentle rains come!
> Oh, Dodo, Dodola! So we can harvest white wheat!
> Oh, Dodo, Dodola! And in the fields, grape vines!
> Oh, Dodo, Dodola! And meadowlands and grasses!

As each chorus is chanted the housewife pours a bucket of water over her. She is presented with a small gift, some flour, bacon, or fruit, and is led on to the next house to repeat the ritual.

THE CHRISTMAS SEASON

Christmas is the holiday children like best. It is not associated with gift-giving, as in most of the Western world. Instead, on two Sundays preceding Christmas there occur *materice* (Mother's Day) and *očevi* (Father's Day). For Mother's Day each mother prepares gifts of cookies, fruit, and perhaps new pairs of mittens for her children and hides them under her mattress. The children creep over to the bed in the morning and bind her legs with string, threatening not to let her loose unless she buys her freedom with the presents they know very well she has hidden out of sight. On Father's Day the children repeat the teasing and in return for their efforts receive a few coins and trinkets from their father or grandfather.

The Orthodox Christmas, *Božić*, falls on January 7 of the modern calendar. Two days before, a pig, ram, or ewe is slaughtered and prepared for the holiday meal. The next day, *Badnjidan*, one of the men of the house sets out through the woods to cut down a young oak tree. Toward nightfall on Christmas Eve the domaćin ceremoniously carries in the *badnjak*, a yule log cut from this tree, and lights the hearth with it. Today it is thrust into the stove, with an end protruding. As he steps over his threshold he cries, "*Hristos se rodi!*" (Christ is born!), and the others call back, "*Vaistinu se rodi*" (Indeed He is born!). He then extends Christmas congratulations and wishes for the health and prosperity of his home. His family reply emphatically, "God grant it!" Two more logs are carried in and put in the oven, and the domaćin bends down to kiss the logs and cross himself three times in the name of the Father, the Son, and the Holy Ghost. Then he recites, "As I have kissed this yule log, may the cow have calves, the ewe lambs, the sow piglets, the hen chicks, and may every soul in my household have luck and a productive year!"

The next ritual is one the children eagerly await. A younger man of the house hoists a large sack stuffed with straw over his shoulder and goes outdoors. The women and children follow, clinging to the sack. Imitating hens, the women cry, "*Kvok, kvok, kvok,*" while the children hop gleefully behind cheeping, "*Piju,*

piju, piju," like young chicks. This procession circles the house three times.

When they return into the house, straw is scattered on the floor, "because Christ was born in the straw," and the family sits down to the last fasting meal—today sometimes the only one—before Christmas. The incense burner is prepared, a tall yellow candle lighted, and everyone prays together before eating. Each member of the family gets a little loaf of bread made especially for him. The females' loaves are usually in the shape of braids and the males' in the form of various types of livestock. In Orašac the meal is traditionally concluded with a special gibanica filled with apples and nuts, and made with sunflower seed oil in place of the prohibited lard.

In most houses in the village all meals are eaten on the straw for three days, and only in a very few is the custom of sleeping on the straw, with all of the members of the family facing East, still followed. The floor is not cleaned or swept during this period, "for if you do there will be a lot of bugs in the summer."

It is felt that an undesirable caller on Christmas morning can bring bad luck to the house. This is counteracted by having someone from within the household, usually a male child, go out and then rap at the door to gain admittance. In this way the family can always be sure of the character of the *polaženik*, or first guest. He enters calling, "Christ is born!" and is warmly received. The domaćica tosses a handful of grain on him as he comes in; the child kneels before the fire and strikes the yule-log with his own branch so that the sparks fly. Then he chants, "As many sparks from this fire, so much health, luck, and good will among the people of our house." Other members repeat the blessing and then, with the child as guest of honor, sit down on the straw to break the Christmas fast.

A special Christmas loaf is baked with a coin in it: whoever gets the coin will be lucky for the coming year. In many Orašac households the coin is later plastered to the ceiling with sticky dough, and it is considered a good omen as long as it remains stuck there. Before the feast, bread is broken in the same manner as for the slava and is placed on the straw along with a sieve of grain and the shell of the hard-boiled egg the polaženik has been given to eat. The meal is traditional holiday fare, with the addition of small square cookies stamped with a waffle pattern, made only for Christmas, and the favorite winter drink, *vruća rakija*, hot sweetened brandy.[3]

Religion, then, is an intimate part of the daily lives of the villagers, taking on a more formalized aspect, with church activities and prescribed rituals, at certain important times during the year. Bound up with it are various folk beliefs which have persisted through time. How the post-war government has affected these customs and the position of the church in the village today are discussed in the following chapter.

[3] This drink is well known in many parts of Yugoslavia as *Šumadinski čaj*, or Šumadijan tea.

CHAPTER 11

GOVERNMENT AND THE VILLAGE

THIS CHAPTER has two purposes: first, to describe the traditional organs of the government in the village, namely the school and the Village Council, and, second, to analyze the effect of postwar government policies on Orašac society. These subjects are, of course, closely interrelated and are best discussed together. Included here are a brief historical review of Orašac during the Second World War and the coming to power of the present government; the village school—a summary of its development and an examination of pre- and post-war educational policies; government action with regard to agriculture, including land reforms, cooperatives, and the state farm; a discussion of a proposed United Nations plan for community development in Orašac; and, finally, the function of the Village Council and the role of the Communist Party in village affairs.

THE SECOND WORLD WAR AND THE EMERGENCE OF THE
FEDERATED PEOPLE'S REPUBLIC OF YUGOSLAVIA

Prior to the Second World War Yugoslavia was a constitutional monarchy in form, although for much of the period between the two World Wars power was concentrated in the hands of King Alexander, and later his cousin, Prince Paul. The formation of a stable democratic government was prevented largely by the bitter rivalry between the Serbs and Croats. On March 25, 1941, Cvetković, the Prime Minister of Yugoslavia, signed the Tripartite Pact, aligning Yugoslavia with the Axis powers. This move was extremely unpopular among the people, and two days later the army overthrew the government, ending Paul's regency by declaring King Peter II of age. General Simović was installed as Prime Minister.

The new government had no chance to prove itself, for on April 6 Hitler declared war on Yugoslavia, and by April 19 the German forces were in control. For the second time in less than thirty years Orašac and the whole of Serbia were occupied by the German Army.[1] Almost immediately after the collapse of the Yugoslav Army, the two rival fighting groups, the Četniks and Partisans, were formed. The former were led mostly by officers in the Royal Yugoslav Army and by some intellectuals, while the majority of the soldiers were Serbian peasants. In contrast, the Partisans under Tito, the pre-war Secretary of the Communist Party, were made up of urban workers and later included peasants as well. Many of their most prominent leaders were pre-war members of the Party. Consequently, many of General Mihailović's Četnik forces were not too mobile and local commanders enjoyed considerable autonomy, while the Partisans were more tightly disciplined and highly mobile.[2] Another difference was that the Partisans were willing to fight the Germans no matter what reprisal they might take on the civilian population, while the Četniks looked toward the day of their ultimate liberation by the Allies.

In 1941 a few attempts were made by the two groups to cooperate, but before long they were fighting each other as well as the Germans. During the early part of the war both forces were aided by the British and Americans, and military missions were maintained at their headquarters. Toward the end of the war Allied support was withdrawn from Mihailović, and in 1945 the United States and Britain recognized Tito's Partisans as the official government of Yugoslavia.[3]

Central Šumadija was the scene of intensive fighting among Germans, Četniks, and Partisans. In Orašac itself, only the im-

[1] Orašac was under Austro-Hungarian occupation from 1915 to 1918.
[2] The Partisans fought all over Yugoslavia while Četnik operations were limited mainly to Serbia.
[3] The precise reasons for these developments are still far from clear. Merely a brief factual background has been attempted here.

mediate area around the mine was occupied, and production was
maintained during most of the war. There was also a German
detachment quartered in Arandjelovac. Although the Germans
retaliated severely on the population in other parts of Šumadija,
especially in its largest city, Kragujevac,[4] their rule in Orašac was
not nearly as harsh. In the early days of the occupation a few villagers were seized as hostages because of insufficient speed on the
part of the peasants in meeting the Germans' demands for grain
and other food supplies. When the material was delivered they were
released. Later several peasants were shot by the Germans because they were found on the road when a German military convoy
was passing through—all Serbs had been ordered to keep out of
sight under penalty of death.

In Orašac there was considerable fighting between the Četniks
and Partisans. In one such clash in 1943, a section of the village
was burned and over a hundred people were made homeless.
Most of the population fled Orašac for a few weeks, seeking refuge
with friends and relatives in other villages. Orašac supplied both
Partisan and Četnik fighters and suffered over a hundred cas-
ualties, including soldiers and civilians. Enmities were created
among clan groups which to some extent still persist today.[5]
By the latter part of 1944, the Četniks had been largely eliminated
and Orašac and the surrounding region came under Partisan
control. A good number of peasants were conscripted for the final
drive against the Germans.[6]

Today there is a monument to fallen Partisans near the Village
Council building, and a small museum in Arandjelovac is devoted
to the history of the Partisans in the Second World War. There
are also other monuments scattered throughout the countryside
commemorating the Partisans' victories. These sites are visited by

[4] Several thousand civilians, including a large number of school children, were
massacred there.

[5] No attempt was made to collect data on this topic, for it is still a very controversial
and highly emotionally charged subject.

[6] According to official estimates, about 200 Orašac men were Partisans and 10 were
Četniks; of this number 45 Partisans and 6 Četniks were killed in fighting outside the
village, and nine more men were killed in fighting within Orašac. Seventy men were
taken as German prisoners early in the war, and all but two eventually returned. The
above figure of 200 Partisans includes men drafted into the Yugoslav Army at the end
of the war.

the school children when they learn about the history of the Partisan Movement and the "National War of Liberation."

THE SCHOOL IN ORAŠAC

The school is one of the main focal points of government influence in the village. Village schools were virtually nonexistent at the time of the First Revolt, but during the first few decades of the nineteenth century a number were established, including one in the neighboring village of Bukovik. The few Orašac children for whom it was possible attended classes there. Despite difficulties an elementary school was established in Orašac in the home of a private peasant in 1856. Plans for a permanent school were further advanced and conservative opposition overcome in an individualistic way. The following account is as revealing with regard to Orašac politics as it is to the history of the school:

Stevan Lukić, the President of the Village Council, raised the question of building a schoolhouse. On his own initiative he ordered every house in the village to contribute ten dinars for the building costs, although such an act was illegal. By 1880 the school had been erected with one classroom and a room for the teacher.[7] Some of the people did not like what Stevan Lukić had done, and they complained to the *Načelnik* [head of the District] in Kragujevac. He came to Orašac personally to conduct an investigation. He reproached Stevan Lukić for building the school in a way which was against the law but told him that he was forgiven because he had done well.[8]

But troubles did not end here because at that time the main support for the school came from the village itself. Teachers were also a problem. They often had very little formal education themselves, on account of the small pay they received. They were appointed by the central government and were frequently transferred. There was also strong sentiment against a girl receiving an education. Most of the peasants, however, were very anxious that their children, especially the boys, receive an education whatever

[7] Now used as teachers' quarters.
[8] This account is part of a manuscript on "The History of the School in Orašac," written by one of the former teachers and deposited in the school archives.

the sacrifices involved. The great desire for schooling and some idea of the difficulties encountered are revealed in this account by the author of Autobiography G, describing his school situation in the 1890s:

All the pupils were boys because at that time nobody even thought about the education of girls. The schoolteachers were often transferred. For example, in my first year of school there were five different teachers. The real time of learning was only two or three months, and the results on tests were next to nothing. From the first to the second grade only I passed, and from the second to the third three passed, and from the third to the fourth there were none, so that for the next year there was no fourth grade.[9]

Teachers usually finished Teacher's School, and some of them had finished *Bogoslovija* [high school for priests], but very frequently they had only four grades of high school. They could be transferred by the President of the Opština or another politician if they did not belong to the same party. No one cared what the children were taught.

Our situation was just a bit better, for while I was in the second and third grades our teacher was an ordained priest who was waiting to receive a parish. When he got his parish he left us, and our teacher in the fourth grade was an old widower with two sons and five daughters and, I think, two grades of high school. His salary was fifty dinars a month, and he was transferred from one part of Serbia to another at least two or three times a year. Under this instruction I finished the fourth grade and was awarded a book for being a good pupil. By the way, I have to say that there were only four of us in the fourth grade.

The building, or should I say the one schoolroom, was uncomfortable, the furniture crude, and the materials of very poor quality. The school was supported by the Opština by means of taxes that were never collected in full or on time. Pupils who finished the fourth grade could not even think about continuing their studies, especially if they came from poor homes. The only thing they could do was to become apprenticed to a merchant or return to work on the land. . . .

After the First World War, as a result of considerable urging on the local level and with contributions both from the village and the national government, a new school was built in Orašac. It was

[9] The school had only four grades.

dedicated by King Alexander on the anniversary of the First Revolt. In 1950 an eight-year school was established in the village, with nine teachers, as compared to three or four before the war. The physical facilities have remained the same.[10] This development has undoubtedly enabled a larger number of children to complete eight years of school than was previously possible.[11]

With the increase in opportunities for education there has been a corresponding decrease in the illiteracy rate. In 1866 only 33 people, or about 3 percent of the population, were literate; by 1953 over 60 percent of the population were in this category. Almost as significant as this increase has been the elimination of the sharp disparity between the sexes. In 1895 the number of literate men outnumbered that of literate women by over 30 to 1. Although the ratio is reaching unity, as shown by Figure 26, by 1953 the number of male literates was still 30 percent greater than that of their female counterparts. Most of the remaining illiterates in 1953 were among the older people, especially the women. The pivotal age for 1953 seems to be forty-five, the overwhelming majority of women over that age not being literate. No one in 1948 had a university education, while twenty-one villagers had completed twelve years of school, i.e., had been graduated from high school. They included the schoolteachers and the priest. Of all villagers over fifteen years of age, 6 percent had completed eight years, and most of the literate village population had four years of schooling. In 1953–54, however, it was estimated that approximately ten students from Orašac were pursuing studies on a university level, chiefly in agronomy and engineering.

In 1953 the local school situation was better than it had been in any years past. In addition to the principal, who did some teaching, there were eight regular teachers, three of them men and five women. One man taught full-time at the auxiliary four-grade schoolroom in the Gajevi neighborhood. In the lower grades one teacher handled the class in all subjects, and specialized courses

[10] Pupils previously had to go to Arandjelovac for the full eight years of high school. Now they go only for the final four years.

[11] Despite this lack of formal educational facilities, from the time of the First Revolt Orašac and other villages throughout Serbia have been the source of many of the army officers, government officials, and professional people of the Serbian nation.

by different instructors were taught in the four upper grades. A seventh-grade program as of February, 1954, included basic courses in history, Serbian, and mathematics, in addition to instruction in biology, chemistry, and physics. At present Russian is the only foreign language taught because there is no teacher qualified for any other. Agriculture, drawing, hygiene, and physical education are also given.

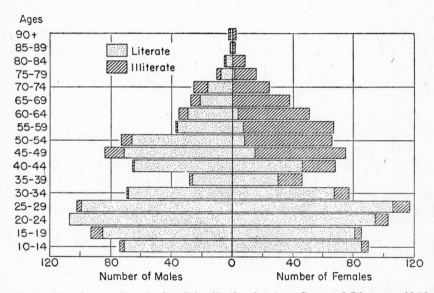

Figure 26. Orašac Population Distribution by Age, Sex, and Literacy, 1953

Source: Serbian Statistical Bureau.

Most of the teachers are young (only two are over thirty) and appear to have considerable interest in their work. The teaching methods used, especially in the upper grades, rely heavily on recitation from memory, based on textbook work. Individualism and special projects are not encouraged. The teachers demand strict discipline and usually get it, and homework is always handed in on time. Classes are held six days a week, and school usually meets in split shifts, so that the teachers have a fairly heavy schedule.

The school building itself is adequate, in fact better than most village schools, having been built as a memorial to the First Revolt. Equipment for classwork, especially visual aids for science courses, is quite up to date. The big lack is in sanitary facilities. The principal was aware of this and frequently complained about it, claiming that plans were under way to alleviate the situation.

One of the most important changes in village education has been in the relationship of school and church. Before the war these two institutions worked together very closely. Customs described in the last chapter and the summary of traditional village observances bear this out. Today the situation is completely different, the basis for the new policy having been proclaimed in Article 25 of the 1946 Constitution:

Freedom of conscience and freedom of religion are guaranteed to citizens.

The Church is separate from the state.

Religious communities whose teaching is not contrary to the Constitution are free in their religious affairs and in the performance of religious ceremonies. Religious schools for the education of priests are free and are under the state.

The abuse of the Church and of religion for political purposes and the existence of political organizations on a religious basis are forbidden.

The state may extend material assistance to religious communities.[12]

In concrete terms applied to the village, this has meant that in the school državni praznici, or state holidays, have replaced all the traditional religious ones. These state holidays are given in the list, "Yearly Activities at Village School." The most important are the First of May (International Labor Holiday), the anniversary of the Day of the Founding of the Republic (November 29, 1943), and New Year's Day (New Style Calendar).

At the same time, school attendance is now compulsory on the day of the pupil's family's slava, Christmas, and other big traditional holidays. On Christmas Day (January 7, 1954) there were very few absences, despite the customary festivities going on at home

[12] Quoted in Kerner, ed., Yugoslavia, p. 491.

Yearly Activities at Village School, Including State Holidays, 1954

New Year's Day
    Party at school, with trimmed tree, candy and
    cookies, singing, plays
	January 1–2

Winter Vacation	January 15—February 1
First of May No school, parade in Arandjelovac	May 1–2

Tito's Birthday
    Special compositions assigned and discussions in all
    classes
	May 25

Summer Vacation	June 20—September 6

Final Examinations
    Mala matura, comprehensive examination for eighth-
    grade graduates, and final examinations for all
    grades
	June 10–20

Repeat Examinations For all grades	End of August
Beginning of New School Term	First Monday in September
Day of the Founding of the Republic No school	November 29–30
Army Day Special lessons prepared	December 22

and the unusually deep snow.[13] The Village Council offices, general store, and kafana were all open as usual, too.

As in the towns, there has been a strong attempt to replace traditional Christmas celebrations with a New Year's festivity. Since the latter occurs a week before the Orthodox holiday, it definitely decreases the importance of Christmas in the eyes of

[13] In practice the smaller children are not punished if they stay home from school for Christmas or the slava, but for those in the upper grades attendance is strictly required. This is part of a government policy which distinguishes between official state holidays and religious ones. To quote Tito on this subject: "If someone in our country wishes to celebrate those holidays which are recognized only by the Church and not the State, this is his own private affair. We, however, cannot pay people in government service for the time spent outside their business offices on holidays which are not recognized by the State. We have a fixed number of State holidays." "President Tito Interviewed by Sherwood Eddy Seminar," *Yugoslav Review,* V, No. 7 (September, 1955), 15.

In Orašac and other villages this is something of a reciprocal relationship, for the authorities clearly realize that should they schedule a meeting at the time of some important religious event they would not be likely to get a sizeable attendance.

most of the children. The last few years have seen the innovation of a trimmed New Year's tree (topped by a red star) and a jolly old man in the form of *Deda Mraz*, or Grandpa Frost, both familiar to Westerners and both very appealing to the children. A party is held at the school and the children receive gifts of fruit, nuts, and candy, purchased with a fund donated by the school and supplemented by the parents. It is a high point of the school year, and all the pupils talk about it for days afterward. To most children, however, it is just an extra bonus, for they participate with enjoyment in all the traditional religious customs and rituals when they return home from school.

When twelve-year-olds were asked to tell about "My Favorite Holiday" in a school assignment, every composition submitted dealt with a state holiday. Had they been written at home and not sponsored by the school, it is probable that the slava, Christmas, or Easter would be high on the list. The purpose in quoting two of them here, however, is to show the influence of the school in molding village children's attitudes.

A. My favorite holiday is New Year's Day. It is celebrated by all the people of our country, all the workers and others. A few years ago New Year's Day wasn't celebrated because of the many wars. Today our people are cultured and they always celebrate the New Year.

A few days ago we celebrated the New Year, and all the workers, miners, and the rest of the people didn't work on that day. We pupils, too, celebrated the New Year, and this time we celebrated the 1954 New Year. All of us gave thirty dinars each. Some didn't give but they took part anyhow. We prepared a decorated fir tree and gift packages at school on New Year's Eve. On Thursday at midnight people in cities and villages waited for the New Year. On New Year's Day we came to the party at school to receive New Year's presents and to attend the eighth grade's performance. We had folk dancing and sang in a chorus. Then we received packages and returned home.

B. Among all the State Holidays I like the First of May best. The holiday of work and victory is celebrated by all our people all over the world. Between 1941 and 1945 we were under German occupation, and on the First of May, 1945, we were liberated and became free. Under the

Germans many workers and peasants secretly went to the forest and there built campfires and celebrated the First of May.

Only after we were liberated from the enemy were we able to freely celebrate the First of May and other state holidays and to begin our Five Year Plan with Comrade Tito at the head. Such were all the movements of our People's Liberation War which united our peoples in the brotherly union, the Federated People's Republic of Yugoslavia. On May First, all the pupils gather near the school and sing and dance with delight. After that the pupils of our school give a performance followed by dancing. Because they got their love for freedom on May First, this day is an important and great holiday. I like the First of May because we were liberated and because it is spring, and spring is the most beautiful season.

The principal of the school and several of the teachers are members of the Communist Party. Great stress is laid on the aims and achievements of the "New Yugoslavia" and the virtues of Tito. Particularly significant for the peasant children is the strong emphasis on the industrialization of Yugoslavia, both in terms of plans and accomplishments. It would not be true to say that agriculture is completely neglected as there is a special course on the subject for the upper grades, but by far the greater stress is on industry. The effect of this schooling is shown in a series of essays written by eighth-graders (fourteen to fifteen years old) on "What I Want to Be and Why."

A. Every year many new factories begin to operate. Every year many shock workers and innovators are proclaimed, and every year we get new and better products for our people, and that is the reason why I have become enthusiastic about our industry which will give man a better life.

As a youth I have become enthusiastic about the accomplishments of our heavy industry, and it has crept into my soul that I would like to learn a trade because I know that our metalworkers were our best fighters in the underground and later on in our War of National Liberation. I have learned about Comrade Tito, and I know that he was a metalworker in a factory for railway cars in Smederevska Palanka, and I know that Djura Djaković also was a metalworker, and Djura Strugar and Rade Končar and many other workers have become national heroes in the war and in peacetime the best fighters for a better tomorrow.

I, as a youth and pupil in the eighth grade, think that when I finish this grade I want to go to learn the trade of the metalworkers, in the tractor factory in Rakovica or in the railway car factory in Smederevska Palanka. From the time when some workers and technicians came to perform a play here in Orašac, I have become enthusiastic about industry, because I have seen that they live in a cultured way and that society has taken care of them. They also work in the interest of society and this is why I am determined, if they accept me as an apprentice, to study one of the metalworking trades, and as such I shall be useful to the Federal People's Republic of Yugoslavia.

B. I entered high school to learn more. As soon as I finish I intend to study to be an electrician, and when I have finished learning my trade I shall take part with my friends in the electrification of the villages and cities as well as in the construction of new hydroelectric plants. The benefit of electrification will be the improvement of every branch of industry in our new socialistic homeland. I shall try to always be among the best. I wouldn't let my friends accuse me of avoiding hard work—No! That won't happen as I am able to work, and I want them to say that I am working as becomes a man who is taking part in the rebuilding of his country. Doing so I shall be of value to my country as well as to myself.

C. When I was a little girl I was hardly able to wait for the time to start school. But I waited and the time finally came. As soon as I began elementary school I began thinking about different occupations such as schoolteacher, doctor, engineer, craftsman, etc. Thinking about these occupations I wanted most to become a schoolteacher. I like this occupation because if I were a schoolteacher I would teach pupils, and by doing so I would spread the new culture to our people. The schoolteacher's work is to emancipate and to make the people literate.

Before the war in the old Yugoslavia a great part of our population was illiterate because there were only a few schoolteachers and only the children of rich parents were admitted to high school. Today in Socialist Yugoslavia much has been done to uproot illiteracy. The children of Socialist Yugoslavia have the right to attend schools without regard to their economic status.

I would like to study to be a teacher because I shall uplift the new generations and lead them to a better future, and in so doing I shall be of great use to myself and to my socialist homeland. That is what I would like to be, but it all depends on my schoolwork and my success.

D. Years go by and my ideas of what I want to become are always changing. After finishing school I shall finally decide what to study, but today I wish I were a sailor.

When I think of a gale I would like to give up the sea, but my wish draws me back when I think that I could go swimming every day. Soon I'll become a sailor and I shall travel on ocean-going ships across the sea and explore the unexplored parts of the world. While the ship will be sailing silently, the sailors busy with some work will hum:

> Through night o'er the seas,
> With the buzz of the motors,
> Onward and onward,
> Sailors of Tito!

So I shall be a faithful son of my homeland and by sailing on the Adriatic Sea I shall guard our borders.

In contrast to the others, the following essay is more reflective and realistic. Of more than twenty compositions submitted, it is the only one that mentions farming as an occupation and that clearly distinguishes between aspirations and concrete possibilities.

E. Years go by and soon I'll be nineteen. Where shall I be studying then, and to what kind of job shall I devote myself? Every occupation is good enough, but a sincere man must do work that will be of help to his people. If we consider that humanity goes forward every day and that nature is no longer the master of man, it is clear that humanity has got to demand a certain quality of work even from the peasant. That doesn't mean that one is to hesitate about doing the work of a peasant because the mechanization of the village has resulted in great progress in cultural affairs as well as in the rebuilding of our country.

If a conscientious man cultivates the land in the proper way, he helps in the rebuilding of the country. If it weren't for agricultural products, all factories would stop. So it is clear that a man is a man whether he works in a village or in a city, and one can't live without the other. If a peasant has difficulty cultivating his land in the proper way he can learn a lot of things through magazines, the radio, and from agricultural experts.

But like the others he, too, has a dream to become a writer—although his dream is perhaps a little more difficult to see come true than the desires of others who wish to become skilled workers or teachers. But unlike the others he realizes that his dream may not be fulfilled.

If I ever do become the writer of my fantasy, and if I meet a friend of mine I would say, "There, friend, my dream came true," or if I remain in the village to be a good farmer I would meet my friend with the words, "There was a fantasy, but it disappeared, and I remained a peasant." But everyday a peasant gets better machines and is in accord with writers and other cultural workers.

If asked, "Why do you like literature?" I would answer that I like it as a tool to make something useful for my people as well as for all peoples, and to show them how to work and how to have a better life in today's world. I like those writers who have traveled around to teach people, to lead them out of darkness and religious things, and the writers who have instructed them in progress and betterment. This is a vast field and everyone can work in it, educated or not. For we know from our experience that one can be educated and still be coarse.

Finally, why I would like to become a writer. Not to become famous but to leave after me a work of help to our people. I would like to enrich our literature because I think the struggle of our people, its childhood, and the darkness of the Turkish period have not been satisfactorily described. Once again I say this is only a fantasy that sometime may come true but that often may be spoiled when we least expect it.

These essays show great variation in style and in objectives, but they all have one thing in common—the theme that one's life work must be concerned with aiding the social and economic progress of the country. If past patterns hold true, only a small minority of those who complete the eighth grade will leave the village. Thus, those who do not continue their schooling or take an apprenticeship but remain in the village will have something of a problem in adjusting to normal village life, particularly since today most of them feel that the term *seljak*, or peasant, is a negative one. At the time of this study, however, it was too early to make any meaningful statements on this matter because the eighth-year class represented the first group of graduates from that grade. That the question may be a significant one in the future is indicated by the school registration figures, which are higher than they have ever been.

Part of the children's attitude is the result of intensive indoctrination, yet there is no question but that it also represents a certain amount of genuine enthusiasm. One of the most important ways in which interest has been stimulated is excursions. These include trips to local Partisan monuments and to factories in Arandjelovac as well as train excursions to Belgrade, Smederevo, and other towns. The cost of such trips is relatively low, so that most parents are able to afford them. Their significance is further heightened when it is realized that although most adults have been to Belgrade at least once, many of them, particularly the women, have seldom been anywhere else outside of the few regional market towns. Descriptions of these school-sponsored visits, such as the following, were included in some of the compositions about most memorable childhood experiences:

When I was in the fourth grade we made an excursion to Belgrade. There we saw Pioneer City[14] and the zoo and visited a circus, which interested us most. We spent four days in Belgrade. On the way back we sang with our teachers on the train. In the fifth grade we made an excursion to Smederevo, where we slept in the school there. We went to the Danube and took a ride on a boat. Later we visited a lead and zinc mine where I saw how the ore is dug. . . .

Even those children who write about things within the village apparently feel obliged to do so in terms of industrialization and "cultural" improvements, as in this essay by a twelve-year-old girl:

Our village is pretty and neat. Behind it there is a little hill and below it a flat plain running to Misača Creek.

The hill is covered with oak trees. In the spring we graze the livestock there. From the other side of the hill one can see Arandjelovac with its factory smokestacks. Many peasants from our village are working there.

In 1952 poles for electricity were erected along the road. Many villages in the county will be electrified. That will be a great event for our people. We will no longer sit in the dark or strain our eyes with kerosene lamps as our brothers, sisters, and parents did. Today electric bulbs will glow in our homes.

[14] A children's summer camp located in a large park outside the capital.

In the middle of our village is our school. This winter the big Cooperative Home will be completed. It is close to the school. In that Home our parents will gather to discuss the progress of our village. We Pioneers, too, shall go to the Home and sing joyous youth songs.

One more indicator of the attitudes and interests of the village school children is their drawings. The upper grades were asked in school to prepare drawings or paintings on any subject they wished. The subject matter ranged from everyday scenes around the village to impressive hydroelectric installations copied from textbooks. Only original drawings were eligible to be submitted in a contest which the principal and we sponsored (although the fourth and fifth pictures included here have elements recognized as being from schoolbooks). The teachers and the children themselves judged the contest, and six of the winning pictures are reproduced on the following pages.

GOVERNMENT AGRICULTURAL POLICIES

The changes in the school have been significant chiefly from an ideological viewpoint. Those in agriculture are mainly economic, but both are connected by a common underlying philosophy of government policy.

After peace had been established in 1945 the government was faced with an enormous task of reconstruction. During this period Yugoslavia was aided by several large grants from UNRRA, in the form of food, agricultural machinery, and other supplies. That the Orašac villagers benefited from this help can be seen from the old cartons and tins bearing the names of General Foods and other concerns, still found in some homes. In addition, one of the tractors used by the state farm, a privately owned seeder, and some small machinery originally came to Yugoslavia under UNRRA auspices.

Generous as all the aid was, it could not, of course, completely reestablish the Yugoslav economy.[15] Basic policies in agriculture were set down in the 1946 Constitution in Article 19:

[15] From the end of the war to 1948, UNRRA expenditures in Yugoslavia totaled $480,000,000.00.

Figure 27. Peasant Woman
Spinning Flax

by Radomir, Seventh Grade

Figure 28. Peasant
Plowing with Cows

by Branko, Seventh Grade

Figure 29. Shepherd Watching His Sheep
by Milena, Sixth Grade

Figure 30. Peasant Plowing with Tractor
by Dragan, Eighth Grade

Figure 31. Miloš Obilić

by **Kosta**, Seventh Grade

Figure 32. The Partisans

by **Dragoslav**, Eighth Grade

The land belongs to those who cultivate it.

The law determines whether and how much land may be owned by an institution or a person who is not a cultivator.

There can be no large landholdings in private hands on any basis whatsoever.

The maximum size of private landholdings will be determined by law.

The state particularly protects and assists poor peasants and peasants with medium-sized holdings by its general economic policy, its low rates of credit, and its tax system.[16]

Under a land reform program instituted in 1945 all arable land above the legal maximum of 25 to 35 hectares was taken over by the state. This program had virtually no effect on Orašac (nor on most of the county) since peasant holdings were well under this size. A government policy which did affect the village was the system of compulsory deliveries instituted soon after the Communists came to power. Quotas at fixed prices were established for grain, livestock products, poultry, and fruit, which were channeled to the government through the purchasing and consumer cooperatives newly established in the villages. The objectives of this program were twofold: first, to ensure a supply of food products for the cities and a basis for the projected program of industrialization; second, to provide the state with a weapon for use against the "kulaks" (the former gazde),[17] who were regarded as one of the chief obstacles to government policies. Proportionately higher quotas were established for the more prosperous peasants, and severe penalties were imposed on those who failed to comply, including jail sentences and confiscation of all or part of their land.[18]

Progressive taxation has also been used as an instrument for altering the economic structure of the village. Tax rates were established locally, according to the estimated income from the

[16] Quoted in Kerner, ed., *Yugoslavia*, p. 490.

[17] The Russian term kulak is now an established part of the peasant vocabulary.

[18] See Autobiography *C* in Chapter 9. Progressive delivery quotas were fixed according to the size of landholdings: in 1948 compulsory deliveries on two to three hectares were 10 to 20 percent of the yield, on three to ten hectares, 15 to 55 percent of the yield. See Rašić, *Agricultural Development in Yugoslavia*, p. 41. This system was abolished in the summer of 1952.

sale of surplus farm products, ranging from seven to thirty-three percent in Orašac. These figures in themselves are not too significant because of the manner in which the assessments were formulated—the local officials assigned the highest assessments to the kulaks.[19] In 1951 a new tax system was introduced. Levies are now assessed according to objective criteria—the size of holding and the quality of land. This is held to be a more satisfactory arrangement, because the former system, where the rate was based on productivity, was considered to have penalized the better farmers. In addition to these taxes there are special ones for wine and rakija.

The peasant can sell any or all of his products to the state at reduced prices, with considerable reduction in taxes, but most villagers prefer to trade on the free market. One result of these policies seems to be increased consumption at home, particularly among the peasants with the largest surpluses, rather than marketing of products. An example of this tendency is the much greater use of wheat flour in the post-war period, compared to earlier times when it was mostly for marketing.

Beginning at the Fifth Congress of the Communist Party in Belgrade in 1948, shortly after the break with the Soviet bloc and continuing until 1952, emphasis was placed on the Peasant Working Cooperatives as a means of bringing about "the socialist transformation of the village." These were in the main the type of cooperative where members pooled their land and retained only a small individual plot for personal use. They were also allowed to keep a limited amount of livestock. The number of such Cooperatives in Yugoslavia grew rapidly, from 1,318 in 1948 to 6,797 in 1951.[20] Yet even at the height of their development, in 1950, all these Working Cooperatives never embraced more than 19.4 percent of the arable land in the country.

[19] This was part of a national policy. To quote an official Yugoslav source, "Thus for instance in 1947, 54.2% of total income tax derived from agriculture was levied from holdings with an income of 50,000 dinars [or more], which accounted for 8.2% of the total number of all holdings, while only 10.7% of all taxes were levied from holdings with a 16,000 dinar income, which were the most numerous." Rašić, *Agricultural Development in Yugoslavia*, p. 41.

[20] Tomasevich, "Collectivization of Agriculture in Yugoslavia," pp. 6–7.

Eighty-seven percent of all agricultural holdings and 61 percent of all agricultural land was in the hands of private peasants.[21] This development was reflected in Orašac and Orašac County. In 1953 6.5 percent of Orašac village households belonged to the local Peasant Working Cooperative.

The Cooperatives were given very favorable tax concessions. In Orašac, for example, the members' households paid under 3 percent of the taxes in the village. The Cooperatives were also supposed to receive credit from the state for the purchase of supplies and machinery.

Despite the generous aid given by the government, these Cooperatives were a failure. There were several reasons for this development, the most important of which was the very strong attachment of the peasant to his land, a bond that was not easily broken. In fact, many of the peasants who supported the government in other matters and who even occupied minor administrative positions were strongly opposed to the cooperative movement and refused to join. Several of those who did join in Orašac were members of the Party, and most of them had little land to begin with (although the Secretary of the local cell owned nine hectares and was a notable exception). Some of the peasants felt that only "lazy people" joined the Cooperative.

The second major factor was that, partly on account of the international situation and partly because of certain currents within the Party, the government was unwilling to use extreme measures of force, such as the Russian Communists did in the early 1930s. In March, 1953, those peasants who wished to were permitted to withdraw. By the end of the year the number of Cooperatives declined to a little over 1,000 for the whole of Yugoslavia. In Orašac, and in most villages in the county, they were dissolved.

This does not mean that all plans for the eventual collectivization of agriculture were abandoned. The official position on this matter has been set forth by Edvard Kardelj, the leading Yugoslav Communist theoretician, in his introduction to the new 1953 Constitution:

[21] Rašić, *Agricultural Development in Yugoslavia*, pp. 39–40.

In theory, therefore, the new Fundamental Law recognizes, first, the sector of social production, on the basis of social ownership of the means of production, i.e., the socialist sector, and, second, the sector of individual handicraft and agricultural production, on the basis of individual implements of work, namely the sector of the individual producer's ownership of the means of production. And this sector under the conditions of a socialist state does not lead necessarily toward capitalism; on the contrary, its gradual socialist transformation without administrative measures and without nationalization, but with the economic help of the socialist sector, is fully possible. Between the two sectors exist of course some transitory forms, whose position must be solved by particular laws on the basis of the provisions of the new fundamental law.[22]

In the furtherance of this policy the law on the "Agricultural Public Fund and the Distribution of Land to Agricultural Organizations" was enacted in May, 1953. Among the official reasons given for this act was that it was designed to prevent the landless peasants who were formerly members of the Peasant Work Co-operatives "from reverting to their former status of hired labourers of the wealthier peasants."[23] Another factor was that it was designed to create a land fund for the establishment of more state farms, intended to "lead the peasant into socialism." This law limited the maximum peasant holding to ten hectares of arable land, and, unlike the earlier reform, it affected a number of peasants in Orašac.[24] Most of these lost a hectare or two. Only three households had more than ten hectares over the maximum.[25] Compensation was provided under this law.

A land fund of some three hundred hectares was thus created from land in Orašac, Misača, Kopljare, and Stojnik,[26] and a state farm was established in the fall of 1953, with headquarters in Orašac. This farm took over the buildings and machinery of the defunct Orašac Working Cooperative. It is not possible to say

[22] Kardelj, "Introduction," in *New Fundamental Law of Yugoslavia*, p. 14.

[23] Rašić, *Agricultural Development in Yugoslavia*, p. 47.

[24] In all, 28 out of 425 households were affected; the largest zadruga, with 22 members and 20 hectares, was permitted to retain its land.

[25] This number was, however, higher than most of the other local villages. Before the reform the largest landowner in Orašac had 40 hectares.

[26] Eighty hectares of this land had previously been confiscated from "enemies of the people."

much about the operation of the state farm since they were planting their first crop when we were last in the village, in the early summer of 1954. Four agronomists were assigned to the project, and an office was set up in the Village Council building in Orašac. According to the chief agronomist, one of the main purposes of the farm will be to show the peasants more modern farming techniques. They also intend to conduct courses at the school.

Judging from the initial reactions of the peasants the agronomists' task will not be an easy one. Many of the villagers fear that the establishment of the state farm is only the prelude to further reforms nationalizing all land holdings over five hectares. These fears have evidently not been limited to Orašac, because Tito and other government leaders have gone out of their way to deny that such measures are planned. Judging by the way other state farms in the area have been managed, the peasants feel that the state operations use poor farming techniques and get a much lower yield than does the average peasant. As one former gazda expressed it, "The government was stupid to take my land. They should have just raised my taxes, for they could get more out of me than they can ever get out of a state farm."

The land itself is of fairly good quality, with forty hectares used as pasture. At present the arable land is scattered in about two hundred different parcels, but the head agronomist said he hoped that before too long it would be consolidated into six or seven places so that machinery could be used to work the land. In addition to cultivating grains the farm also plans to raise livestock. At present they have about thirty pigs. Within six years they intend to have a herd of over a hundred cattle and several thousand chickens.

Currently twenty farm hands are employed full time in addition to the agronomists and several clerks. About half of the workers are from Orašac, the other half coming from Stojnik. During the peak season in summer it is expected that as many as two hundred people may be employed on a part-time basis. They would also like to have two additional agronomists so that they could be permanently assigned to Stojnik and Kopljare villages. There are now three state farms of this type in Orašac County.

A UNITED NATIONS PROJECT IN COMMUNITY DEVELOPMENT

The attempts of the government to reorganize agriculture and to raise living standards in the village have not been limited to collectivization and the organization of state farms. One of the most important innovations has been a series of community development projects sponsored jointly by the Yugoslav Cooperative Union and the Technical Assistance Administration of the United Nations. This program envisions one village community in each of the six republics which would serve as a demonstration center for a project which involves improving health and sanitation and the introduction of methods of canning fruits and vegetables for home consumption. Better methods of marketing agricultural produce and technical advice in the breeding of livestock are also included in the program. The village of Orašac was chosen to be the demonstration center for the Republic of Serbia.[27]

An American agronomist with considerable experience in community development was employed by the United Nations under this program. Preliminary surveys were made of all the selected villages in the country in the spring of 1953, and in September a conference in Slovenia was attended by "community leaders," a man and a woman chosen by the local Cooperative[28] in each of the villages. At this conference films were shown, lectures given, and discussions held in an effort to acquaint the trainees with the objectives of the program. The United Nations expert later visited Orašac on several occasions, at which times open meetings were held in order to stimulate interest and a desire for participation among the villagers. The chief point stressed by the United Nations agronomist was that this was not going to be a program where the peasants would be given equipment and told what to do, but rather a program under which they would learn to help themselves achieve a higher standard of living.

Among the specific objectives of the program were the establish-

---

[27] Another program sponsored by the United Nations Technical Assistance Administration is taking place in the nearby villages of Gornja Šatornja and Jarmenovci. The major emphasis in this second program is electrification.

[28] General purchasing and consumer Cooperative, not related to the older Peasant Working Cooperatives.

ment of a community canning center, where, with the aid of pressure cookers and Mason jars, the peasant women would be taught how to preserve fruits and vegetables; a small pasteurizing plant, to enable villagers to market milk instead of using it for cheese; a small medical station and the building of more sanitary wells and outhouses. The community activities were to be centered in the Cooperative Home which also contains the local tavern and general store.[29]

The discussion periods themselves sometimes turned into occasions for the airing of grievances against government policies and various officials. Some peasants also put forward their own desires for improvement, but no definite moves were made and little stir seems to have been created in the village. The average peasant's conception of the program became quite different than what had been intended. While one of the central themes of the project was the de-emphasis of elaborate machinery as a means for raising living standards and an emphasis on self-help, it was nevertheless decided to give each of the villages in the project a gift of a motion picture projector to promote good will for the United Nations. The net result was that the peasants came to regard the projector and the subsequent possibility of regular movies in the village as the most vital part of the project. There was also considerable confusion as to what "UN" meant. Most villagers thought the projector was part of the American aid program to Yugoslavia and most attempts to explain the difference between the *U.S.* and the *UN* met with little success.

No concrete action was taken on the program during 1954, and as far as can be determined the program has evidently been discontinued (1957).[30] Undoubtedly one of the big difficulties has

[29] In villages all over Yugoslavia, the Cooperative Home was originally intended as a center for government-sponsored community activities. Construction of many of them was begun in the burst of enthusiasm during the first Five-Year Plan and was later abandoned after the break with the Cominform in 1948. The peasants donated both money and labor to the building in the early stages. The Home in Orašac (Zadružni Dom) was completed with substantial government assistance in early 1954, in part because of the United Nations project but also because of the celebration of the One Hundred Fiftieth Anniversary of the First Revolt, in February, 1954, when many important government officials visited the village.

[30] The electrification project (in Šatornja and Jarmenovci) has been making slow but steady progress; by early 1955 the transmission lines had been erected and some of the equipment installed.

been whether a government ideologically committed to the social-
ization of agriculture should be aiding the private peasant.

However, several tentative steps in this direction have been
taken, one being the extension of more liberal credit terms to the
private peasants. In this respect a recent statement by Tito is
interesting:

> Our policy is to promote and secure in the largest possible degree, the
> cooperatives and State farm enterprise which we already have, to mecha-
> nize them to the largest possible extent and increase the productive
> capacity of the land.
>
> This does not mean to say that we leave unaided the small farm enter-
> prises whose produce is small or even nil, sometimes even becoming a
> burden. We have not abandoned the idea that Yugoslavia will succeed
> some day in uniting her small farms and that a *modus vivendi* in this respect
> will be found. A solution to this must be worked out because at the present
> time, we have to import much of our bread. We do not wish to use forcible
> methods. However, we are trying to convince our peasants that this
> method of individual cultivation is not advantageous either to them or
> the country.[31]

GOVERNMENT-SPONSORED IMPROVEMENTS

There have been a number of small projects which have had a
significant impact on the life of the villagers. The earliest of these
was the establishment of an *ambulanta,* or first-aid station, at the
mine in 1944. It is in charge of a man who has had some schooling
and was apprenticed to a doctor for four years. Although he is
not able to take care of serious cases he is of considerable help to
the miners and many villagers as well.

Another development was the formation of a maternity ward in
the small hospital in Arandjelovac in 1950. Since that date a very
small but increasing number of peasant women have been having
their children born there. In the first year of operation one out of
seventy-three Orašac births occurred there; in 1954 the proportion
was 20 percent. Utilization of both the County Hospital and a
health clinic in town has increased in recent years but almost all

---

[31] "President Tito Interviewed by Sherwood Eddy Seminar," *Yugoslav Review,* V,
No. 7 (September, 1955), p. 15.

the use has been by the mixed peasants. The pure agriculturalists, who constituted almost 60 percent of the population of Orašac in 1953, made proportionately little use of these facilities. For example, of the 172 Orašani who visited the clinic in 1954, only 13 percent were pure agriculturalists. This is because they must pay for these services, while mixed agriculturalists who work for the state, and their families, receive free medical care. The matter is not entirely financial, since many peasants still feel that one goes to a hospital only to die.

The biggest single improvement was, of course, the completion of the Cooperative Home. In addition to housing the kafana and store it provides the village with a large assembly hall and with rooms which will eventually serve as community library, discussion rooms, and offices.

Some progress has also been made in the electrification of village homes. This has proceeded very slowly, not only because of the shortage of materials but also because each peasant must pay the full cost of connecting his home to the main line running alongside the road as well as for the installation outlet. Since most of the houses are scattered at some distance from the road this has proved quite a problem. Once the initial cost has been paid the peasant household profits in the long run because the cost of electricity is low and much cheaper than kerosene. Power stoppages are frequent, however, since the plant in Arandjelovac is not adequate to supply both the local industries and private homes. This is not too important to the villager. He uses the electricity only to light his home, one room at a time, and in a few cases for a radio as well, but even so he always has a kerosene lamp handy.

Other activities were chiefly of an educational nature and were connected with the school. These include courses in hygiene and homemaking, given to girls in their mid-teens who had completed school but were not yet married. The sessions were conducted by one of the women teachers, and the emphasis was on proper nutrition and care of babies.[32] A recent addition has been a series of lectures, given by one of the male teachers, on the dangers of aerial bombing and bacteriological warfare. This is presented to adult

---

[32] Similar courses were also given before the war.

villagers by groups, and attendance is compulsory. Literacy courses
are given to some of the older people in the wintertime. There is
also a Red Cross Society, to which a few of the women belong,
which is concerned with matters of health and hygiene. One of
the women teachers is chairman. A Cultural Society, led by the
school principal, maintains a small circulating library (about one
hundred books).

OTHER GOVERNMENT ORGANIZATIONS IN THE VILLAGE

In addition to the school and state farm there are three other governmental organizations in the village: the Communist Party,[33]
the General Cooperative, and the Village Council. The Party is
the most important, although its activities and influence are difficult to define in a precise way since in the village as in the towns
it still retains something of its pre-war secretive character. Thus
not only is its exact composition unknown to the general public,
but since it is rather an elite and carefully chosen group, the average peasant does not go out of his way to inquire in any detailed
way about its membership or activities.[34]

Certain matters were fairly obvious to the majority of peasants,
however. In spite of the fact that the number of Party members
was not common knowledge, many of the most important village
Communists freely admitted their membership. These included
almost all of the village intelligentsia—the principal, most of the
younger teachers, the agronomists, and the director of the coal
mine. The chief exceptions were the older teachers and the priest,
none of whom had much voice in village politics. Many of the
elected and appointed officials and clerks were also members,
although this was not universally true. In Orašac the President
and Secretary of the Village Council were not members of the
Party. But the President of the General Cooperative was, while

[33] The Party is formally not a part of the government on the national level; it is
included here because in the village it very definitely acts as an organ of the government in the sense that it supports its policies and attempts to see that they are carried
out.
[34] Nor did we attempt any detailed investigation of its affairs as such an act would
have prejudiced our continued residence in the community. The comments made here
are based on unsolicited information obtained from local officials as well as on general
observations.

the local Chairman of the Party had previously been President of the Village Council for the maximum of two terms.[35]

As far as rank and file membership is concerned, as might be expected, it came chiefly from the mixed peasants, particularly those who were miners. Age did not seem to be an important factor. Many of them were, however, former Partisans, for during their army service the men receive intense indoctrination, and a number of them return home much more sympathetic to the government, if not members of the Party.

Undoubtedly elements of ambition and expediency are motives for some of the men who join. Some of the members sincerely believe that their belonging will help advance progress in the village, and a few even go to the formerly unheard-of extreme of being painfully honest with the tax collector.

Sacrifices are sometimes demanded of Party members. Shortly after the war, for example, there was a shortage of workers at the mine, and all members were requested to work there. As a result, some resigned. On the other hand, a few who followed instructions now occupy influential positions in local affairs.

In general, the Party is most active during political campaigns for elections for local or national offices and during times of internal drives or foreign crises. During elections Party members play a prominent role in nominating candidates, many of them serving as candidates themselves. They also supervise the elections. Until recently there has been only one slate of candidates, but in the 1953 elections there were two contenders for a single office, that of regional delegate to the Republic of Serbia Parliament. One of them was a former Partisan and Secretary of the County Party Organization. The other was a woman who was principal of a high school in Kragujevac. Here traditional forces came into play: most people, both in the village as well as in the town, thought that women have no place in politics. Her defeat was a foregone conclusion, and she lost by a large majority. Nevertheless, great interest in the outcome of this contest was displayed by Party members and officials in both Orašac and Arandjelovac.

[35] Most of the village offices and clerical positions appear to have rotated among a limited number of men.

Communists also explained to the villagers the meaning of the new type of elections to the Council of Producers, established by the 1953 Constitution. Here representatives are elected by various sectors of the economy rather than by geographic units. Only peasants who are members of the General Cooperative (about 95 percent of the villagers) were permitted to participate.

In the 1953 elections, for the Federal Assembly on November 22 and for the Council of Producers on November 24, voting took place at the village school. Rooms used for the occasion were especially decorated with bright woven blankets hung on the walls, serving as a background for pictures of Tito framed with bowers of oak branches. Glasses of autumn flowers stood on every desk and ballot box. An election board composed of officials from Arandjelovac and local peasants supervised the voting, sitting at long tables similarly draped with colorful blankets. Approximately 90 percent of the Orašac population eligible to vote[36] participated in the first election and a somewhat lower percentage voted in the second. As the individual villager entered he was registered and given a ballot to mark and place in a slot in the box. It was explained that this type of election is more democratic than earlier ones because now there is only one ballot box. Formerly there was a separate box where negative votes were cast. According to some of the school teachers and officials, "our elections are an example of the unity of the peoples of Socialist Yugoslavia." They further claimed that now elections are very orderly and well managed, whereas pre-war elections were often hotly contested and violent affairs. Both election days were holidays of a sort in the village. Many former Partisans and others appeared at the school in their best outfits, proudly displaying war medals.

The Trieste Affair of October, 1953, illustrates how the local Communist Party functions in regard to an external crisis. When news reached Orašac that the United States and Great Britain had issued a joint declaration saying they were turning Zone A of the long-disputed Free Territory of Trieste over to Italy, the village cell immediately became active. Neighborhood meetings were organized in individual peasant homes, and all villagers were

[36] All citizens over the age of eighteen.

told to attend. The teachers, agronomists, and other Party members acted as discussion moderators and explained the unfairness of the act as they interpreted it. Fiery resentment was displayed by most Party members, while the villagers themselves seemed chiefly concerned that there would not be another war. An interesting commentary on the effectiveness of this discussion group medium is that on the following day, at a graveyard feast, a man who had attended one of the meetings carefully examined the scapula of the roast sheep served at the meal and declared, "Everything will be all right with Trieste."[37]

As many high-ranking government officials have admitted, there is a very significant gap between local intelligentsia and the majority of the peasants. An illustration of this situation was provided at one of the meetings in an Orašac peasant home, where a female teacher was addressing a group of men and telling them of the need for greater participation of the village women in local affairs. While this was going on, the wives of several of them peered cautiously at the proceedings from the doorway of a smaller room, afraid to enter and disturb their menfolk.

Supplementing the Party is the local branch of the Socialist Alliance, the mass organization for the propagation of government policy, embracing approximately 80 percent of the villagers. Meetings are usually held about once a month.

Most of the activities of the General Cooperative, the Consumer and Purchasing Cooperative, have already been referred to under various contexts, but little has been said about its organization.[38] It is run by a full-time, annually elected President who serves as general manager. His staff includes a bookkeeper, two clerks in the general store, a man who runs the kafana, and a combination watchman and janitor for the Cooperative Home. In recent years some of the activities of the Cooperative have declined, namely

[37] Although there was much official resentment directed against America and England and demonstrations in Belgrade during which the American and British Information Centers' windows were smashed, no ill feelings were expressed nor action taken against the author and his wife in the village. The local officials continued to be friendly but were eager to discuss the question and justify their attitudes.

[38] The General Cooperative has the largest membership of any organization in Orašac, with some 414 households and 1,110 adult members in 1954. (A Purchasing Cooperative existed before the war, but on a much smaller scale.)

those connected with compulsory deliveries of agricultural products and livestock.

Other activities, however, have shown a steady increase. This applies particularly to the tavern and the store, both of which have doubled their income between 1950 and 1954.

The Cooperative by no means enjoys a monopoly in the field of purchasing agricultural produce; in addition to state organizations which come to Orašac to purchase fruit in season, the weekly *pijac* in Arandjelovac still remains the chief outlet for most peasants.[39]

The job of carrying out most government policies falls to the Village Council. This is an old institution dating back to an organization of village elders which had considerable autonomy at the time of the Turkish conquest. Soon after Serbia achieved her independence, however, village government was transformed into an organ of the national government. So it has remained to the present day.

The present Village Council is selected from among forty-two candidates chosen at a meeting open to all Orašani. The twenty-one who receive the highest number of votes are elected to the Council, and the one with the largest number is chosen as President for a three-year term. The Council meets about once a month to make decisions on local affairs. Its members include the director of the mine, the President of the Cooperative, several employees of the Cooperative, a few miners, and several ex-Partisans in addition to peasants who have no governmental or organizational affiliations. All of the members are peasants who were born in Orašac. Only seven are Communists. Some of the other members do not appear to be fully in sympathy with all government programs, although they are not likely to speak their minds on these topics at Council meetings.

The permanent staff of the Village Council, besides the full-time salaried President, includes an appointed Secretary, two

[39] A few of the more prosperous peasants with larger surpluses sometimes go as far as Belgrade or even to the Vojvodina. The latter is an especially favorable market because it has a surplus of corn and wheat but a relative scarcity of wine. There the Orašac peasant is able to conclude advantageous barter arrangements or receive a better price for his wine and brandy than in Arandjelovac. The government places no restrictions on such trade other than the regular taxes.

clerks and a combination janitor and errand boy. Unlike the President of the Cooperative, who has more than enough work to keep him busy since he is the manager of two business enterprises in addition to his other activities, the duties of the President of the *odbor* are more of a ceremonial and social rather than administrative nature. Most of the work is handled by the Secretary and his two assistants, although this situation may vary somewhat from village to village depending on the personalities involved. The President greets visitors, seeks to sound out opinion among the peasants, performs the civil marriage ceremonies, presides at meetings, and acts as something of an intermediary between the local population and county officials. It is the special duty of the Secretary to see that the taxes are collected, and one of the clerks is in charge of recording vital statistics. In addition, all petitions on legal matters concerning divorce, division of zadrugas, and other matters first pass through the Village Council before they are referred to the County Court. They also issue the permits required for the sale of livestock.[40] Arrangements for attendance at courses, the showing of films, and the celebration of state holidays are other functions of the Village Council.[41]

There is no militia stationed in Orašac, so all serious infractions of the law, including political crimes, are handled by the police in Arandjelovac.

What conclusions are possible concerning post-war government activities in Orašac? Crucial to an understanding of this problem is the realization that the peasant's interest is primarily focused on economic matters.[42] That is, he is dissatisfied with the price he receives for his products relative to the cost of the consumer goods and farm tools he wishes to buy. One of the most frequent comments heard about the United Nations project was, "If the government would lower prices, that would raise our standard of living more than any project." There are indications that the

[40] Similar permits were required before the war.

[41] They also sponsored the "donations" of food and money by the peasants to help with arrangements for the big celebration held on the anniversary of the First Revolt.

[42] Perhaps this attitude is conditioned by the fact that the peasants see no probability of fundamentally altering the political structure of their country but do believe that some economic changes are possible.

government plans to pursue such a policy. Some prices have already been lowered, and a long-range program emphasizing consumer goods rather than heavy industry seems to be a very definite possibility.[43]

As far as the church is concerned, it is still comparatively free to function. Attendance is not restricted in any way, although religious processions outside the churchyard have been banned. Participation is largely an individual matter although a member of the Party or the village government is not likely to be seen attending services. Immediately after the war an attempt was made to limit church collections to within the church itself, but this matter was soon dropped. The Church Council still meets although there have been no new elections since the war, and the members are not likely to advertise their positions. One of the most revealing indices of church activity in the post-war period is given in Table 15, which gives a comparison of records of births and mar-

Table 15. Comparison of Births and Marriages Recorded by Church and Village Council, 1949–53

	NUMBER OF BIRTHS RECORDED[a]		NUMBER OF MARRIAGES RECORDED	
Year	*Village Council*	*Church*	*Village Council*	*Church*
1949	46	44	33	[b]
1950	72	54	27	19
1951	49	48	19	11
1952	60	59	22	12
1953	39	39	25	15

Source: Records of Orašac Village Council and church christening records.
[a] Excluding births in maternity ward in Arandjelovac.
[b] Data not available.

riages kept by the church and the Village Council. Almost every baby has been christened, while only something over half of the marriages have been performed in church. We have already seen that the church rites are not the most important part of a peasant wedding. On the other hand, being christened and having a kum seem to be indispensable parts of Serbian tradition. Indeed, in 1953 every baby born, including two to Communist fathers, was christened in church.

[43] Raymond, "Yugoslavs Shift Economic Policy," New York *Times*, October 2, 1955.

Some matters which most peasants consider Communist are by no means peculiar to members of the Party, for in the village the Party is often the agent of urban trends which originated earlier in Western Europe and which were later incorporated into Marxist and Leninist philosophies. For example, disregarding formalized religious observances is regarded as one of the characteristics of a Communist. When we did not cross ourselves upon entering the church, it was at first thought that we were members of the Party. Similarly, many Communists feel that they ought to celebrate individual birthdays rather than the family slava. According to the Orašac priest, however, there are less than ten households (or two percent of all village houses) which do not call him to bless the water for their slava.[44] Yet there is virtually no household in the village which does not celebrate its saint's day. Those where there are Party members may dispense with the priest's service and may not invite very many guests, but a pig is roasted and a feast enjoyed nevertheless. At memorial graveyard feasts the families of certain Party members have been observed performing all the rituals and customs, although the men themselves were not present.

The status of the gazda has altered a great deal in the post-war period. He has lost his political power and much, although by no means all, of his social influence in the village. His taxes have been high, and in some instances a part of his land has been taken away. In most cases he is regarded as something of a social outcast by government officials. Some of his basic attitudes have changed, too. He often tries very hard today to make himself seem poorer than he is, not only to the tax collector but to his fellow villagers, with the hope of achieving thereby a little protective coloration. Despite all these changes the gazda has not been eliminated— although economic differences have certainly been reduced they have not been abolished. A man with eight or nine hectares, who manages his household well, is still looked up to and envied by one who has only three or four, but he is not respected to the extent that he would have been before the war.

Today most peasants conceive of a higher standard of living in terms of advancing their own individual farms, increasing their

[44] In a few cases the priest is asked to come while the man of the house is not home.

livestock, and building a new house and perhaps a better barn. Few think in terms of buying more land simply to have larger holdings. The experience with the Peasant Working Cooperatives and their subsequent dissolution has strengthened this viewpoint.

Not all the peasants' hostility is a result of present government policies but is related to long-standing complaints which have been carried over into the post-war period. One of these is the result of the strong resentment of bureaucracy, often voiced by pre-war peasant parties. Another reason for distrust stems from peasant reaction to various policies of the inter-war government. They claimed that many of the politicians of that period were dishonest and corrupt but went unpunished. Today many villagers with grievances or doubts are not likely to air them. Instead they shrug their shoulders and say, "I just want to work my own little piece of land, mind my own business, and stay alive."

This does not mean that their attitude toward the government has been a completely negative one. Many government improvements have been welcomed by all. These include the Cooperative Home, the eight-year school, and electrification. The policy of developing the country industrially has evoked considerable enthusiasm in the village, even though there is the feeling that it has proceeded too fast and at the expense of agriculture, an observation by no means limited to Orašac. Some of the younger women have also been favorably inclined toward a few of their new legal rights, such as those regarding divorce and voting as well as the generally proclaimed (but, in the village, ineffectual) concept of women being the economic equals of men. The mixed agriculturalists have come to regard pensions and free medical care as an established part of their lives.[45] Many also feel that now they have an opportunity for work which was not present in pre-war Yugoslavia and that they are no longer dependent on the whims of the gazde.

It is not intended here to make any fundamental evaluation of the social and cultural implications of Yugoslav Communism. Aside from being far beyond the scope of a community study, it seems a little premature to make judgments on a government

[45] Pensions existed in pre-war Yugoslavia but were not often granted to peasants.

which has existed for only a little over a decade and which, during that period, has undergone many changes. The basic policies and beliefs of the Yugoslav Communist Government do not seem to have changed; however, at the same time, neither have those of the peasants of Orašac or their counterparts throughout Yugoslavia. The government is becoming increasingly aware that no progress in agriculture is possible without the willing cooperation of the peasantry. As Tito himself has said, perhaps a *modus vivendi* will be found.

CHAPTER 12

THE ORAŠAC VILLAGER
AND THE WORLD OUTSIDE

THE UNIVERSE of the Orašac peasant centers on his house-hold, his neighborhood, his clan, and his village. The world outside the village is of secondary importance, although he is very much aware of it and interested in it. Toward each larger and more distant sphere of influence and association, from the relation of Orašac to its surrounding village and market town, to Šumadija and Serbia, to the rest of Yugoslavia, and to the vast world beyond, his feelings become less intense.

NEIGHBORING VILLAGES AND THE MARKET TOWN

Part of the peasant's fervent attachment to his own plot of land is projected to his immediate surroundings. Not only does he invariably say that his village is the best in the area, but he also feels that he personally would not be happy living elsewhere. People are inherently proud of what is theirs, an attitude brought out in conversations on almost any subject. Despite constant instruction on the values of industrialization, and professed desires to leave the village in order to better serve their country, this attitude is even reflected in the essays of many of the school children, who speak of their birthplace with the greatest attachment and affection.

It is not uncommon to hear a man from Orašac declare emphatically that he could never live in neighboring Kopljare village

"because it is too flat there," and for the Kopljare man to reply
that he could not possibly settle in Orašac "because of the hills,"
although a casual traveler finds it hard to see any great difference
in the topography of the two villages.

When Orašac girls and youths meet young people from other
villages at dances or at the market, they tend to identify with and
be identified by their own village. They even make up songs and
jingles, flattering to themselves as Orašani and derogatory to people from other villages. Admittedly these are chanted in fun. Two
composed on the spot went like this: "*Vrbica selo na velikom glasu—
momci riju a devojke pasu*" (Vrbica is a famous village—its young
men grovel and its girls graze) and "*Cveto bagrem na šljivi. Stojničani
vašljivi; Orašani lutke bele, pobedu odnele*" (Acacia is blossoming on
the plum tree. The people of Stojnik village have lice; the people
from Orašac are white dolls and won the victory). But this works
both ways—one against the Orašani goes: "*Džigerice i ti li si meso?
Orašani i vi li ste ljudi?*" (Can you call liver meat? Can you call
the Orašani men?).

Inter-village rivalry has had more serious implications. One
incident occurred about twenty years ago, over a bitterly contested
election to the Church Council. Some of the men from Orašac
were determined that those from Kopljare, with whom they share
the parish, did not deserve to be represented. Harsh words were
exchanged, and there were a few fist fights before a compromise
was finally reached. More recently a similar event took place.
The Orašac villagers are extremely proud that the First Revolt
occurred in their village. Under the influence of one rakija too
many, some openly flaunt the fact that that distinction therefore
makes them just a little bit better than the others. This feeling
came to the surface during the celebration on the occasion of the
one-hundred-fiftieth anniversary of the Revolt, when people from
nearby villages resented this attitude. The result was a free-for-all
brawl involving young men from several villages and the smashing
of windows in the newly opened Cooperative Home.

A new settler is not quickly accepted by the traditional villagers. Some smaller clans have been in Orašac almost twenty-
five years but are considered newcomers. There are also two fam-

ilies who moved to Orašac thirty years ago, from a Serbian village near the Bulgarian border. They are still referred to as "The Bulgarians." The ethnic German miners and the few Slovenes are thought of as temporary residents and have limited contact with the villagers. For the most part they do not venture away from the kolonija into the village proper. The village priest is known as *Crnogorac,* Montenegrin, since he recently came to Orašac from there, and a schoolboy whose parents were born in Bosnia is called *Bosanac* and ridiculed by his classmates because he speaks a slightly different dialect.

The Orašac peasant is parochial but in no sense isolated. His greatest degree of contact with the world outside the village, other than via the national institutions present in the village, is through Arandjelovac.[1] At least one and often two members of most households go to the market town every Friday. Some villagers have special customers to whom they bring a specified amount of kajmak, wine, or brandy each week, but most bring their produce to trade on the open market. Peasants buy and sell to one another as well as to the townsfolk. This is especially true in the sale of livestock. Continuing the theme of inter-village rivalry, a peasant will sooner trust a fellow villager than one from another hamlet. Before a livestock transaction occurs, the first question is not on the qualities of the animal under consideration but, "Which village are you from?"

The long, narrow row of shops lining the town's main street is occupied by various private craftsmen and several state-controlled stores. The peasants' purchasing of staples and certain consumer goods has already been discussed, but much of their town business is at the sandal-maker's, potter's or tanner's. The town has always supported a much greater variety of craftsmen than has the village. The variety of crafts still operating today reveals the extent to which the peasants depend on them. Other reasons for a trip to town are errands at the County Seat, the Court, the health clinic, or a visit to a relative.

---

[1] Orašac County is similar to most others in Šumadija in that it consists of a group of twenty or so villages oriented toward one small town which acts as both market and administrative center.

The most important events attracting villagers into town are the *vašari*, the county fairs and livestock markets which occur several times a year. The fairs are arranged in a patterned fashion, with specified spots for the various activities. The Friday market-place functions as usual, but the vacant lots and hills beyond are filled with the overflow of carts piled high with bulk produce, with a turbulent mass of squealing pigs, placid cows, and animated villagers, clinching bargains, amidst shouting and hand-slapping. Temporary stands are set up to sell household goods, such as tin and wooden utensils, made and sold by craftsmen from the South. The main feature of the fair is the amusement section, complete with games of chance and Gypsy musicians. Afterwards there is traditionally a dance for the young people, around the town churchyard on another hill overlooking the market scene.

ŠUMADIJA AND SERBIA

Beyond the scope of the surrounding villages and market town, the peasant thinks in terms of Šumadija and Serbia. Within this sphere the Orašac peasant will insist that the region of the Jasenica basin is the best part of Šumadija.[2]

Šumadija in general has been a very homogeneous area during the last century and a half, although the composition of the population has altered slightly since the war. Most of the non-Serb population is concentrated in the towns. They include factory workers from other areas, a few Tsintsar merchants and a small group of Jewish professional and business people. Before the war the number of Jews was considerably higher, and many refugees were hidden in peasant cottages during the German occupation. In contrast to the traditions of distrust and anti-Semitism which exist in other parts of Eastern Europe, the Serbs in the towns and the peasants who came in contact with the Jews thought of them as clever, rich, and with "good souls." Two peasant households in Orašac still correspond with Jews whom they had sheltered in their homes and who later went to Israel.

[2] The peasants of the Jasenica region regard those to the north, in the Kosmaj area, as not being true Šumadijans, calling them *Šijaci*. They consider themselves to be *Eroji*, true descendants of the Dinaric herdsmen, while they, in turn, are regarded as Šijaci by people further south.

There is one group of people counted in the official census as of
Serb nationality and Orthodox religion whom the peasants nevertheless consider outsiders. It is the *Cigani*, the Gypsies. In Šumadija
there are actually two kinds of Gypsies, the kind the Orašani refer
to as "our Gypsies" and the type that live in more southern parts
of Šumadija and other areas of Serbia who are wandering smiths
and entertainers.

The Gypsies of the first type are sedentary. There are none in
Orašac village, but there is a settlement of them in Ranilović, a
small group in Kopljare, and a *Ciganska Mala*, or Gypsy Quarter,
in Arandjelovac. They live much as the Serb peasantry does,
speaking Serbian, observing slavas, and practicing both agriculture and herding to some extent. They are easily distinguished by
their darker skin and other physical features. Despite their seeming
adaptation to peasant life, they are rarely successful farmers and
usually occupy the most marginal land. Their homes are shabby
even when compared to the poorest peasant house. They supplement their income in other ways. The men make and repair various types of metal cooking utensils, and fashion such items as wool
combers, wooden mixing troughs, spoons, spindles, and cheese
boxes. In so doing they fulfill a distinct economic need and yet
do not compete with any of the village or town craftsmen. This is
also true of their other major occupation, that of serving as musicians, entertainers, and fortunetellers. Whatever else the peasant
may say about Gypsies, he is full of admiration for their ability
as musicians, and the larger weddings in the village are frequently
classified according to the number of Gypsy musicians hired for
the event.

The other type of Gypsies, the nomadic ones, are also craftsmen
and entertainers. Once or twice a year a caravan of several Gypsy
families passes through Orašac to sell kettles and frying pans and
to tell fortunes by reading the future in a ball of fuzz plucked from
the "client's" clothing. There is one group that brings a chained
toothless dancing bear to the villages each year, making the animal
perform in return for flour, bacon, beans, and dried meat. Money
is rarely given. In the scattered villages of Šumadija, where enter-

tainment is limited, the coming of these wandering Gypsies is eagerly anticipated.

Despite the fact that the peasants consider the first type as their Gypsies, all Gypsies in general are regarded with condescension and suspicion. They are thought to be lazy, unreliable, and thieves. Villagers explain that they rarely leave their cottages unoccupied "because of the Gypsies," and children are told, "If you're not good we'll give you to the Gypsies" or "The Gypsies will come and take you away."

To the Orašac villager Serbia is the logical extension of Šumadija, and he speaks with pride of Šumadija as the heart of Serbia. Although geographically this is so, the peasants have a somewhat different explanation, based on cultural traits. In the first place, "Šumadija is the most desirable part of Serbia, the richest, most attractive area, and the home of the most *kulturni* people." In addition, peasants and townsfolk alike point out that it was in Šumadija that both the First and Second Revolts began, and that the Šumadijans have always been the bravest fighters defending their homeland, drawing examples from the time of the Turks up to the last war, when many parts of the region were the scenes of some of the earliest battles against the Germans. During a discussion of this question, one man concluded, "We Šumadijans also speak the purest form of the language"; "and have the finest bearing," added another; "and are the greatest lovers," concluded one more. The peasant's feelings about his Šumadija are expressed in the popular song, *Šumadijo, Rodni Kraju* (Šumadija, My Birthplace).

> Šumadijo, rodni kraju,
> U tebi je ko u raju,
> Divne šume i planine,
> Svud' livade i doline.
>
> Ti neguješ lepe momke,
> Lepe momke i devojke.
> Šumadince, Šumadinke,
> Crnooke i visoke.

U livadi i u gori,
Čobanska se pesma ori.
Mome srcu najmilija,
Jer je peva Šumadija.

Šumadija, my birthplace,
You are like paradise,
Wonderful woods and mountains,
And everywhere meadows and valleys.

Handsome youths, from Šumadija,
Handsome youths and pretty maidens.
Šumadijan men, Šumadijan women,
Black-eyed and tall.

Through the meadows and on high,
Shepherds' songs echo back.
My heart is happiest,
When the song is of Šumadija.

This feeling for their native place was also expressed in some of
the songs sung by Šumadijan Partisans in the last war:

Šumadinci mi smo Partizani,
Mi volimo svoj rodni kraj.
Tanaska Rajića, mi smo potomci,
Za slobodu naroda, bijemo boj!

We are Partisans from Šumadija,
We love our native place.
Descendants of Tanasko Rajić,[3]
Our battle is for liberty!

The second part of this song equates Mihailović with the Germans and the Fascists, but the sentiments of the first stanza are
by no means peculiar to the Partisans. It is interesting to note,
however, that even though the Partisans were an urban-dominated
Communist organization they utilized group loyalties. The peasants

[3] A hero of the First Revolt.

recruited from this area formed the Šumadijan Brigade, and today there is a large organization of its veterans. Their annual meetings are usually the occasion for important political rallies. In October, 1953, a mass meeting in their honor was held in Mladenovac at which Vice-President Ranković made a speech.[4]

Being a Šumadinac, the Orašac peasant feels himself to be something of a privileged character, but basically he considers himself a Serb. He is passionately proud of his Serbia and will fight to defend it against all enemies, as has been amply demonstrated in the past one hundred and fifty years. This great pride in nationality is no doubt due in part to the origin of Serbia as a peasant state.

Although the Orašani conceive of Šumadija as an integral part of Serbia it does not follow that they similarly conceive of Serbia as a part of Yugoslavia. Yugoslavia is a political creation of the First World War, compounded of two small independent states, Serbia and Montenegro, and parts of the defunct Turkish and Austro-Hungarian Empires. The common bonds in all Yugoslavia are much less obvious than in the case of Serbia alone, or even Serbia and Montenegro, where the great majority of the people share a religion and historical tradition. Since the Serbs are by far the largest national unit in Yugoslavia, and also because they were an independent state for almost a hundred years before the creation of Yugoslavia, it has been rather difficult for them to think of Yugoslavia as a federal or multinational state. This led to severe tensions in the inter-war years. Although the present government is a federal state with individual constituent republics and although open conflict has been eliminated, the problem has by no means been completely solved.

The patriotism and pride exhibited by the Orašani are characteristics of all Serbs. They feel themselves to be much more than simply inhabitants of Serbia. They are the creators and the defenders of their country. "We *are* Serbia." This binding identity with their homeland has been reinforced over generations by the

---

[4] Both the songs and military groups are, of course, found in other regions throughout Yugoslavia but are mentioned here because they help reinforce traditional attitudes already present.

chanting of the heroic epic poems, instilling in almost every child a knowledge of, and love for, his country which he retains throughout life.

The villager, proud as he is of his land, accepts the fact that sometimes his is not really the best of all possible situations and reserves the privilege of criticizing it. On the one hand he boasts about how fine everything is, and on the other frequently offers two explanations for why things are not even better. These are that they were "almost five hundred years under the Turks" and that "every twenty years there is another war on our land." Yet a sublime faith in the virtues of his country persists.

Despite the fallacies possible when making generalizations, and allowing for individual differences, there are nevertheless several distinct traits by which the Orašac villagers, and for the most part all Šumadijans, may be characterized. In three broad groups, they include a fervent love of one's land and people, a vigorous and demonstrative personality, and a belief in the concept that a man must work in order to survive.

The bearing of the Orašac villagers is erect and proud. This is not only due to military training but also to their feeling they must bow to no one. Almost every man in Orašac has served in the army (often twice and sometimes even three times). It gives him a common link with the ancestors of whom he is so proud; like them, he has helped shape the country, fight for it, and give it its independence. When a Serbian king visited the village, the peasants shook his hand rather than bowed to him. A king or high official was respected, not venerated. He was not considered too different from the ordinary man, capable of the same good deeds and human failings. According to one saying, "Even the Holy Patriarch, when hungry, will steal a piece of bread."

Despite the one-party system today, the Orašani sometimes speak their minds openly regardless of the consequences. An old grandmother lectured a group of militiamen conducting a security investigation in Orašac by telling them their mothers should have had more sense than to bring them up to be policemen. In interpersonal relations, with an exception in the case of nicknames, the villager is direct and informal. When asked a question he takes

great pains to answer it precisely and accurately, and he will freely
admit his ignorance if he is not sure of the answer. This is not to
say, of course, that he is incapable of concealing information on
matters which he believes might adversely affect his welfare.

Hospitality and a cooperative nature are also part of his out-
going personality. The Orašac peasant will give you the shirt off
his back but will expect the same from you when he needs it.
But he is also a *tvrdoglav*, hard-headed and stubborn. His vigor is
frequently explosive when he cannot give in or when a situation
annoys or distresses him. His feelings give rise to a remarkable
series of curses for which the Serbs are well known in other parts
of Yugoslavia. He will curse his bread, impure blood, one hundred
crosses, God, the sun, or anything else that strikes his fancy. In
Orašac this cursing is so much a part of the local idiom that young
children parrot their elders in everyday speech and enjoy it hugely.
After giving vent to his feelings a villager may easily go to the other
extreme of displaying uninhibited emotions. In talking about his
grandchild, his own plot of land, or his sweetheart he might describe
his affection in terms of a love stronger than his two eyes, his right
hand, or his soul.

Čovek mora da radi (a man must work)—this is the most basic
credo of the villagers. A very high premium is placed on industry
and capability, and, in fact, the standard greeting when one villager meets another is, "*Jesi vredan?*" (Are you working hard?) or
"*Ti si poranio!*" (You're up early!). An old proverb goes: *Vinograd
ne ište molitve nego motike* (Vineyards do not need prayers but hoes).

The great value of work is not so much in the idea of working
to achieve success but essentially in that of working to stay alive.
Despite the attitudes of self-confidence so often expressed, there is
a very real insecurity, for the weather is a most important factor
in the success or failure of crops and the reason for a definite element of uncertainty. The dodola rite is still practiced, and people
accept long periods of drought "because God wills it," but these
attitudes are not as strong today as they once were. Today unfavorable meteorological conditions are thought of primarily in terms of
economic losses which must be sustained or at least lessened.

Among the pure agricultural households of Orašac one of the

strongest causes for insecurity is the fact that the mixed agricultural peasants are assured regular wages, pensions, medical care,
and other benefits under government policies. Although the two
groups are not clearly defined as yet, real feelings of antagonism
have begun to develop. Recent government land reforms and
taxation policies have also had their effect, and references to worry
and struggle (*mučiti*) are often heard in the village.

Yet, in spite of these factors making for insecurity, the Orašac
peasant, proud realist that he is, soon retorts with another pat
village expression, "*Nije lako, ali ako*" (It isn't easy, but so what,
we'll manage). And, he concludes, "*Neka je živ i zdrav*" (The most
important thing is to live and be well).

In the village there is great faith in progress for its own sake.
This is certainly due in part to the pioneering nature of the settlement of Šumadija and to the complete transformation of that
frontier within a century and a half. Orašac peasants feel very
strongly that their tools and methods are primitive and do not
hesitate to say, "Look at us. We work as though we were in the
Stone Age." They say that they have to work this way, knowing
that it is more primitive and "a hundred years behind Western
Europe and America," because their present methods are all they
have available. Their reasons for this again include comments
about the centuries of Turkish control and constant warfare.

The desire for progress is also shown by the villagers' attitude
toward education. To be illiterate, for a man especially, is a marked
sign of social inferiority and often presumed to be an indication of
mental incapacity as well. Those who are illiterate are very conscious of this stigma. Closely connected with the value placed on
education is the idea that any person can advance himself through
his own efforts, once he has provided his most basic needs of livelihood. The ideal is no longer to be the biggest gazda in the village
but to alter one's status by increased education and cash income.

Both the values placed on progress in itself and the desire for
individual advancement are shown in the great wish for electrification and other home improvements. During an open meeting
held to discuss the United Nations program there was comparatively little debate as to the desirability of the aims of the project.

Attention was centered on how it would be financed and suggestions for specific programs.

The desire for technological progress is not, of course, universal among all the villagers, nor does it apply to all types of change, especially in those areas where some theoretical knowledge is required to understand the merit of such change. While it is easy to see that an electric bulb is brighter than a kerosene lamp, it is not so obvious why it is necessary to wash one's hands before eating or to go to the expense and trouble of building an outhouse. But hygiene in the abstract is, however, very highly valued, and an extra whitewashing of cottage walls is often justified on this basis. If the item in question has prestige associations its acceptance is often facilitated. Thus if a toilet is presented as a sign of "culture," the peasant will often be anxious to comply—much as an American can be induced to buy a toothpaste or gasoline because it contains a new, "scientific" ingredient; both only dimly understand the relationship.

THE REST OF YUGOSLAVIA

The inhabitants of Orašac are aware that they are formally citizens of Yugoslavia, but only the village intellectuals would speak of themselves as Yugoslavs or of their language as Serbo-Croatian. It is possible that this attitude will gradually change, for the idea of a united Yugoslavia and "the brotherhood of our peoples" is very strongly emphasized by the school and government organizations.

But there is no doubt that today the villagers regard the other South Slavs as different. The Macedonians, although considered very closely akin to the Serbs, most of them sharing as they do a common religion, are nevertheless thought of as rather poor and backward. A similar opinion is held of the Bosnians. Those who are Moslems are called "Turks," although they are Slavs who accepted Islam at the time of the Turkish conquest.

There is at the same time something of a common feeling particularly with the Montenegrins, Macedonians, and some of the Bosnians. Serbs regard Croats as a different people, however, chiefly because of their Roman Catholic faith, even though they speak almost identical forms of the same language. It would not be correct to say that the Serbian peasant views the Croats with hatred, despite the fact that many members of the Serbian minority communities in Croatia were killed by the Ustaši (Croatian Fascists) during the last war. Rather, their attitude is more of suspicion and distrust. A Croat who married an Orašac girl later returned to Orašac to live. He was the waiter at the kafana for a time. When his job was taken away from him he claimed it was sheer prejudice, although the President of the Cooperative insisted it was because he did not do his job properly.

As far as the Slovenes are concerned, they are regarded as complete strangers. Added to the differences in religion and historical development is the fact that they speak a different language and have by far the highest standard of living in the whole of Yugoslavia. In fact, Serbian peasants refer to Slovenes as *stranci*, foreigners.

These attitudes do not seem to have been lessened but rather strengthened as a result of contacts during army service.

And, of course, the stereotypes for each of the South Slav groups still persist as strongly as ever among Serbs who have never been to other parts of the country or have never met any fellow Yugoslavs. A traveler through Serbia will be warned to enjoy all the good food he can, for he will not get it in Croatia; to realize that people will not be as helpful and friendly in Slovenia, that in Macedonia he will see people living *kao stoka*, like animals; and so forth.

In contrast to peasants in other parts of Yugoslavia, the Šumadijan feels that he is a *žurac*, a hurrier, a go-getter. The villagers frequently compare themselves to people from the Vojvodina, who, they claim, take their time about everything. "Not us," they assert, "we know what must be done." Perhaps this is an explanation for the fact that the Orašac villager never fails to ask the exact time of day when he passes someone wearing a watch, even though he does not work by the clock. A saying used often in the village to get children to hurry off to their chores is "*Slaninu pod haljinu pa beži u planinu*" (Tuck some bacon under your clothes and run to the hills).

ORAŠAC AND THE WORLD BEYOND YUGOSLAVIA

Less than six copies of the two main Belgrade newspapers are received in the village each day, and there are only about twenty radios or crystal sets, so it is not surprising that the villagers' news of world developments is rather sketchy. At the same time, despite the fact that they are most preoccupied with earning a living and with local affairs, they have a very definite interest in other parts of the world. To fail to mention this interest and indicate some of their feelings and attitudes on the subject would be to neglect a limited but significant aspect of their culture.

One of the primary stimuli for this interest has been the considerable periods spent by many village men abroad, as a result of military service. In the First World War they participated in campaigns in Albania and Greece, and by their imprisonment in Czechoslovakia they saw something of a different way of life. In the Second World War seventy Orašac men spent the war in German prison camps with British, French, and American soldiers, while others fought with the Partisans when they cooperated with the Russians. This, added to the fact that Orašac itself has twice in this century been occupied by German armies, could not very well help but affect the outlook of the whole village. In the last century there were, of course, the wars against the Bulgarians and Turks.

In spite of two wars with the Germans and the especially hard occupation, from 1941 to 1945, the Orašani do not hate Germans as bitterly as do some other European peoples. Those who have spent considerable time in Germany proudly display their linguistic ability. They have also brought back with them an admiration for the Germans' technical superiority and higher standard of living. German massacres in Šumadija have not been forgotten, of course. Respect for Germany's industrialization was not strong enough to prevent most Orašac prisoners of war from returning home—in 1954 all but two had come back.

In contrast to the Germans, the Russians are considered to be little better than barbarians. It is admitted that they are good

fighters, but their culture and general standard of living are felt
to be of a very low order. One can hear countless tales of how
Russian soldiers drank kerosene and raped grandmothers. There
is also a local legend concerning the gluttony of a Russian platoon
which, in passing through Orašac, asked to be fed. The story as-
serts that the villager who provided the food was urged to eat and
drink with them. He is said to have died of his exertions a short
time later, while the Russians marched on to battle. Orašani are
conscious of their Slavic kinship, but one of the big motivating
factors behind their attitudes seems to be a fear of Russian domination, especially of the type that existed until the Cominform break
in 1948.

The Italians are looked upon as good singers but very poor
soldiers. At the time of the Trieste Affair even those peasants who
were not particularly interested in the issue itself felt that if it
ever came to war they would have no trouble winning. "They eat
cats" is a common way people in Orašac describe the Italians.
Other expressions heard in the village are "*On je glup kao Francuski
doktor*" (He is stupid like a French doctor), that is, very smart, and
"*U redu kao u Beču*" (Good as in Vienna) (everything is fine).
The English seem to be regarded as rather impersonal and unin-
teresting people by the Orašac men who met them in prison camps.
Reactions to both Albanians and Bulgarians are primarily negative
since they have been enemies of the Serbs in several wars. Attitudes toward the Turks and Turkish influence have been discussed
in other parts of this study.

In describing peasant attitudes more material is available about
America since we had frequent opportunity to observe the villagers'
reactions to ourselves as citizens of the United States.

To the Šumadijan peasant, America is a kind of bounteous
paradise where all good things come true.[5] This feeling is so strong
that peasants speak of Šumadija as being the best place in the
world after America, or they proudly refer to Šumadija as "a
little America," with proportionately rich resources and essentially

[5] Very few Šumadijans migrated to America, largely because their area was recently
settled and is not as seriously overpopulated as other places. Only two Orašac households have relatives in the United States. The only direct contact which the village
itself has had has been a Junior Red Cross parcel received by the school.

the same kind of people. This attitude has been in part engendered by the massive American aid which Yugoslavia has received since the end of the Second World War.[6] Even though only a small part has reached the village the people are very much aware of the significant role that this aid has played in the post-war economy.

Although at present direct contacts with America are of practically no importance, there are many forms of indirect contact. Every peasant is familiar with Nikola Tesla, who left Yugoslavia as an emigrant boy to become a famous scientist in America. Today the largest Yugoslav radio factory bears his name. Another form of contact is the radio, for "Voice of America" can occasionally be heard over one of the few village radios. One day in the Orašac kafana, in the course of a conversation with some village men on the beauties of regional folk music, one of them turned on Radio Belgrade to prove his point, and out blared the American jazz tune, *Rag Mop*. Serbian folk melodies and folk-patterned popular music predominate in the village, but some of the school girls have learned from their teachers the Serbo-Croat versions of such songs as *Jingle Bells*, *My Darling Clementine*, and *Magic is the Moonlight*. The words *džip* and *najlon* (jeep, nylon) are part of the local vocabulary.[7]

Many of the younger villagers have been to the movies in Arandjelovac, where they have seen foreign films, including American ones. Their contacts are much more limited than those of the town children, however, for the latter were familiar with the term *kauboj* (cowboy) while village children had no idea what it meant. It is possible that with film showings at the village Cooperative Home there will be more consciousness of foreign countries in general.[8] The films have the greatest effect on the younger generation. Many of the older people have never seen a motion picture and

[6] It is difficult to estimate the exact amount since some of the figures, notably those for military aid, are secret; a rough estimate of American assistance in all forms, including that of UNRRA, would be more than one and a half billion dollars.

[7] In Orašac *najlon* is an adjective for anything fine and durable. A sturdy oak table was praised as a *najlon sto*, and a hearty old man was called a *najlon deda*.

[8] As part of the United Nations project a series of health and agricultural films were shown. An added treat was a technicolor travel film on Yellowstone National Park and a Disney cartoon, both of which made as much if not more impression than the community development films.

have no desire to do so, particularly since they must pay for the privilege.

Despite attitudes of extreme friendliness and contact between American and Serbian soldiers in Germany, little is known in a factual way about the United States. Most men, however, had a high opinion of Roosevelt and knew that Eisenhower was the current President. In addition to being known as a very rich country, America is also considered to be a place where "no one works with his hands because everything is done by machine." There was eager curiosity at all levels of the population about different aspects of American life. Questions ranged from those of old women, who wanted to know if there were cats, dogs, potatoes, or a moon in America, to those of the younger people, who were curious as to whether there were really buildings a hundred stories high. Some peasants wanted to know about farming conditions and the ways in which American government agricultural policies differ from those in Yugoslavia. When the average size of American farms was explained, and the fact that they were usually operated by machinery, many of the peasants found it hard to conceive of them as being individually owned and not operated by the state. A few men offered large sums of money for the purpose of having tractors or jeeps sent. They were also curious about the religion of most Americans, and it was with difficulty that they were convinced that there is a form of Christianity which was neither Catholic nor Orthodox.

In contrast, the schoolteachers were primarily interested in political and economic matters, such as the foreign policies of the late Senators McCarthy and Taft. Casual discussions on comparative economic systems usually resulted in emphatic recitations on the part of the teachers as to why their way was better.

CHAPTER 13

SOME THOUGHTS ON A SERBIAN VILLAGE

THE BASIC emphasis in this book has been on history and social change as reflected in the culture of Orašac. The following comments, written by a more perceptive villager, sum up some of these changes and express his attitude toward them.

Ever since I can remember there have been radical changes in the way of living as well as in the social life. The forests were cleared, and the people changed their way of life. Old houses fell into decay and new ones were built, healthier and stronger than the older ones. Many roads were cut, and railways laid down. I remember when there was only one railway, from Belgrade to Caribrod,[1] by way of Niš. There were no cars nor any motor vehicles. There was no electric current, or wagons with iron axles, or wagons made with iron parts.

The social life of the village changed, and so did the costumes and food. Bachelors took the girls, and the girls married according to their own free will, the zadruga almost disappeared, and the religious ceremonies were neglected. People stopped fasting, they didn't go to church anymore, and they didn't believe in anything. The oath was no longer held.

There are no more rich people who have too much or poor people who depend entirely on them. Nutrition has improved, corn bread is very rarely eaten, and instead of it [corn flour] we use white flour. There is work for everyone who is healthy and strong. There is no superstition and fanaticism, all that is being forgotten.

Before the wars[2] there were no educated men from Orašac, and now there are some in every profession. The schoolrooms are adequate and so

[1] Present-day Dimitrovgrad on the Bulgarian border.
[2] Before 1912.

are the number of teachers. There **is** electric current, a room for movies, radio sets, and all of this came so suddenly that I hardly can believe everything could change so much in my lifetime. The death rate of children has dropped greatly, and the life of old people is made longer with the help of doctors. There are no whole families who die from contagious diseases, nor epidemics which wipe out entire counties. There still is some backwardness, but this will soon be improved.

The well-known proverb, "There is something good in every evil," one can see everywhere. Maybe there are some things which are not very good compared to what was in the past, but if you consider everything there is quite a difference between the present and the past, concerning the way of living, customs and habits, dealings between people, culture, education in the home and school, as well as the conditions of land cultivation and livestock breeding.[3]

Human culture is by its very nature dynamic. There is virtually no culture in the world the content of which remains completely static. This has been particularly true in the past few years when the effects of industrialization have been making themselves felt to an increasing extent in all parts of the world. There are, however, very great differences in rates of change in Orašac and in those areas where most of basic patterns were laid down a long time ago. In Orašac change seems to be one of the central themes of the culture. Perhaps this is so because the establishment of the village preceded the Industrial Revolution by only a short period. Also significant has been Orašac's location in Šumadija, a region which has constantly been exposed to outside influences, both political and cultural.

Over the past century and a half there have been a number of important changes in Orašac. There was, first, an increasing centralization of power in the hands of the national government, with a subsequent decline in the importance of local authorities. Second, the villager has been drawn more and more into a cash economy, primarily on account of increasing taxes but also because the expanding towns required more food from the countryside, while the peasant himself has been developing new tastes and needs.[4] Third,

[3] Written by the author of Autobiography G.
[4] A completely natural or self-sufficient economy never existed in Orašac.

there has been the state's increasing regulation of the peasant's life, by taxes, laws, military service, and other obligations. Fourth, as a result of increasing participation in a cash economy, technology and the material culture of the village have begun to change at a faster rate than ever before. Fifth, changes are also reflected in the nonmaterial culture, as in the decline of the zadruga. Sixth, some villagers have begun to migrate to the town and to derive income from sources other than agriculture. Basically, these changes are all an outgrowth of the influence of the Western commercial and industrial revolution, which over the past seventy-five years has made an increasing impact on rural Serbia.

Other conclusions which can be drawn from this study concern the relationship of the peasant to the state and to the urban governing classes. As we have seen, the withdrawal of the Turks left something of a vacuum which was eventually filled by political leaders and merchants newly emerged from the ranks of the peasantry. This type of development differs from that which took place in other parts of the world, where there exist class differences of long standing.

Since a great deal of the theory concerning the implications of rural-urban differences has been based on field work in Latin America, it may be well to examine some of these concepts in the light of the Serbian material. In an article on folk culture based largely on extensive experience in Latin America, Foster writes:

a folk society is not a whole society, an isolate, in itself. It is a "half society," a part of a larger social unit (usually a nation) which is vertically and horizontally structured. The folk component of this larger unit bears a symbiotic spatial-temporal relationship to the more complex component, which is formed by the upper classes of the pre-industrial urban center. In this sense folk and urban are not polar concepts; rather, they are integral parts of the definition of a certain type of socio-cultural unit in which the pre-industrial city is a focal point. Far from threatening the folk society, this type of urban unit is a precondition for its existence.[5]

It is certainly true that without urban centers there can be no folk, that is, villagers who are members of a national state. But

[5] Foster, "What is Folk Culture?" *American Anthropologist*, Vol. 55, No. 2 (April–June, 1953), p. 163.

what would seem to follow logically from Foster's remarks—that urban upper classes are a precondition for the existence of folk society—does not necessarily always hold, at least not in the case of Serbia. This concept appears to be somewhat static in that it does not clearly make the point that the folk is the more basic element of the two. The urban upper class can be replaced by another ruling group from outside, or, more specifically, as happened in Serbia, a ruling and commercial class can emerge from the folk itself. It seems unlikely that there is any instance in which the urban upper class or classes remained while the peasantry was replaced by another group, for the folk can become subsistence farmers or herdsmen, but an urban class requires a constant food supply for its existence.

In *The Little Community* Redfield, writing about peasant cultures, makes a statement that might well apply to the situation in Orašac:

So, in thinking about peasant communities or about partly urbanized rural communities, we begin to shape a form of thought that will conceive of primitive, folk, or peasant life as a general and abstract kind of living, as an imagined total structure, qualitatively different from the kind of living that comes to characterize towns and cities. We could perhaps see in the village two kinds of abstractly distinguishable kinds of life and kinds of communities, and see these, right in the village, in relationship to each other. The interpenetration of town and country can be conceived not only as a system of differentiated activity-fields but also . . . as an intermingling of two styles of life. This interpenetration, this intermingling, occurs within the village, within, indeed, the individual villager himself.[6]

To be a peasant villager is most basically a state of mind reinforced by common residence. The practice of agriculture, although almost always present, varies greatly in degree of importance. Those villagers who have spent most of their lives working as clerks, miners, or craftsmen have still remained fundamentally peasants. These peasant-workers (the "mixed" agriculturalists of this study) are a common phenomenon throughout Yugoslavia and undoubtedly in many other parts of the world as well. A good example of the combining of rural and urban traditions is provided

[6] Redfield, *The Little Community: Viewpoints for the Study of a Human Whole*, p. 131.

by the lignite mine in Orašac. It appears that working in the mine has enabled many peasants, who might otherwise have been forced to leave the village because of a lack of economic opportunity, to remain on the land. This blending of influences has no doubt been substantially aided by the absence of a landless class.

It is also true, however, that in Orašac differences are beginning to emerge between pure and mixed groups, in terms of political attitudes and state benefits, but these are not very significant at present. Attitudes toward family, clan, and traditional observances appear to be quite similar regardless of the household's sources of income. It is therefore not a simple question of peasants becoming acculturated into an urban pattern but instead a matter of the degree to which various elements predominate. This is not true in all respects, however. Although many peasants have experienced urban life to some degree, they all share a common set of values distinct from those of the urban dwellers. These values are derived from such absolute factors as permanent residence in the village (allowing for temporary residence elsewhere), strong association with a large kin group and attachment to a piece of land which may or may not be of economic value.

There is no question but that the major current of influence has been from the town and the city to the village, but the relationship between these entities has certain elements of reciprocity. There are two aspects to this problem. One is, as Foster points out, that there are many elements of rural culture present in the city. This is particularly true in Serbia where almost all city dwellers have relatives in the village. These relationships are usually kept up for two generations after a peasant's departure from the village, and often for a longer period. Another aspect is that in Serbia the peasants, composing as they do the great majority of the population, have always had a very significant voice in politics, even though their chosen representatives have often been something less than attentive to the wishes and desires of their constituents.

During the post-war period the best example of the peasants' influence has been the government's revision of its agricultural program. Other examples are popular songs dealing with village life and folk themes, the commercialization of peasant crafts for tourist purposes, and the organization of professional folk dance groups.

This study of a village in Serbia has a very definite relationship to dynamic events occurring throughout Eastern Europe. Forced collectivization of agriculture seems to have been abandoned in Yugoslavia and perhaps in other countries as well, but whether there will be a positive program of agricultural developments and social improvements remains to be seen. In any case, the Yugoslav government will have to find some way to solve its recurring agricultural crises. Although small, scattered peasant holdings are uneconomical in the light of modern agricultural techniques, it also appears evident that little effective social progress can occur without the active support of the people themselves.

GLOSSARY OF SERBIAN WORDS USED IN TEXT

baba	grandmother or any woman over forty-five
banka	ten-dinar note
beba	infant under one year
čiča	familiar term for uncle or old man
čovek	mature man
dečko	boy
deda	grandfather or any man over forty-five
devojka	maiden
dinar	unit of currency (300 to $1 in 1953–54)
djak	pupil
domaćica	wife of head of household, housewife
domaćin	head of household
gazda	prosperous peasant
gibanica	greasy pastry filled with cheese
gozba	celebration
gusle	one-stringed national instrument
hajduk	highwayman in Turkish times
harač	head tax in Turkish times
janičar	Turkish mercenary of Christian origin
kafana	tavern
kajmak	loose cheese made of compressed, salted skins of boiled milk
knez	prince or local headman
kolo	Serbian national dance
kolonija	small mining colony in Orašac
komišanje	cooperative corn-husking bee

komšiluk	neighborhood
kuća	hearth, house, household
kultura	standard of living
kum	godfather
majstor	craftsman
marveni vašar	livestock market and fair
mlada	bride
mladoženja	bridegroom
moba	cooperative work group
momak	youth, bachelor
napola	share-cropping
odbor	post-war name for Village Council
opanci	leather peasant sandals
opština	pre-war name for Village Council
pashaluk	Turkish province
pasulj	bean gruel, village food staple
pijac	market
pobratim	blood-brother
pop	village priest
porodica	nuclear family
pozajmica	labor loan
prelo	spinning bee
prijatelj	friend or in-law
proja	cornbread
rakija	any strong colorless fruit brandy; in Orašac specifically plum brandy (*šljivovica*)
rayah	Turkish term for Christian peasantry
sarma	stuffed cabbage
seljak	peasant
slatko	sweet preserves offered guests
slava	feast day of patron saint
starešina	household elder, head of zadruga
šubara	fur peasant hat
torba	woven carrying sack
vajat	small outbuilding serving as sleeping quarters
vamilija	clan
varoš	market town
vračar	dispenser of folk medicine, formerly including shamanistic activities

zadruga	joint family; also, general Consumer and Purchasing Co-operative (*Opšta Zadruga*)
Zadrunži Dom	Cooperative Home
žena	mature woman, wife
žito	ceremonial cake of wheat, nuts, and sugar

SELECTED BIBLIOGRAPHY

Arsenijević, Batalaka. Istorija Srpskog Ustanka (History of the Serbian Revolt). Vol. I. Belgrade, 1898.

Brashich, Ranko M. Land Reform and Ownership in Yugoslavia, 1919–1953. New York, 1954. Mid-European Studies Center publication No. 17.

—— Taxation in Yugoslavia's Agricultural Policy. New York, 1953. Mid-European Studies Center mimeographed series No. 4.

Bratanić, B. "Oraće Sprave Centralnog Dijela Balkanskog Poluotoka" (Plowing Implements of the Central Part of the Balkan Peninsula), in Zbornik Etnografskog Muzeja u Beograda, 1901–1951. Belgrade, 1953. Pages 42–57.

Bulletin of Information and Documentation, Belgrade, Glavni Zadružni Savez FNRJ.

Coon, Carleton S. "Racial History," in Robert J. Kerner, ed., Yugoslavia. Berkeley, University of California Press, 1949. Pages 24–32.

Cvijić, Jovan. Balkansko Poluostrvo i Južnoslovenske Zemlje (The Balkan Peninsula and South Slav Lands). Vol. I. Belgrade, 1931.

—— Cvijićeva Knjiga (Cvijić's Book). Belgrade, 1927. Srpska Književna Zadruga publication No. 201.

Djaja, Aleksandar. Ishrana Seoske Porodice: Selo Rajković (Nutrition of the Inhabitants of the Village of Rajković). Belgrade, Institut za Izućavanje Ishrane Naroda, 1951.

Djordjević, Dragoslav, ed. Šumadija u Prošlosti i Sadašnjosti (Šumadija in the Past and Present). Subotica, Izdanje Jugoslovenskog Dnevnika, 1932.

Djordjević, Tihomir. Iz Srbije Kneza Miloša: Stanovništvo-Naselja (From the Serbia of Prince Miloš: Population-Settlements). Belgrade, 1924.

—— Kulturne Prilike od 1815 do 1839 (The Cultural Situation from 1815 to 1839). Belgrade, 1922.

Djurić, Janićije. "Skupština u Orašcu" (The Meeting in Orašac), in Glasnik Društva Srpske Slovenosti, IV (1852), 113–15. Reprinted in Istoriska Citanka (Historical Reader). Belgrade, 1949. Pages 96–97.

Drobnjaković, Borivoje M. Jasenica: Antropogeografska Ispitivanja (Jasenica: Anthropogeographic Investigations). Vol. XIII of Naselja i Poreklo Stanovništva. Belgrade, Srpska Kraljevska Akademija, 1923.

—— Smederevsko Podunavlje i Jasenica (Smederevo Podunavlje and Jasenica). Vol. XIX of Naselja i Poreklo Stanovništva. Belgrade, Srpska Kraljevska Akademija, 1925.

—— "Stanovništvo u Srbiji za Vreme Prvog Ustanka" (The Population of Serbia at the Time of the First Revolt), in Srpsko Geografsko Društvo, special publication No. 32. Belgrade, 1954. Pages 36–52.

—— "Sur la composition ethnique de la population de Šumadija," in Comptes rendus de III Congrès des Géographes et Ethnographes Slaves en Jugoslavie, 1930. Belgrade, 1932.

—— Upitnik za Prikupljanje Gradje o Pokućanstvu (Questionnaire for the Gathering of Material on Household Utensils). Belgrade, Srpska Akademija Nauka, 1949.

Erdeljanović, Jovan. Etnološka Gradja o Šumadincima (Ethnological Notes on Šumadijans). Vol. LXIV of Srpski Etnografski Zbornik. Belgrade, Srpska Akademija Nauka, 1951. Published posthumously.

Fewkes, Vladimir J. "Neolithic Sites in the Moravo-Danubian Area," *American School of Prehistoric Research Bulletin*, No. 12 (May, 1936), pp. 5–82.

Filipović, Milenko S. "Selo u Srbiji Krajem 18 i Početkom 19 Veka" (The Village in Serbia at the End of the Eighteenth and Beginning of the Nineteenth Century), in Srpsko Geografsko Društvo, special publication No. 32. Belgrade, 1954. Pages 74–89.

Foster, George. "What Is Folk Culture?" *American Anthropologist*, LV, No. 2 (April–June, 1953), 159–73.

Gavrilović, Jovan. Rečnik, Geografsko-Statistički Srbije (Geographical and Statistical Dictionary of Serbia). Belgrade, 1846.

Georgevitch, Tichomir. "National Superstitions and Traditions," in Alfred Stead, ed., Servia by the Servians. London, William Heinemann, 1905. Pages 158–68.

Grdić, Gojko. "Razvoj Privrede Srbije i Vojvodine od Oslobodjena od Turaka" (The Development of the Economy of Serbia and the Vojvodina from the Liberation from the Turks), in Kosta Mihailović, ed., Proizvodne Snage NR Srbije (Productive Resources of the People's Republic of Serbia). Belgrade, Ekonomski Institut, 1953. Pages 1–64.

Jovanović, Branislav. "O Šumama Srbije Početkom XIX Veka" (The Forests of Serbia at the Beginning of the Nineteenth Century), in Srpsko Geografsko Društvo, special publication No. 32. Belgrade, 1954. Pages 17–35.

Jovanović, Jovan. "Dve Stare Crkve u Kosmaju" (Two Old Churches in Kosmaj), *Starinar*, 1908.

Karadžić, Vuk S. Iz Istorije Prvog Srpskog Ustanka (From the History of the First Revolt). Edited by Radosav Perović. Belgrade, Narodna Knjiga, 1954.

Kardelj, Edvard, Concerning Some Problems of Our Village Policy. Belgrade, Glavni Zadružni Savez FNRJ, 1953.

—— "Introduction," in New Fundamental Law of Yugoslavia. Belgrade, Union of Jurists' Association of Yugoslavia, 1953.

Kerner, Robert J., ed. Yugoslavia. Berkeley, University of California Press, 1949.

Kojić, Branislav. "Novija Seoska Kuća u Srbiji" (The Newer Peasant House in Serbia), in Zbornik Radova. Belgrade, Srpska Akademija Nauka, 1950. Pages 293–307.

—— Stara Gradska i Seoska Arhitektura u Srbiji (Old Town and Village Architecture in Serbia). Belgrade, Prosveta, 1949.

Kostić, Cvetko. Seljaci—Industriski Radnici (Peasants—Industrial Workers). Belgrade, 1955.

Lodge, Olive. Peasant Life in Jugoslavia. London, Seeley, Service & Co., Ltd., 1941.

Lutovac, Milisav. Privredno-Geografska Karakteristika Sliva Jasenice (Economic-Geographic Characteristics of the Jasenica Basin). Belgrade, 1951. Geografski Institut publication No. 3.

—— "Privredno-Geografske Prilike i Saobraćajne Veze Srbije Prvog Ustanka" (Economic-Geographic Conditions and Communications in Serbia at the Time of the First Revolt), in Srpsko Geografsko Društvo, special publication No. 32. Belgrade, 1954. Pages 53–74.

Mihailović, Kosta, and Emilija Verčon. "Stanovništvo" (Population), in Kosta Mihailović, ed., Proizvodne Snage NR Srbije (Productive Resources of the People's Republic of Serbia). Belgrade, Ekonomski Institut, 1953. Pages 65–97.

Mijatović, Chedo. Servia of the Servians. London, Sir Isaac Pitman & Sons, 1911.

Miličević, M. Kneževina Srbija (The Kingdom of Serbia). Belgrade, Državna Štamparija, 1876.

Miličević (*Continued*)
—— Život Srba Seljaka (Serbian Peasant Life). Belgrade, Srpska Kraljevska Akademija, 1894.
Mosely, Philip E. "Adaptation for Survival: The Varžić Zadruga," The Slavonic and East European Review, XXI, No. 56 (March, 1943), 147–73.
—— "The Distribution of the Zadruga within South-Eastern Europe," in Jewish Social Studies Publication, Vol. V (1953). Pages 219–30. Joshua Starr Memorial Volume.
—— "The Peasant Family: The *Zadruga*, or Communal Joint-Family in the Balkans," in Caroline Ware, ed., The Cultural Approach to History. New York, Columbia University Press, 1940.
Myers, Paul F., and Arthur A. Campbell. The Population of Yugoslavia. Washington, D. C., Government Printing Office, 1954. U.S. Bureau of the Census, International Population Statistics Reports, Series P-90, No. 5.
Neal, Fred Warner, "The Reforms in Yugoslavia," *American Slavic and East European Review*, XIII, No. 2 (April, 1954), 225–44.
Novaković, Stojan. Ustanak na Dahije, 1804 (Revolt against the Turks, 1804). Belgrade, 1954. Srpska Književna Zadruga publication No. 324.
Noyes, George P. "The Serbo-Croatian Language," in Robert J. Kerner, ed., Yugoslavia. Berkeley, University of California Press, 1949. Pages 279–301.
Nuttonson, M. Y. Agricultural Climatology of Yugoslavia and Its Agro-Climatic Analogues in North America. Washington, D. C., American Institute of Crop Ecology, 1947. International Agro-Climatological Series, Study No. 4.
Pavlović, Jeremije M. Život i Običaji Narodni u Kragujevačkoj Jasenici u Šumadiji (Peasant Life and Customs in Jasenica Region of the Kragujevac District of Šumadija). Vol. XXII of Srpski Etnografski Zbornik. Belgrade, 1921.
—— Život i Rad Ženskinja u Kragujevačkoj Jasenici (Women's Life and Role in the Jasenica Region of the Kragujevac District). Belgrade, 1930. Etnografska Biblioteka publication No. 3.
Petrović, Aleksandar, Banjane: Socialjno-Zdravstvene i Higijenske Prilike (Banjane: Social-Health and Hygiene Conditions). Belgrade, Biblioteka Centralnog Higijenskog Zavoda, 1932.
—— Rakovica: Socialjno-Zdravstvene i Higijenske Prilike (Rakovica: Social-Health and Hygiene Conditions). Belgrade, Biblioteka Centralnog Higijenskog Zavoda, 1939.

Petrović, Petar Ž. Upitnik za Ispitivanje Narodnih Poljoprivrednih Sprava (Questionnaire for Investigations of Peasant Agricultural Implements). Belgrade, Srpska Akademija Nauka, 1949.

—— Život i Običaji Narodni u Gruži (Life and Customs of the People of Gruža). Vol. XXVI of Srpski Etnografski Zbornik. Belgrade, Srpska Akademija Nauka, 1948.

Petrovitch, W. M. Serbia, Her History and Customs. London, 1915.

Popović, Dušan. Srbija i Beograd. Belgrade, Srpska Književna Zadruga, 1950.

"President Tito Interviewed by Sherwood Eddy Seminar," *Yugoslav Review*, V, No. 7 (September, 1955), 3–28.

Proizvodne Snage NR Srbije (Productive Resources of the People's Republic of Serbia). Edited by Kosta Mihailović. Belgrade, Ekonomski Institut, 1953.

Protić, Ljubiša. Razvitak Industrije i Promet Dobara u Srbiji za Vreme Prve Vlade Kneza Miloša (The Growth of Industry and Trade in Serbia at the Time of the First Reign of Prince Miloš). Belgrade, Rad, 1953.

Prvi Rezultati Popisa Stanovništva u NR Srbiji od 31 Marta, 1953 (First Results of the Population Census of the People's Republic of Serbia as of March 31, 1953). Belgrade, Zavod za Statistiku i Evidenciju NR Srbije, 1953.

Prvi Srpski Ustanak (The First Serbian Revolt). Katalog Izložbe. Belgrade, 1954.

Prvi Srpski Ustanak: Narodne Pjesme iz Zbirke Novice Saulića (First Serbian Revolt: Folk Songs from the Collection of the Novica Saulić). Belgrade, Narodna Knjiga, 1954.

Prvi Ustanak: Srpske Narodne Pesme (The First Revolt: Serbian Folk Songs). Edited by Nada Stanić. Belgrade, Dečja Knjiga, 1954.

Ranke, Leopold. History of Servia and the Servian Revolution. Translated by Mrs. Alexander Kerr. London, John Murray, 1847.

Rašić, Petko. Agricultural Development in Yugoslavia. Belgrade, 1955.

Raymond, Jack. "Yugoslavs Shift Economic Policy," New York *Times*, October 2, 1955.

Redfield, Robert. The Little Community: Viewpoints for the Study of a Human Whole. Chicago, University of Chicago Press, 1955.

Sanders, Irwin T. Balkan Village. Lexington, University of Kentucky Press, 1949.

Schevill, Ferdinand. The History of the Balkan Peninsula. New York, Harcourt, Brace & Co., 1922.

Škerlj, Božo. "Yugoslavia, an Anthropological Review for 1952–54," in Yearbook of Anthropology, 1955. New York, Wenner-Gren Foundation for Anthropological Research, 1955.

Stanovništvo Narodne Republike Srbije od 1834–1953 (Population of the People's Republic of Serbia from 1834 to 1953). Belgrade, 1953. Zavod za Statisktiku i Evidenciju, Series B, Vol. I, June, 1953.

Stoykovitch, Velimir N. "The Economic Position and Future of Yugoslavian Agriculture," in O. S. Morgan, ed., Agricultural Systems of Middle Europe. New York, The Macmillan Co., 1933.

Temperley, H. W. V. History of Serbia. London, G. Bell & Sons, Ltd., 1917.

Tomasevich, Jozo. Collectivization of Agriculture in Yugoslavia. N. p., 1955. Conference of Collectivization of Agriculture in Eastern Europe (mimeographed).

—— Peasants, Politics, and Economic Changes in Yugoslavia. Stanford, Stanford University Press, 1955.

Tomasić, Dinko. Personality and Culture in Eastern European Politics. New York, George W. Stewart, 1948.

Tomić, Dušan, and Jovan Šević. "Poljoprivreda" (Agriculture), in Kosta Mihailović, ed., Proizvodne Snage NR Srbije (Productive Resources of the People's Republic of Serbia). Belgrade, Ekonomski Institut, 1953.

Trajković, Ljubica. Serbia. Belgrade, Putnik, 1953.

Trouton, Ruth. Peasant Renaissance in Yugoslavia, 1900–1950. London, Routledge & Kegan Paul Ltd., 1952.

Troyanovitch, Sima. "Manners and Customs," in Alfred Stead, ed., Servia by the Servians. London, William Heinemann, 1905. Pages 169–98.

Turney-High, Harry Holbert. Château-Gérard: The Life and Times of a Walloon Village. Columbia, University of South Carolina Press, 1953.

Vasić, Pavle. "Srpska Nošnja za Vreme Prvog Ustanka," in Istoriski Glasnik, 1–2. Organ Istoriskog Društva NR Srbije. Belgrade, 1954. Pages 149–92.

Vasović, Milorad. "Šumadija," in Zemlja i Ljudi (The Land and People). Belgrade, 1953. Pages 16–26. Srpsko Geografsko Društvo, publication No. 3.

Warriner, Doreen. "Some Controversial Issues in the History of Agrarian Europe," Slavonic and East European Review, XXXII, No. 78 (December, 1953), 168–86.

West, Rebecca. Black Lamb and Grey Falcon. New York, The Viking Press, 1943.

INDEX

Adolescence, 179–98; clothing of, 121, 218–19; organization of special youth groups, 145
Adult, young, 180–98
Adult education, 273–74
Adultery, 214, 216–17, 223
Aged, the, 203–4
Age structure of Orašac population, 43
Agricultural equipment, 59–64
Agricultural laborers, 49n, 90, 91
Agriculture, 9, 49–51, 56–96; collectivization of, 145, 265–69, 306; crops, yields, and holdings, 56–59; division of labor in, 69–71, 143–44; effect on social organization in Orašac, 134; government policies, 261, 265–72; increasing number in, 89–96; in nineteenth century, 24, 25, 26; present attitude toward, 256–61; seasonal cycles and, 64–69, 72; as source of cash income, 78–87; sources of income outside private, 89–96; teaching of, 252; technology in, 59–64; see also Mixed agriculturists; Pure agriculturalists
Agronomists, 74n, 88, 269
Albania, 297
Albanians, 3; attitude toward, 297, 298
Aleksandar Karadjordjević, prince of Serbia, 36
Alexander, king of Yugoslavia, 211n, 246
America, see Latin America; United States of America
Andrić clan, 150–53
Anić clan, 12, 32, 151
Anti-Semitism, absence of, 287
Arandjelovac, 5 (map), 7–8, 27, 39; county fairs in, 186–87; households in, 135,

136 (tab.); industry in, 88; market in, 86–87, 286; nationalities in, 46; Orašac peasants in, 95; population of, 45, 50 (tab.); prices of selected consumer items in, 1953, 84, 85
Archangel Michael's Day, 31, 238
Aristocracy, absence of, 15, 166
Art, children's, 14, 261, 262–64 (figs.)
Artisans, 89, 91; see also Craftsmen
Austro-Hungarian influence, 3
Austro-Turkish wars, 10–11, 29
Autobiographies of Orašac peasants, 204–23, 250; see also Children, essays by

Ballads, 14–15, 32, 227–28; see also Folksongs
Banjane, xvii
Bee-keeping, 55, 97–100
Belgrade, 2 (map), 5 (map); early history of, 9; effect of increasing demands of market, 88; Orašac peasants in, 95
Belgrade Pashaluk, 11, 16, 21n, 29–30, 33
Beliefs and customs, folk, 241–45
Birth control, 140, 201–2
Birth rate, 43–45
Births: comparison of, recorded by Church and Village Council, 1949–53, 280; decrease in number of, 138–40; in hospitals, 272
Bjelo Polje, 12
Blood-brotherhood, 162–63
Bosnia-Herzegovina, 2 (map), 3–4, 101, 295
Brandy (rakija), 26, 59; defined, 67; implements used in production, 60, 63 (fig.), 64; making of, 67; as source of

IV-e   9/20/58

DATE DUE

GAYLORD   PRINTED IN U.S.A.